A Research Agenda for Peace and Tourism

A Research Agenda for Peace and Tourism

Edited by

ANNA FARMAKI

Assistant Professor, Department of Tourism Management and Hospitality, Cyprus University of Technology, Cyprus

Elgar Research Agendas

Cheltenham, UK • Northampton, MA, USA

Published by
Edward Elgar Publishing Limited
The Lypiatts
15 Lansdown Road
Cheltenham
Glos GL50 2JA
UK

Edward Elgar Publishing, Inc.
William Pratt House
9 Dewey Court
Northampton
Massachusetts 01060
USA

A catalogue record for this book
is available from the British Library

Library of Congress Control Number: 2023949661

This book is available electronically in the **Elgar**online
Geography, Planning and Tourism subject collection
http://dx.doi.org/10.4337/9781803927978

MIX
Paper | Supporting
responsible forestry
FSC   FSC® C013604
www.fsc.org

ISBN 978 1 80392 796 1 (cased)
ISBN 978 1 80392 797 8 (eBook)

Printed and bound by CPI Group (UK) Ltd, Croydon, CR0 4YY

I dedicate this book to my husband Panagiotis, who has always supported and encouraged me, as well as to our children Ioannis Alexandros and Sergios.

I would also like to dedicate this book to the memory of my grandfather, Sergey Ivanovich Klesarev, who fought in the Second World War.

Contents

List of editor and contributors   ix
Preface   xiii
Acknowledgements   xix

1   Critical debates surrounding the peace and
     tourism nexus   1
     Anna Farmaki

2   Times of warfare and peace: tourism as
     a peace-builder?   17
     Maximiliano E. Korstanje

3   Media, animosity and peace through tourism   35
     Anna Farmaki

4   Peace, social justice and the preservation of
     cultural heritage in tourism   49
     Craig Webster

5   Dark tourism acceptance and peacebuilding in
     troubled destinations   69
     *Vasilis Papavasiliou, Elena Malkawi and Maria
     Hadjielia Drotarova*

6   The ecclesial cultural parks in Italy as places of
     inner peace: an investigation of the perceptions of
     stakeholders   89
     Filippo Grasso and Marco Platania

7   The peace and conflict duet: a complex systems
     perspective   105
     Jalayer Khalilzadeh

8   Reflections on researching tourism and peace   121
        Jack Shepherd and Mónica Guasca

9   The metaphorical perceptions of tourism students
        on the relationship between tourism and peace   139
        Dilara Bahtiyar Sari and Metin Sürme

10   Women and peace: a gender approach to peace
        through tourism   157
        Fiona Bakas and Anna Farmaki

11   Peace prospects through border and cross-border
        tourism   175
        Rohit Chauhan

12   Corporate social responsibility: a contributor to
        peace in conflict-ridden destinations?   193
        Anna Farmaki and Dimitrios Stergiou

Index   207

Editor and contributors

Editor

Anna Farmaki is Assistant Professor in Tourism Management at the Cyprus University of Technology, Cyprus. She holds a doctorate (PhD) in marketing from Nottingham Trent University. She has published extensively in reputable, peer-reviewed academic journals such as *Tourism Management, Annals of Tourism Research, Journal of Business Research* and *International Journal of Hospitality Management* among others and has presented her work in various international conferences, seminars and workshops. Dr Farmaki is a Fellow of the Higher Education Academy (UK) and a member of the Management Committee in several COST Actions. In addition, she is Associate Editor in Tourism Review and sits on the Editorial Board of several journals including the *International Journal of Contemporary Hospitality Management, Tourism Management Perspectives, Tourism Planning and Development*, the *Journal of Hospitality and Tourism Management* and the *Journal of Service Theory and Practice*. Her research interests lie primarily in the areas of tourism planning and development with emphasis on sustainable tourism, and tourist behaviour.

Contributors

Fiona Bakas is a tourism lecturer at Lusófona University, Lisbon and a visiting lecturer at Dalarna University, Sweden. She is a collaborating researcher at the University of Coimbra, the University of Aveiro and the University of the Aegean as well as a scientific advisor for the American College of Greece and an active member in the COST Action Women on the Move. She is an associate member of the NGO 'Equality in Tourism' and an elected member of the environmental and cultural development NGO 'Lousitanea'. Her research interests are creative and cultural tourism, gender in tourism labour, events and festivals, qualitative and action-research methodologies, cultural mapping, female entrepreneurship, ecotourism and travelling as an intention to learn a foreign language.

Rohit Chauhan is an Assistant Professor of tourism in School of Hotel Management and Tourism at Lovely Professional University India. He has earned a doctorate in tourism on the topic of sustainable rural tourism. His research interests focus upon rural tourism, peace through tourism, gastronomy, tourism experiences and social tourism.

Maria Hadjielia Drotarova works as a head of research, and senior lecturer in the field of tourism and hospitality at CTL Eurocollege in Limassol. She is a UNESCO Peace Speaker. Her research combines the fields of education and tourism, using qualitative research methods. Her research interests focus on topics such as educational research, adult learning, hospitality, and heritage tourism: dark tourism and cultural tourism, and innovative technologies in tourism. The research work of Dr Hadjielia Drotarova has been published in leading academic journals such as the *International Journal of Hospitality Management, Technological Forecasting and Social Change* and the *Journal of Heritage Tourism.*

Filippo Grasso teaches Market Analysis at the University of Messina (Sicily). In his scientific studies he deals with the territorial tourism system for the governance and management of flows and promotion of tourism in the territories. He is a tourism expert and is a regular member of the International Association of Scientific Experts in Tourism, Swisse.

Mónica Guasca is a doctoral researcher at the Division of Geography and Tourism at the University of Leuven (KU Leuven), Belgium. She currently studies the role of bottom-up tourism initiatives in peacebuilding in Colombia, exploring the linkages between tourism, power, and the spatial reconfigurations that underlie the so-called post-conflict period. Her research interests lie primarily in the (uneven) socio-economic development of societies recovering from war, and in the connection between space, agency and peace.

Jalayer (Jolly) Khalilzadeh has a passion for network and [complex] system science research in general, and their applications in hospitality and tourism in particular. His works have been published in top-ranked academic journals. He has various editorial positions in international blind peer-reviewed journals. Currently, he serves as an Assistant Professor of Tourism at East Carolina University (ECU).

Maximiliano E. Korstanje is Reader at the University of Palermo, Buenos Aires Argentina. Korstanje was Visiting Professor at CERS, University of Leeds, UK, University of la Habana (Cuba) & University of Las Palmas de Gran Canaria (Spain). In addition, he serves as book series editor of Advances in Hospitality, Tourism and Service industries (IGI Global, USA) and Tourism Security Safety and post conflict destinations (Emerald Group, UK).

Elena Malkawi spent her early career at the Novosibirsk University of the Consumer Cooperation, Russia, where she was an assistant professor of economics. Since 2010 Elena has been a member of Business Faculty in CTL Eurocollege, where she has taught a range of courses on economics and management to MBA level students. Elena is an active member of CTL Eurocollege research team and her areas of interest include behavioural economics and digitalization.

Vasilis Papavasiliou's research interests lie in (i) the meaning of touristic experiences, (ii) interpretation of 'places/spaces', (iii) heritage management (iv) depictions of authenticity, theming and nostalgia, (v) social memory, politics/representations of the past, (vi) nationalism, ethnic conflict and (vii) borders, trauma and memory. After completing his PhD at the Hong Kong Polytechnic University, he has given various presentations and participated in a number of events and expositions. He has launched his own Cyprus tourism and promotion webpage and gives regular educational tours around the island. He is also assisting the Cyprus Deputy Ministry of Tourism regarding promotion and agrotouristic events. Currently he works at the Ctl Eurocollege as a lecturer teaching tourism and hospitality courses.

Marco Platania teaches Tourism Economics at the University of Catania (Italy) and is a Visiting Research Fellow at the University of Winchester (UK). He deals with regional economy, tourism economics and sustainability.

Dilara Bahtiyar Sari graduated from Adnan Menderes University, School of Tourism and Hotel Management, Travel Management and Tourism Guidance Department in 2014. She received her master's degree from Akdeniz University Social Sciences Institute, Tourism Management Department in 2017. In 2022, she completed her doctorate at Akdeniz University, Institute of Social Sciences, Tourism Management Department with her doctoral thesis on 'Efficiency in Professional Tourist Guides: Scale Development Study'. Sari has published national and international articles in the field of tourism and currently works as Assistant Professor at Gaziantep University, Vocational School of Tourism and Hotel Management.

Jack Shepherd is a researcher at the European Tourism Research Institute at Mid Sweden University, Östersund, Sweden, and a Visiting Research Fellow at the University of Wakayama, Japan. His research tries to bridge insights from both tourism and peace studies in order to explore the relationship between tourism and peacebuilding, with most of his work focusing on the Israeli-Palestinian conflict. Jack's research often employs creative forms of narrative inquiry, and such work has featured in *Annals of Tourism Research*, *Tourism Geographies* and *Journal of Sustainable Tourism*.

Dimitrios Stergiou is Vice-Dean and Associate Professor in Tourism Management at the School of Social Sciences at the Hellenic Open University. He completed an MSc in Tourism Management & Marketing at Bournemouth University and a PhD on tourism education and management from the University of Surrey. He is the Assistant Editor of the *Journal of Air Transport Studies* and Member of the Editorial Board of *Tourism Review*. Alongside his academic duties he has worked with government and private organisations on tourism projects. His research interests lie in the areas of tourism education, tourism management, and theoretical/methodological issues related to tourism.

Metin Sürme graduated from Mersin University School of Tourism and Hotel Management in 2013. He received his master's degree from Gaziantep University, Institute of Social Sciences, Department of Tourism Management in 2015. In 2019, he completed his doctorate at Gaziantep University, Institute of Social Sciences, Department of Business Administration with his doctoral thesis on 'The Effect of Perceptions on Refugees in Destinations on Personality Image, Attitude, Satisfaction and Behavioral Intention towards the Destination'. Metin has published many national and international articles in the field of tourism and currently works at Gaziantep University Vocational School of Tourism and Hotel Management.

Craig Webster (PhD) is an Associate Professor of Hospitality and Food Management in the Department of Applied Business Studies at Ball State University, USA. His research interests include the political economy of tourism, robots, and artificial intelligence in service industries and fringe events. Dr Webster has published in many peer-reviewed journals. His most recent book is *Robots, Artificial Intelligence and Service Automation in Travel, Tourism, and Hospitality*, co-edited with Stanislav Ivanov (Emerald, 2019).

Preface

As I sit at my desk writing the preface for this edited volume on Peace and Tourism, I can't stop thinking about the number of events that have emerged in the last couple of years that have greatly impacted our lives. Terrorism attacks, wars, health crises, inflation and natural disasters are among the incidents that have erupted in the span of a few years changing the world significantly. By extent, these events have had a profound effect on the global tourism industry. Tourism is generally vulnerable to crises, as evidenced by innumerable studies examining the susceptibility of the tourism industry to the changes brought about by exogenous shocks (e.g., Papatheodorou et al., 2010; Pappas, 2021; Ritchie et al., 2014; Sönmez et al., 1999; Zeng et al., 2005). Extant literature concludes that, at times of uncertainty, tourism demand falls as travel intentions are negatively affected by crises (Blake & Sinclair, 2003; Pappas & Farmaki, 2022; Wang, 2009), due to the worsening of the perceived image of destinations in light of negative events (Ahmad et al., 2021; Li et al., 2018). Even so, tourism has proven resilient to externalities with destinations managing to recover over time (Biggs et al., 2012; Dahles & Susilowati, 2015; Gurtner, 2016).

In recent years, what is particularly noticeable and quite alarming is the rise of political instability and conflict worldwide which threatens global peacefulness (Farmaki & Stergiou, 2021). Even though in the post-Second World War era the majority of conflicts recorded represent civil conflicts erupting mainly in the Middle East and Africa (UCDP/PRIO, 2018), the military advance of the Russian army to Ukraine in February 2022 acts as a reminder of the threat of interstate conflict in the West and evidence of the rise in international tensions. Incidents of political instability and conflict impact international tourism flows negatively (Perles-Ribes et al., 2019). Unsurprisingly, the importance of peace has been recently highlighted, with peace being recently included as a sustainable development goal (SDG) in the United Nation's Agenda 2030. Peace represents a significant goal of intergovernmental organisations and nations worldwide that has been long sought after although still hard to attain.

In this context, tourism was heralded as a potential contributor to peacebuilding especially in destinations affected by conflict. Expressing commitment to the achievement of peace, the World Tourism Organization highlighted the potential of tourism to bridge differences by improving mutual understanding among people via travel-induced contact. Indeed, there is a burgeoning number of studies advocating the peace through tourism stance (e.g., D'Amore, 2009; Higgins-Desbiolles et al., 2022; Kim & Crompton, 1990). Undoubtedly, tourism is valuable in changing perceptions previously held by visitors of a hostile community. Nevertheless, with much of pertinent literature yielding inconclusive results of the peace through tourism tenet (Farmaki, 2017), the question remains: can tourism bring about peace in a destination that has experienced or is experiencing conflict?

In some cases, it seems that perceptual and attitudinal aspects are improved following visitation to a hostile community (e.g., Becken & Carmignani, 2016; Durko & Petrick, 2016), whereas in others they remain stubbornly unchanged leading to the conclusion that tourism benefits peace rather than contributing to it (Pratt & Liu, 2016). Evidently, the nexus between peace and tourism is a complex one. There are social, economic and political factors that interfere with the peace goal including animosity, mistrust of a hostile community, political tensions and economic competition between divided societies, among others (Farmaki, 2017). Indeed, it has been argued that global tourism may promote inequalities that sustain a conflict and inhibit peacebuilding (Farmaki & Stergiou, 2021). Tourism, for instance, has been accused of being a divisive factor preventing meaningful contact between host communities and tourists (Farmaki, 2017) as well as limiting the potential socio-economic benefits that may be acquired by the local community and which are necessary to eliminate existing inequalities that perpetuate conflict. Equally, there are various stakeholders involved in the peace and tourism nexus and whose contribution is vital for the peace through tourism goal to be effectively achieved. These include but are not limited to policymakers, tourism businesses, non-governmental organisations, educators, visitors and researchers.

Evidently, for research to be truly reflective of the peace and tourism interrelationships it must shift focus on specific issues pertinent to tourism dynamics, forms and conditions that may contribute to reconciliation and peacebuilding. Despite the insightful contributions of extant literature on peace and tourism, the dynamic nature of their nexus entails that there are still important aspects to be uncovered. There remains a fruitful ground on which tourism and peace research may grow further and it needs to grow if we seek to gain a deep understanding of the potential opportunities and challenges surrounding this intricate relationship. Thus, this book aims to act as a stepping-stone for a renewed discussion of issues important to peace and tourism research and which, insofar, have not been extensively addressed in past studies. Through a collection of empirical and conceptual chapters, this edited volume aims to contribute to the ongoing debate surrounding the peace and tourism relationship by critically analysing a variety of topics such as potential tourism forms that may benefit peace and the role of certain stakeholders in peacebuilding.

In Chapter 1, Anna Farmaki discusses the critical debates surrounding peace and tourism research whilst offering directions for future research in an attempt to enable interested parties to better address the controversies underpinning relevant literature. Maximiliano Korstanje then takes the lead in Chapter 2 to critically examine the role of tourism as a peacebuilder by laying the foundations towards a new understanding of human violence. Chapter 3 by Anna Farmaki examines the role of media in developing and/or strengthening animosity, discussing the related implications on peace through tourism. In Chapter 4, Craig Webster critically reflects on the Black Lives Matter uprising to present the issue of social justice and cultural heritage as relevant to peace and tourism. An interesting contribution is that of Vasilis Papavasiliou, Elena Malkawi and Maria Hadjielia Drotarova who, in Chapter 5, discuss acceptance of dark tourism sites in troubled destinations as a potential peacebuilding tool. Chapter 6 by Marco Platania and Filippo Grasso introduces the concept of inner peace as a prerequisite to social peace by presenting the role of ecclesiastical cultural parks launched in Italy.

Jalayer Khalilzadeh then examines, in Chapter 7, the peace and conflict duet from a methodological perspective whilst, in Chapter 8, Jack Shepherd and Mónica Guasca provide a reflective account from their experience researching peace and tourism in Colombia and Palestine. Moving on, in Chapter 9 Dilara Bahtiyar Sari and Metin Sürme discuss the role of peace in tourism education by drawing from the metaphorical perceptions of Turkish tourism students. Chapter 10, by Fiona Bakas and Anna Farmaki, explains the importance of women in peacebuilding before analysing their role in peace through tourism using a feminist economics approach. Rohit Chauhan discusses in Chapter 11 the peace prospects in Kashmir and Gilgit-Baltistan through border and cross-border tourism. Last, in Chapter 12, Anna Farmaki and Dimitris Stergiou present findings from Cyprus to examine the role of corporate social responsibility in peacebuilding.

The list of topics presented and discussed in this edited volume is not exhaustive of the important theme of peace and tourism which is more pressing nowadays than ever. Yet, by bringing these issues forward this book aspires to lay out the extent of the potential of tourism in building and maintaining peace as well as to identify the requirements needed by destinations wishing to benefit from this contribution. In so doing, the book may be of use not only to researchers wishing to investigate the interface between peace and tourism but also to policymakers and industry practitioners in destinations affected directly or indirectly by conflict.

References

Ahmad, A., Jamaludin, A., Zuraimi, N. S. M., & Valeri, M. (2021). Visit intention and destination image in post-Covid-19 crisis recovery. *Current Issues in Tourism*, *24*(17), 2392–7.

Becken, S., & Carmignani, F. (2016). Does tourism lead to peace? *Annals of Tourism Research*, *61*, 63–79.

Biggs, D., Hall, C. M., & Stoeckl, N. (2012). The resilience of formal and informal tourism enterprises to disasters: reef tourism in Phuket, Thailand. *Journal of Sustainable Tourism*, *20*(5), 645–65.

Blake, A., & Sinclair, M. T. (2003). Tourism crisis management: US response to September 11. *Annals of Tourism Research*, *30*(4), 813–32.

Dahles, H., & Susilowati, T. P. (2015). Business resilience in times of growth and crisis. *Annals of Tourism Research*, *51*, 34–50.

D'Amore, L. (2009). Peace through tourism: the birthing of a new socio-economic order. *Journal of Business Ethics*, *89*(4), 559–68.

Durko, A., & Petrick, J. (2016). The Nutella project: an education initiative to suggest tourism as a means to peace between the United States and Afghanistan. *Journal of Travel Research*, *55*(8), 1081–93.

Farmaki, A. (2017). The tourism and peace nexus. *Tourism Management*, *59*, 528–40.

Farmaki, A., & Stergiou, D. (2021). Peace and tourism: bridging the gap through justice. *Peace & Change*, *46*(3), 286–309.

Gurtner, Y. (2016). Returning to paradise: investigating issues of tourism crisis and disaster recovery on the island of Bali. *Journal of Hospitality and Tourism Management*, *28*, 11–19.

Higgins-Desbiolles, F., Blanchard, L. A., & Urbain, Y. (2022). Peace through tourism: critical reflections on the intersections between peace, justice, sustainable development and tourism. *Journal of Sustainable Tourism*, *30*(2–3), 335–51.

Kim, Y. K., & Crompton, J. L. (1990). Role of tourism in unifying the two Koreas. *Annals of Tourism Research*, *17*(3), 353–66.

Li, F., Wen, J., & Ying, T. (2018). The influence of crisis on tourists' perceived destination image and revisit intention: an exploratory study of Chinese tourists to North Korea. *Journal of Destination Marketing & Management*, *9*, 104–11.

Papatheodorou, A., Rosselló, J., & Xiao, H. (2010). Global economic crisis and tourism: consequences and perspectives. *Journal of Travel Research*, *49*(1), 39–45.

Pappas, N. (2021). COVID19: holiday intentions during a pandemic. *Tourism Management*, *84*, 104287.

Pappas, N., & Farmaki, A. (2022). Attributes attitudes and chaordic travel intentions during COVID-19. *Current Issues in Tourism*, *25*(24), 4014–30.

Perles-Ribes, J. F., Ramon-Rodriguez, A. B., Such-Devesa, M. J., & Moreno-Izquierdo, L. (2019). Effects of political instability in consolidated destinations: the case of Catalonia (Spain). *Tourism Management*, *70*, 134–9.

Pratt, S., & Liu, A. (2016). Does tourism really lead to peace? A global view. *International Journal of Tourism Research*, *18*(1), 82–90.

Ritchie, B. W., Crotts, J. C., Zehrer, A., & Volsky, G. T. (2014). Understanding the effects of a tourism crisis: the impact of the BP oil spill on regional lodging demand. *Journal of Travel Research*, *53*(1), 12–25.

Sönmez, S. F., Apostolopoulos, Y., & Tarlow, P. (1999). Tourism in crisis: managing the effects of terrorism. *Journal of Travel Research*, *38*(1), 13–18.

UCDP/PRIO (2018). *Uppsala Conflict Data Program*. Available at https://ucdp.uu.se/ (accessed 3 October 2022).

Wang, Y. S. (2009). The impact of crisis events and macroeconomic activity on Taiwan's international inbound tourism demand. *Tourism Management*, *30*(1), 75–82.

Zeng, B., Carter, R. W., & De Lacy, T. (2005). Short-term perturbations and tourism effects: the case of SARS in China. *Current Issues in Tourism*, *8*(4), 306–22.

Acknowledgements

The editor has a number of acknowledgements she would like to make that have contributed to the development of this book. First and foremost, I would like to thank all the contributors to this edited volume who have trusted me with their chapters. I appreciate the time they spent in writing the chapter as well as their understanding and patience with my requests for adjustments throughout the revision process. I would also like to thank Stephanie Hartley, senior assistant editor, who entrusted me with this project. Her assistance and guidance throughout the development of the book was invaluable. Last, I am grateful to the staff at Edward Elgar Publishing for their patience and support from the preparation of the book proposal to the submission of the final book content.

1 Critical debates surrounding the peace and tourism nexus

Anna Farmaki

Introduction

Tourism represents an important sector of the global economy. The travel and tourism industry contributes more than 10 per cent to global gross domestic product (GDP), which amounts to US$1.8 trillion, and employs around 10 per cent of the global workforce (WTTC, 2020). The tourism industry also supports other sectors, such as agriculture, as tourist arrivals creates demand for other products and services. Consequently, residents of tourist destinations enjoy a higher standard of living and improved well-being (Proença & Soukiazis, 2008). Although tourism has been heralded as a significant economic contributor to destination, it is also a social activity that allows hosts and guests to interact (King et al., 1993) and embark on a mutual exchange of cultural aspects. In this context, it was suggested that tourism may act as a potential contributor to reconciliation and peacebuilding (D'Amore, 1988).

The rationale behind the peace through tourism proposition lies on the fact that travel yields contact between tourists and the host community which, supposedly, leads to improved perceptions and relations between people in destinations that have or are experiencing conflict. Several studies have been published examining the effects of travel-induced contact, centring mostly on a comparison between visitors' pre- and post-visit perceptions and attitudes following visitation to a hostile community (e.g., Kim et al., 2007; Pizam et al., 1991). However, findings of relevant studies remain inconclusive of the ability of tourism to improve people's understanding of each other and lead to peace (Farmaki, 2017). Indeed, critics of the peace through tourism proposition have questioned the ability of the industry to contribute to peace, suggesting that tourism actually benefits from peace rather than the other way around (Litvin, 1998; Pratt & Liu, 2016). Much of the criticism against the peace through tourism tenet is based on the fact that the structure of tourism – especially global mass tourism – limits meaningful contact between hosts and guests. Likewise, the profit-oriented nature of tourism implies that the industry may in fact worsen social and economic inequalities between social groups and, in turn, further fuel a conflict (Farmaki & Stergiou, 2021).

The ongoing debate on the peace and tourism interface calls for further academic attention on this important topic. The increasing political instability noted around the world in recent years (Farmaki & Stergiou, 2021) entails that it is timely and more pressing than ever to re-examine the peace and tourism relationship. As the number of tourist flows worldwide is expanding (WTO, 2020), the tourism industry may potentially emerge as not only a significant pillar of the global economy but also a hopeful force that may contribute to peace. After all, the goal for peace is long pursued by intergovernmental organisations and international agents whereas its inclusion as a sustainable development goal (SDG) in the United Nation's Agenda 2030 signifies the value placed on peace as a way to promote sustainable development (UN, 2022). In this regard, it is important to examine all potential tools that may enable the achievement of peace, including tourism.

Thus, the aim of this chapter is to identify and analyse the various debatable issues related to the peace and tourism nexus in order to uncover the potential opportunities and challenges influencing the relationship. The rest of the chapter is organised as follows. First, the notions of conflict and peace are explained with reference to relevant theories in order to provide an understanding of the background in which peace through tourism takes place. Then, the peace through tourism research is reviewed and discussed to identify the key issues surrounding the debate of the peace and tourism nexus. Last, the chapter concludes with a discussion of the conditions influencing peace and tourism and offers directions for future research with the aim of progressing the research agenda on this important topic.

Conflict and peace: two sides of a coin

There cannot be a discussion of peace without reference to conflict, and vice versa, as the two represent two sides of a coin. The nature, context and duration of a conflict are influential on the prospects of achieving and maintaining peace. Therefore, it is important to analyse both concepts and understand the theoretical background prescribing each before considering the role of tourism in peacebuilding.

Conflict

Conflict is defined as the "struggle over values and claims to scarce status, power and resources in which the aims of the opponents are to neutralise, injure and eliminate rivals" (Coser, 1957: 7). It arises between two or more entities with mutually opposing interests while it requires the presence of resource scarcity as well as behaviour aimed at harming opponents (Mack & Snyder, 1957). Therefore, contradiction between two parties is not adequate for conflict to emerge; rather, it manifests as the overt and coercive behaviour of one party which leads to an attempt of retaliation by the other party (Bar-Tal, 2011). Nonetheless, conflict is not always shown with acts of violence (Boulding, 1962) as some conflicts are passive. According to Peleg (2006) a conflict is dynamic and may go through phases of escalation or de-escalation, thereby becoming active or passive at some point in time.

Much of conflict studies have concentrated on analysing why conflicts happen. Various theories have been proposed to explain the causes of a conflict. These theories may be classified into two categories: agency and structural theories (Table 1.1). The first type of theories suggests that conflict emerges due to societal factors related to individual and collective perceptions which influence human behaviour (Farmaki, 2017). Agency theories are then further classified into micro-level and macro-level theories depending on their behavioural perspectives. Micro-level theories such as social identity theory propose that conflict arises from the psychological need of people to distinguish themselves from others while macro-level theories (i.e., game theory, social conflict theory) propose that conflict emerges due to the inequalities between social groups which lead to power struggles and potentially discriminatory behaviour against the less-dominant group (Farmaki, 2017). On the contrary, structural theories place the emergence of conflict in a political and economic context where resource competition and institutional factors may lead to conflict (Wolff, 2006).

Table 1.1   Theories of conflict causation

Agency theories	Structural theories
• Trace the causes of conflict into perceptions at the individual and collective agency level	• Seek explanation of behaviour in terms of the economic and political context in which behaviour occurs
• Some scholars propose that conflict emerges at the *micro-level* due to the psychological need of individuals to differentiate themselves	• Postulate that political and institutional factors and resource-based competition lead to conflict
• Others propose that conflict emanates from intergroup interactions at the *macro-level*	

Nonetheless, both types are inadequate on their own to appropriately explain conflict emergence. In this regard, a meso approach (e.g., human needs theory, greed and grievance theory) has been preferred in more recent conflict studies as a lens of examining conflict situations as they consider micro-level conflict dynamics in the wider context of political, economic and social processes. Indeed, Hoeffler (2012) suggested that the dynamics of conflict should be viewed in relation to the context in which it emerges and in light of its causes which, according to the literature, may be summarised into ethnic differences, resource competition and political factors (Farmaki, 2017). Nevertheless, a conflict is rarely caused by one factor only. For example, it is not enough for ethnic divisions to exist; political and economic factors will typically exacerbate ethnic or social differences and are usually required to mobilise a conflict. This explains why in some contexts societal differences (i.e., religious divisions) do not lead to conflict and different social groups live peacefully with each other while, in other situations, homogeneous groups fight against each other at a point in time. In addition, the causes of a conflict will often shape its duration with some being temporary while others being characterised as protracted and very difficult to resolve. Given that in recent years there has been a rise in conflict worldwide (Farmaki & Stergiou, 2021), it is not surprising that peace has become an important goal for policymakers.

Peace

Conflicts and wars can have devastating effects on countries and societies in economic, social and psychological terms. In this regard, peace has become a long-pursued goal for intergovernmental organisations and international agents; yet, it is a goal that is still not achieved in many parts of the world.

In this context, a burgeoning number of studies has been devoted trying to understand how peace can be achieved and maintained, with pertinent literature distinguishing between various types of peace. Perhaps the most widely known conceptualization of peace is that of Galtung (1964) who argued that there is a negative and a positive form of peace. The first is understood as the absence of war and violence. However, this form of peace has been criticised as being short-term oriented, ignoring the long-term goal of building a just and inclusive society which may leave the door open for conflict to re-emerge (Diehl, 2016). The second form of peace – positive peace – has been recognised as a process that allows "the integration of human society and the provision of basic human needs to all members of the society" (Galtung, 1964: 2). Positive peace, therefore, requires justice, inclusivity, collaboration, harmony, sympathy and freedom. To achieve positive peace, it is thus necessary that the causes of a conflict are addressed. As such, it is not enough to merely settle or resolve a conflict as these approaches imply a temporary cessation of violence. Rather, to achieve positive peace the conflict context needs to be transformed at the social structure (Farmaki, 2017). Figure 1.1 illustrates the relationship between peace and conflict resolution approaches.

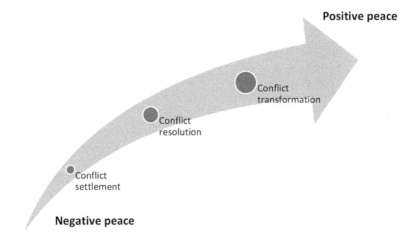

Figure 1.1   Conflict resolution approaches and peace forms

Specifically, for the achievement of positive peace the structural inequalities present in the conflict context must be addressed otherwise the door for conflict re-emergence will remain open. In so doing, it is important that economic, political and social inequalities are eliminated and that justice is restored to ensure a more inclusive and equitable society. According to Kerr and Mobekk (2007), peace and justice go hand in hand as they have mutually reinforcing objectives. Justice can be achieved through various activities, namely through the establishment of distributive, procedural and restorative justice activities. Distributive justice involves the fair and equitable distribution of resources and economic benefits to local communities. Procedural justice can be achieved when inclusive decision-making processes are in place and governance is transparent and effective whilst restorative justice emerges when activism and education restore perceptual biases in the society, allowing disadvantaged groups to share their point of view of events (Jamal & Camargo, 2014). Ultimately, justice is about righteousness (Johannsen, 2017) and for reconciliation to occur it is necessary that justice is given to those deprived of it, that the rule of law is supported, that healing and reconciliation is promoted, and that accountability is established (Kerr & Mobekk, 2007).

The perspective that a positive form of peace is required to transform conflict contexts is shared by the United Nations which recently included peace as one of the SDGs in its Agenda 2030. Representing SDG16, sustainable peace – as it was coined – has been acknowledged as a prerequisite for the sustainable development of nations and the well-being of societies (UN, 2022). The inclusion of peace in the Agenda 2030 gives it a long-term perspective while it recognises that it needs to exist at the local, regional, national and international levels, and involve different groups of actors (Farmaki & Stergiou, 2021). In particular, it is necessary for various groups of actors to be involved in peacebuilding, each carrying out their own set of responsibilities. For instance, the role of diplomats and politicians (known as Track I actors) are essential to settle a conflict and to end the violence. Track II actors such as civil society groups and conflict professionals are also needed to address structural and cultural violence through the organisation of workshops and the provision of seminars. The role of Track II actors is important in resolving a conflict. However, to truly transform the conflict context Track III actors are required in addition to Track I and II stakeholders. Track III actors refer to non-governmental organisations and other entities providing humanitarian aid whose activities are vital for transforming the social structure of a society by creating peace constituencies (Farmaki, 2017). The achievement of positive peace, evidently, requires a holistic inclusive approach at various levels starting from the bottom up and the commitment of agents from several sectors. One sector that has been recognised as contributing to peacebuilding is tourism.

Peace and tourism: a long-standing debate

Tourism has been proposed as a potential tool for achieving reconciliation and peace. The idea of the peace through tourism notion was first introduced by D'Amore (1988) in a conference that took place in Vancouver, Canada. The proposition rested on the rationale that travel and tourism brings people from various parts of the world together and, hence, this contact yields improved perceptions and attitudes towards one another. Since then, a burgeoning number of studies has been published examining pre- and post-visit perceptions and attitudes of a group of tourists visiting a hostile out-group (e.g., Anastasopoulos, 1992; Durko & Petrick, 2016; Kim & Prideaux, 2006; Milman et al., 1990; Pizam et al., 2002). These studies, however, yield inconclusive results with some supporting the peace through tourism argument while others opposing it.

On the one hand, there is research that provides hopeful evidence of the potential contribution of tourism to peace. Relevant studies drew mostly from post-conflict contexts and examined tourist perceptions after visiting destinations considered as opposing or hostile (e.g., Durko & Petrick, 2015; Yu & Chung, 2001). These studies reported a positive change following visitation in terms of visitor perceptions and attitudes, concluding that travel and tourism can potentially alleviate negative biases and stereotypes and contribute to reconciliation efforts. Indeed, several scholars have suggested that tourism may act as a Track II diplomacy activity and a confidence-building measure that can enhance the interaction between divided communities and improve mutual understanding while strengthening cooperation potential (Kim & Crompton, 1990; Sonmez & Apostolopoulos, 2000). In this regard, Causevic and Lynch (2011) came up with the term "phoenix tourism" to illustrate the power of tourism in normalising relationships in post-conflict situations.

On the other hand, the existence of studies that yield unfavourable results questions the efficacy of the peace through tourism rationale. This pool of research identifies various factors as inhibiting the peace through tourism potential. For example, in his study of Greek visitors to Turkey, Anastasopoulos (1992) found that perceptions do not improve after visitation to a nation considered a traditional enemy. Likewise, Kim and Prideaux (2006) reported minimal interest on behalf of South Koreans in visiting Mount Gumgang due to political tensions. Indeed, political influence was acknowledged as a key obstacle in the peace through tourism goal by several studies which conclude that tourism is often used as a political tool aimed at enhancing the socio-psychological gaps between divided groups (Farmaki et al., 2019; Scott, 2012). Nationalistic sentiments and resentment against an outgroup were also identified as inhibiting the effectiveness of peace through tourism as they reduce willingness to visit a hostile outgroup (Farmaki et al., 2019) and mistrust between divided communities seems to prohibit tourism cooperation (Selwyn & Karkut, 2007). Such sentiments may be prolonged due to respective governments' attempts to exploit heritage sites and communicate a specific narrative which reinforces ethnic polarization (Poria & Ashworth, 2009).

In this context, Farmaki and Stergiou (2021) identified tourism as a potentially divisive factor in post-conflict contexts. Specifically, the authors suggested that tourism may deepen the injustices present between divided communities rather than bridging them. The rationale behind this argument lies in the fact that tourism is an economic industry as well as a social phenomenon with subsequent implications in terms of the economic and social benefits and/or costs it may exert on communities. For instance, the structure and nature of global mass tourism implies that local communities are often excluded from tourism revenues (Bianchi, 2018). In the context of divided communities, tourism may possibly lead to the marginalisation of ethnic minorities in terms of employment, investment and an equitable distribution of economic resources and gains. On a similar note, tourism may widen the socio-cultural gaps between divided communities through polarised heritage interpretation and social exclusion which prohibits the process of reconciliation. In fact, a key argument against the peace through tourism tenet is that organised mass tourism does not allow meaningful contact between people (Tomljenovic, 2010); hence, the full capacity of tourism in increasing mutual understanding and alleviating negative stereotypes is not realised. Tourism is also associated with political institutions responsible for decision-making processes relevant to development and investment. In this regard, tourism may become a catalyst for the exercise of political relegation of certain ethnic groups that may be excluded from governance mechanisms (Farmaki & Antoniou, 2017).

In light of these arguments, critics of the peace through tourism tenet suggest that tourism benefits from peace rather than contributing to it (Litvin, 1998; Pratt & Liu, 2016). This is partly true considering that for tourism to flourish, a stable and peaceful environment is required. There is plenty of evidence showcasing the adverse effects of wars, conflicts and terrorist attacks on tourist arrivals and intention to visit a destination (Hamadeh & Bassil, 2017; Seabra et al., 2020). Likewise, opponents of the peace through tourism tenet have posited that much of past research that reported a positive contribution of tourism to peacebuilding relies on samples of students visiting a hostile out-group as part of an educational programme (Farmaki, 2017). Even so, the hopeful evidence that exists and which suggests a potential positive link between tourism and peace entails that further exploration of the peace through tourism tenet is worthwhile. Whilst the factors prohibiting the peace through tourism goal have been discussed and acknowledged in pertinent research, the conditions in which tourism may contribute to peace have received less attention. The section below presents and discusses the requirements that need to be in place for peace through tourism to flourish, as recognised by the literature.

Peace through tourism: the way forward

It is axiomatic that regardless of the presence of barriers inhibiting the peace through tourism goal, the pursuit for the achievement of peace should not cease. The goal of peace is becoming increasingly important as the number of conflicts and wars around the world have increased (Dupuy & Rustad, 2018). Thus, an understanding of the conditions under which tourism may contribute to reconciliation and peace is required. According to Farmaki (2017), the question should not focus on whether tourism contributes to peace but rather what tourism may offer to peacebuilding. In answering this pivotal question, it is necessary to examine the conditions under which a positive perceptual and attitudinal change is noticed in post-conflict settings following visitation. In addition, it is important to acknowledge that peacebuilding requires activities and tactics beyond the interaction of visitors and hosts. Therefore, discussion on peace through tourism cannot ignore the role of tourism as an industry, a political tool and a social activity alongside the costs and benefits it may offer to the political, economic and social spheres.

In terms of the first requirement, a foray into pertinent literature reveals that for a positive effect on perceptual and attitudinal change to occur in post-conflict settings the following conditions are necessary: intergroup cooperation towards a common goal, equal status between hosts and tourists, and governmental support for the initiative, all vital for the effectiveness of contact between divided societies (Farmaki, 2017; Pettigrew & Tropp, 2006). In addition, the use of a common third-party language was recognised as a positive influence on intergroup dialogue (Pilecki & Hammack, 2014). While these conditions may be present in cases of student groups visiting a hostile outgroup as reported by studies yielding favourable results in terms of peace through tourism, in reality tourism rarely meets the aforementioned conditions due to the inequalities it often promotes (Farmaki, 2017). For tourism to contribute to peacebuilding it is necessary that contact between people is meaningful, that stakeholders at all levels in both the public and private sector are supportive of the initiative and that tourism brings benefits to the political, economic and social realms. Such a goal requires the restoration of injustices done to minorities in the past as well as the elimination of economic inequalities that may be present in a divided society.

Given the structure and nature of global tourism and the competitiveness characterising the industry, which requires the extensive use of resources, it is difficult for the industry to bridge any inequalities that may be present between tourists and the host community and/or among ethnic groups in a divided society. In this regard, various niche and/or alternative tourism forms such as eco-tourism and community-based tourism have been acknowledged as contributing to peace since their focus is rooted in gaining benefits for the community and restoring justice. For example, Alluri (2009) identified cultural and environmental preservation as a way to develop peace in Rwanda. Farmaki (2017) agreed that such types of tourism forms are important in peacebuilding contexts as they elicit an active behaviour among participants and reinforce intergroup contact whilst offering economic and social benefits to vulnerable groups. Although research on alternative tourism forms such as community tourism and eco-tourism exists, its focus is more on the socio-economic benefits derived by the local community or certain social groups like women (e.g., Agyeman et al., 2019; Makandwa et al., 2023) rather than social cohesion and peace.

However, community-centric tourism development is inextricably linked to social stability and peace. Peace parks and museums, for instance, have been recognised as important in alleviating animosity and promoting social inclusion whilst encouraging the process of forgiveness as a prerequisite for reconciliation (Watson, 2014). Likewise, volunteer tourism has been identified as another way of promoting intergroup contact and peace (Everingham et al., 2022). In relation to this point, tourism presents itself as a complementary educational tool which can be used as a means of reconciliation and peace (Farmaki & Stergiou, 2021). On a similar note, Antoniou (2022) pointed out that peer-to-peer accommodation platforms may act as a peacebuilding tool as they encourage meaningful interaction between hosts and guests.

Notwithstanding, through community-centric tourism development the existing economic, political and social inequalities that may be present among ethnic groups could be eradicated given that policies for equal employment opportunities and transparent governance mechanisms are put in place. Correspondingly, training programmes need to be promoted to help minorities bridge the gap in terms of employment whereas investment programmes may be helpful in fostering entrepreneurial activities (Joseph & Van Buren, 2022). In this context, Farmaki and Stergiou (2021) identified the role of the private sector as influential on peace through tourism. Specifically, the corporate social responsibility (CSR) activities of international tourism and hospitality companies are integral in promoting reconciliation and peace (Jamali & Mirshak, 2010). Thus, tourism needs to be placed in a wider context of political, economic and social factors that shape a conflict setting and examined in terms of its benefits, costs, effects and influences on a society beyond the economic realm.

Conclusion

Arguably, the question whether tourism contributes to peace remains one of the most debatable ones in tourism research. Overall, the literature informs us that tourism can be either a divisive factor in reconciliation and peacebuilding processes, due to the structure and nature of the industry (Bianchi, 2018), or a promoter of socio-economic exchanges between divided groups that may, ultimately, help in the alleviation of negative perceptions and attitudes in post-conflict settings and restore socio-economic inequalities that prolong conflicts (D'Amore, 1988). Much of the debate surrounding the peace through tourism tenet revolves around the limitations of the contact hypothesis used in past research as a lens for examining perceptual and attitudinal change in tourists visiting a hostile outgroup as well as the fact that most previous studies have drawn from student group samples (Farmaki, 2017). Therefore, the methodological and theoretical approaches used in analyses of the tourism and peace interface need to be reconsidered by future research.

While proposals have been put forward identifying alternative niche tourism forms centring on community well-being as integral for the peacebuilding process in a post-conflict situation, little academic attention has been paid to these tourism forms in the context of peace. Evidently, academic attention needs to shift towards the capacity of such tourism forms to bring and maintain peace in a society by minimising the socio-economic and political inequalities that may be present as well as promoting intergroup contact. As such, related projects and initiatives may be worth exploring further in terms of the degree of their contribution to peacebuilding. In addition, as heritage is an important component in conflict it needs to be further explored by tourism scholars in relation to the ability of heritage sites to foster peace. For example, rather than focusing on how museums and cultural heritage sites can promote polarising views in a divided society (Farmaki & Antoniou, 207), future research can shift the discussion on what type of sites can be developed to promote intergroup contact, reconciliation and peace.

There are other research routes, beyond community-centric tourism development, worth exploring with regard to the tourism and peace interface. Despite
the burgeoning literature accumulated on the sharing economy, for instance,
there is scant attention paid to its relevance to peace. In addition, researchers
could explore the effects of policymaking processes, economic initiatives and
CSR on peacebuilding as these present a fruitful ground for understanding the
role of various tourism stakeholders in the achievement of peace (Farmaki &
Stergiou, 2021). Similarly, research should not ignore analyses of the effects of
external factors (i.e., pandemics) on peace processes as the vulnerability of the
tourism industry implies that these will shape to a great extent peacebuilding
efforts through tourism activities. In relation to this point, it is important to
mention that cases studied so far have specific conflict settings that vary in
terms of the duration and stage of conflict; hence, any attempt to examine the
tourism and peace relationship needs to consider context-specific factors.

Understanding how tourism can be an agent of peace is the question that
needs to preoccupy researchers, with future investigation shifting away from
attempts to answer whether tourism contributes to peace and focusing on what
and how tourism can contribute to reconciliation and peacebuilding. Despite
the debatable issues underlying the tourism and peace nexus and the argument
that tourism promises more than it can deliver, the research agenda on the
tourism and peace nexus needs to progress if our aspirations to build a sustainable future for a global society are to be achieved. As tourism arrivals continue
to grow worldwide, travel may provide great opportunities in bridging the gaps
dividing societies. Knowledge of how this may evolve and how obstacles to
the peace through tourism effort can be minimised is, therefore, valuable and
necessary should the unhidden potential of tourism be realised.

References

Agyeman, Y. B., Yeboah, A. O., & Ashie, E. (2019). Protected areas and poverty reduc-
tion: the role of ecotourism livelihood in local communities in Ghana. *Community
Development*, 50(1), 73–91.
Alluri, R. M. (2009). *The role of tourism in post-conflict peacebuilding in Rwanda*. Bern:
Swisspeace.
Anastasopoulos, P. G. (1992). Tourism and attitude change: Greek tourists visiting
Turkey. *Annals of Tourism Research*, 19(4), 629–42.
Antoniou, K. (2022). Peer-to-peer accommodation as a peacebuilding tool: commu-
nity resilience and group membership. In A. Farmaki et al. (Eds.), *Peer-to-peer
accommodation and community resilience: implications for sustainable development*
(pp. 111–22). Wallingford: CABI.

Bar-Tal, D. (2011). Challenges for constructing peace culture and peace education. In E. Matthews, D. Newman, & M. Dajani (Eds.), *The Israel Palestine conflict: parallel discourses* (pp. 209–23). London: Routledge.

Bianchi, R. (2018). The political economy of tourism development: a critical review. *Annals of Tourism Research, 70*, 88–102.

Boulding, K. E. (1962). *Conflict and defense: a general theory*. New York: Harper Torchbooks.

Causevic, S., & Lynch, P. (2011). Phoenix tourism: post-conflict tourism role. *Annals of Tourism Research, 38*(3), 780–800.

Coser, L. A. (1957). Social conflict and the theory of social change. *The British Journal of Sociology, 8*(3), 197–207.

D'Amore, L. J. (1988). Tourism—a vital force for peace. *Tourism Management, 9*(2), 151–4.

Diehl, P. F. (2016). Exploring peace: looking beyond war and negative peace. *International Studies Quarterly, 60*(1), 1–10.

Dupuy, K., & Rustad, S. A. (2018). Trends in armed conflict, 1946–2017. *Conflict Trends, 5*. https://www.prio.org/publications/11181.

Durko, A., & Petrick, J. (2016). The Nutella project: an education initiative to suggest tourism as a means to peace between the United States and Afghanistan. *Journal of Travel Research, 55*(8), 1081–93.

Everingham, P., Young, T. N., Wearing, S. L., & Lyons, K. (2022). A diverse economies approach for promoting peace and justice in volunteer tourism. *Journal of Sustainable Tourism, 30*(2–3), 618–36.

Farmaki, A. (2017). The tourism and peace nexus. *Tourism Management, 59*, 528–40.

Farmaki, A., & Antoniou, K. (2017). Politicising dark tourism sites: evidence from Cyprus. *Worldwide Hospitality and Tourism Themes, 9*(2), 175–86.

Farmaki, A., Khalilzadeh, J., & Altinay, L. (2019). Travel motivation and demotivation within politically unstable nations. *Tourism Management Perspectives, 29*, 118–30.

Farmaki, A., & Stergiou, D. (2021). Peace and tourism: bridging the gap through justice. *Peace & Change, 46*(3), 286–309.

Galtung, J. (1964). A structural theory of aggression. *Journal of Peace Research, 1*(2), 95–119.

Hamadeh, M., & Bassil, C. (2017). Terrorism, war, and volatility in tourist arrivals: the case of Lebanon. *Tourism Analysis, 22*(4), 537–50.

Hoeffler, A. (2012). *On the causes of civil war*. Oxford handbook of the economics of peace and conflict. Oxford: Oxford University Press.

Jamal, T., & Camargo, B. A. (2014). Sustainable tourism, justice and an ethic of care: toward the just destination. *Journal of Sustainable Tourism, 22*(1), 11–30.

Jamali, D., & Mirshak, R. (2010). Business-conflict linkages: revisiting MNCs, CSR, and conflict. *Journal of Business Ethics, 93*(3), 443–64.

Johannsen, K. (2017). *A conceptual investigation of justice*. London: Routledge.

Joseph, J., & Van Buren III, H. J. (2022). Entrepreneurship, conflict, and peace: the role of inclusion and value creation. *Business & Society, 61*(6), 1558–93.

Kerr, R., & Mobekk, E. (2007). *Peace and justice*. Cambridge: Polity Press.

Kim, Y. K., & Crompton, J. L. (1990). Role of tourism in unifying the two Koreas. *Annals of Tourism Research, 17*(3), 353–66.

Kim, S. S., & Prideaux, B. (2006). An investigation of the relationship between South Korean domestic public opinion, tourism development in North Korea and a role for tourism in promoting peace on the Korean peninsula. *Tourism Management, 27*(1), 124–37.

Kim, S. S., Prideaux, B., & Prideaux, J. (2007). Using tourism to promote peace on the Korean Peninsula. *Annals of Tourism Research*, *34*(2), 291–309.

King, B., Pizam, A., & Milman, A. (1993). Social impacts of tourism: host perceptions. *Annals of Tourism Research*, *20*(4), 650–65.

Litvin, S. W. (1998). Tourism: the world's peace industry? *Journal of Travel Research*, *37*(1), 63–6.

Mack, R. W., & Synder, R. C. (1957). The analysis of conflict: toward an overview and synthesis. *Journal of Conflict Resolution, l.(Haziran)*, *212*, 248.

Makandwa, G., de Klerk, S., & Saayman, A. (2023). Culturally-based community tourism ventures in Southern Africa and rural women entrepreneurs' skills. *Current Issues in Tourism*, *26*(8), 1268–81.

Milman, A., Reichel, A., & Pizam, A. (1990). The impact of tourism on ethnic attitudes: the Israeli-Egyptian case. *Journal of Travel Research*, *29*(2), 45–9.

Peleg, S. (2006). Peace journalism through the lens of conflict theory: analysis and practice. *Conflict & Communication*, *5*(2). https:// www .researchgate .net/ publication/ 264725593 _Peace_Journalism _through _the _Lens _of _Conflict _Theory _Analysis _and_Practice.

Pettigrew, T. F., & Tropp, L. R. (2006). A meta-analytic test of intergroup contact theory. *Journal of Personality and Social Psychology*, *90*(5), 751.

Pilecki, A., & Hammack, P. L. (2014). Negotiating the past, imagining the future: Israeli and Palestinian narratives in intergroup dialog. *International Journal of Intercultural Relations*, *43*, 100–113.

Pizam, A., Fleischer, A., & Mansfeld, Y. (2002). Tourism and social change: the case of Israeli ecotourists visiting Jordan. *Journal of Travel Research*, *41*(2), 177–84.

Pizam, A., Jafari, J., & Milman, A. (1991). Influence of tourism on attitudes: US students visiting USSR. *Tourism Management*, *12*(1), 47–54.

Poria, Y., & Ashworth, G. (2009). Heritage tourism: current resource for conflict. *Annals of Tourism Research*, *36*(3), 522–5.

Pratt, S., & Liu, A. (2016). Does tourism really lead to peace? A global view. *International Journal of Tourism Research*, *18*(1), 82–90.

Proença, S., & Soukiazis, E. (2008). Tourism as an economic growth factor: a case study for Southern European countries. *Tourism Economics*, *14*(4), 791–806.

Scott, J. (2012). Tourism, civil society and peace in Cyprus. *Annals of Tourism Research*, *39*(4), 2114–32.

Seabra, C., Reis, P., & Abrantes, J. L. (2020). The influence of terrorism in tourism arrivals: a longitudinal approach in a Mediterranean country. *Annals of Tourism Research*, *80*, 102811.

Selwyn, T., & Karkut, J. (2007). The politics of institution building and European co-operation: reflections on an EC TEMPUS project on tourism and culture in Bosnia-Herzegovina. In P. M. Burns & M. Novelli (Eds.), *Tourism and politics: global frameworks and local realities* (pp. 123–45). Amsterdam: Elsevier.

Sonmez, S. F., & Apostolopoulos, Y. (2000). Conflict resolution through tourism cooperation? The case of the partitioned island-state of Cyprus. *Journal of Travel & Tourism Marketing*, *9*(3), 35–48.

Tomljenovic, R. (2010). Tourism and intercultural understanding or contact hypothesis revisited. In O. Moufakkir & I. Kelly (Eds.), *Tourism, Progress and Peace* (pp. 17–34). Wallingford: CABI.

UN [United Nations] (2022). Goal 16: promote just, peaceful and inclusive societies. Available at https:// www.un.org/ sustainabledevelopment/ peace-justice/ (accessed 25 October 2022).

Watson, I. (2014). Rethinking peace parks in Korea. *Peace Review*, *26*(1), 102–11.

Wolff, S. (2006). *Ethnic conflict: a global perspective*. Oxford: Oxford University Press.

WTO [World Tourism Organization] (2020). Tourism data dashboard. Available at https://www.unwto.org/tourism-data/unwto-tourism-dashboard (accessed 24 October 2022).

WTTC [World Travel and Tourism Council] (2020). Economic impact reports. Available at https://wttc.org/research/economic-impact (accessed 25 October 2022).

Yu, L., & Chung, M. H. (2001). Tourism as a catalytic force for low-politics activities between politically divided countries: the cases of South/North Korea and Taiwan/China. *New Political Science*, *23*(4), 537–45.

2   Times of warfare and peace: tourism as a peace-builder?

Maximiliano E. Korstanje

Introduction

Over recent decades, scholars have questioned to what extent the tourism industry remains as one of the main peace-builders globally (Litvin, 1998; D'Amore, 1988). At a closer look, the peace-building process cannot be duly understood without discussing warfare and conflict (Farmaki, 2017). As Moufakkir and Kelly (2010) put it, from its outset the industry was widely catalogued as a vehicle of economic prosperity, political stability and, of course, peace. However, some evidence suggests that tourism per se is not a peace-builder (Cho, 2007). Although a valuable human aspiration, peace is a very hard concept to grasp. As authors acknowledge, peace should not be defined as the lack of conflict but as a hierarchical concept deciphered on two levels: positive and negative peace. While the former signals to those states or groups who collaborate looking for mutual benefits, the latter refers to the lack or suppression of physical violence. Consequently, they say that the axiom that punctuates tourism as a successful instrument that corrects social maladies (e.g., poverty or racial segregation) – leading towards a state of warfare – should be at least revisited. In consonance with this, Jacqueline Haessly (2010) argues convincingly that the culture of peace can be successfully ensured through an efficient education process. Different cultures and languages refer to peace as a presence, a term mainly marked by human (temporal) under-standing among leaders. Haessly highlights that peace greases the rails of other desirable conditions – such as justice, harmony, equity or freedom, to name only a few – towards a durable time of understanding. The paradox lies in the fact all these values are justified in the name of war. Not surprisingly, wars start when some population feels its integrity or freedom threatened or, what is more important, when war is overtly declared in the name of peace and justice.

Whatever the case may be, there is a manifest desire to care for the common good when peace is ultimately invoked. As the author goes on to write:

> A culture of peace will be achieved when citizens of the world understand global problems, have the skills to resolve conflicts and struggles for justice non-violently, live by international standards of human rights and equity, appreciate cultural diversity, and respect the Earth and each other. Such learning can only be achieved with systematic education for peace' [...] Peace education is a lifelong process by which attitudes, values, knowledge and skills are passed on between people across the generations, and is essential for both understanding the world in which people live and for learning to live well with others in this world. (Haessly, 2010: 11)

Following from this, a large segment of the specialized literature aims to discuss the problem of peace-building ignoring the vital role played by warfare. Having said this, one of the methodological problems of peace tourism research seems to be associated with a resistance to seeing how the tourism industry derived historically from bellicose events or the sinew of war. The end of the Second World War not only led to technological revolutions in the fields of production and transport, paving the way for the rise of modern tourism, but also allowed a strong financial administration efficiency which enabled lasting economic prosperity. The present chapter is structured according to three clear axes. The first section gives readers a snapshot of the long-lasting impacts of conflict in tourism and society. The second section is reserved to debate the contributions and methodological limitations of tourism peace studies. Over many years, scholars have developed different viewpoints and models to understand the role of tourism as a peace-builder. In the third section I examine the literature with a focus on post-disaster tourism, a fertile ground that today has captivated many professional researchers. Post-disaster tourism is situated as a new theoretical paradigm which escapes the idea that tourism is a classic articulator of harmony and peace. Rather, tourism catalyzes to reconstruct cities and communities in a post-conflict context. Ultimately, we look for a historical diagnosis that helps readers to understand the nature of the modern tourism industry and its intersection with warfare. Based on the legacies of Norbert Elias and Miguel Angel Centeno, the section dissects the real nature of tourism as an emerging phenomenon that historians dubbed the interwar period which ranges from the First to the Second World War.

Tourism and peace: a short companion

Over time, the tourism industry has faced countless situations, risks and challenges showing a great level of resilience to different external crises (e.g., the COVID-19 pandemic). At the same time, some voices have valorized the tourism industry as a natural articulator of political stability and peace (Isaac, 2019). Of course, these voices applauded enthusiastically the belief that those democratic societies which adopted tourism have further possibilities to construct a climate of durable peace than under-developing or undemocratic regimes. Not only political stability but also respect for the law as well as constitutional guarantees seem to be vital to achieve a resilient process which leads to peace (Richter, 2007; Farmaki & Stergiou, 2021). As Girish Prayag (2019) eloquently notes, resilience, which is known as the capacity to recover from adversity while coping with adaptive abilities, is an inherent part of the tourism industry. Building destination resilience is not an easy task to perform. Prayag differentiates two types of resilience: planned and adaptive resilience. Planned resilience evokes the need to employ existing resources and planning capacity to mitigate the effects of disaster in the community, whereas adaptive resilience speaks of the natural capacity to adapt the community to unexpected global dangers. Adaptive resilience emerges in the context of extreme chaos outside the plans of experts. It should be noted that undemocratic countries often had fewer possibilities to adapt their institutions to global risks simply because they fail in the information campaign.

Against this backdrop, so-called failed states as well as under-developed economies have fewer probabilities to boost their economies through tourism (Honey, 2009). In *Ethnicity Inc.*, Jean and John Comaroff enumerate a combination of problems generated by the tourism industry, which includes inter-ethnic conflicts, ethnic cleansing and even warfare, in societies mainly marked by political instability or a history of conflict (Comaroff & Comaroff, 2009). The point of entry was brilliantly addressed by historian Sasha Pack who showed how in Franco`s Spain, modern tourism not only was successfully administered but boosted the economy. In a closer look, the belief that tourism cultivates a climate of mutual understanding, peace and economic prosperity should be revisited in the light of historical facts. Tourism has been administered, developed and successfully manipulated by dictatorships to legitimate their regimes (Pack, 2006). Hence, it is important to mention that some voices toy with the idea that the modern tourism industry, like many technological transport revolutions – far from placating the state of warfare – is a direct result of two world wars (Mansfeld, 1999; Mansfeld & Korman, 2015). This begs a more than interesting question: is tourism an agent that ensures the necessary conditions for a durable peace or not?

The present chapter centers on efforts in deciphering different aspects, viewpoints and case studies revolving around the intersection between tourism with peace and war. Secondly and most importantly, it is essential not to close doors without discussing the rise of a new niche dubbed postwar or post-conflict tourism worldwide as well as its contributions and methodological limitations. Recently, some interesting studies have emphasized the importance of studying peace and war in perspective. Both are two sides of the same coin. In this respect, post-conflict and war tourism offer a fertile ground to expand the current understanding of peace-building, or, what is more important, the direct contribution of tourism in a much deeper peace-building process. Although the literature on peace tourism has advanced greatly, it systematically overlooks the role of conflict and war in peace-building. In *The Better Angels of Our Nature: The Decline of Violence in History and Its Causes*, Steven Pinker (2011) provides interesting statistics and information on the reduction of violence worldwide. Combining qualitative and quantitative methods, he shows that the expansion of capitalism, as well as the increase in travel and tourism, has created a climate of empathy and understanding for the "Other" which has led to a drastic reduction in violence. This does not mean that globalization creates peace, but it cements stable political institutions to foster democratic governments. Although warfare remains alive in human culture, no less true is that violence declined in the twentieth century by more than 70 percent in comparison with earlier centuries. There is a pacification process which merits discussion, as hinted at eloquently by Pinker.

Peace tourism studies

It is difficult to resist the impression that the question of peace was enthusiastically adopted in the fields of tourism research (Var, Ap & Van Doren, 1998). Peace tourism studies emphasized the importance of embracing sustainable forms of consumption to lead communities to a climate of economic prosperity, mutual understanding and durable peace (Leslie, 1996; Cho, 2007; Haessly, 2010; Farmaki, 2017). Some authors have lamented that inter-ethnic contact generates situations that break the peace (Korstanje, 2011). As Comaroff and Comaroff (2009) have documented, some under-developed economies where some ethnic minorities have remained on the periphery of economic production, often incorporate tourism as poverty relief. Though the project is successful in the short run, the imposition of heavy taxes by the central administration leads the community into a state of extreme violence. In this vein, Renata Tomljenovic (2010) overtly acknowledges that the industry often erects some barriers to maximize its profits; when this happens, host–guest relations are simply put under strain. At a first glimpse, inter-ethnic disputes tend to dilute when ethnocentrism is disarticulated. Based on Gordon Allport's contact theory, she holds the thesis that the quality of contact is determinant for tourists to avoid hosts. Having said this, tourists' psychological motivation, as well as their characters, play a leading role in the creation of national barriers that affect human relations. It is noteworthy that language and cultural barriers remain the most adverse effects on the quality of contact. Additionally, some studies have found interesting evidence that proves that previous historical national disputes (among states or nations) condition directly host–guest relations, in some cases leaving negative attitudes (prejudice) behind (Isaac & Platenkamp, 2010; Maoz, 2010) but in others aggravating much deeper culturally rooted ethnocentrism. Some historical geopolitical long-dormant discrepancies are certainly triggered by the arrival of foreign tourists. When the question of previous inter-state conflict or rivalry between two or more nations is remains unresolved, tourists from the non-host nation are catalogued as a potential enemy (Gelbman, 2008, 2010; Korstanje, 2011; Pratt & Liu, 2016).

Those advocates of tourism as peace-builder center considerable efforts in highlighting how overseas trips open travelers' minds; as a literary genre, travel writing not only captivated the attention of European readerships but also created more open and democratic societies (Kim, Prideaux & Prideaux, 2007; Wohlmuther & Wintersteiner, 2014; Mansfield, 2017). For the lens of specialized literature, the introduction of tourism as a main economic driver not only sanitizes the economy, diluting previous inter-ethnic conflicts (Crouch & Ritchie, 1999; Pennnings, 2004; Levy & Hawkins, 2009) but also cultivates education for new social institutions oriented to enhance political stability and sustainability (Evans, 1976; Salazar, 2006). Whenever the involved stakeholders infer that they have much to gain with stability and the profits generated by tourism, the conflict also disappears (Fallon, 2001; Honey, 2009; Bramwell, 2011). In a seminal paper, Susanne Becken and Fabrizio Carmignani (2016) interrogate further to what extent the evidence, which is obtained from applied research, does not show the fact that tourism is a force for peace. To fill the gap, they offer a model that tests events associated with conflicts in almost 126 countries from 1995 to 2010. The adoption of a tourism industry in some destinations has stabilizing effects for peace, but results are far from being determinant. Becken and Carmignani state eloquently that an increase in international/domestic tourist arrivals in a given year seems to be directly significant with conflict reduction in the next year. At the same time, developed economies that had more prolonged peace times have more probability to attract more segments than failed states mainly marked by war and conflict. This suggests preliminarily two important axioms; on the one hand, the tourism industry provides a firm basis for the avoidance of conflict and warfare over time. On the other hand, this does not mean to say that tourism gives a destination any certain immunity to a state of conflict. The incidence of conflict is based on the persistence of peace/war status in the previous year.

To put this in other terms, while being at war increases notably the probability of remaining in war, it appears no less true that an increase in international arrivals should be used as a promising cure to achieve a long period of stability.

In a nutshell, the theoretical paradigms revolving around the impact of tourism on political stability has gradually varied over time. In the 1990s, scholars enthusiastically applauded the idea that tourism – through poverty relief – assisted local communities to enhance cooperation and political harmony (Crouch & Ritchie, 1999; Moscardo, 2011; Bramwell & Lane, 2011). Nonetheless, some founding events, accelerated by the fall of the Soviet Union and the end of the Cold War, put this paradigm under the critical lens of scrutiny. These global events include the end of the U.S.S.R., followed by the Kosovo War, the attacks on the World Trade Center in 2001, the global financial crisis of 2008, the COVID-19 pandemic, and the multiple natural disasters provoked by the ecological crisis. All these major risks not only conspired directly against the belief that rational-planning may potentiate geopolitical relations among states (towards a perpetual peace as imagined by Kant), but began with the end of certainties. From that moment on, specialists recognize that in a complex and ever-changing war, a post-conflict destination is the best instrument to revitalize areas devastated by conflict and warfare. This means that the idea of prevention sets the pace for post-conflict consumption (Çakmak & Isaac, 2012; Isaac, Çakmak & Butler, 2019; Séraphin, Korstanje & Gowreensukar, 2020a; Séraphin, Butcher & Korstanje, 2017). In the next section, I discuss the main contributions and limitations of post-conflict destinations as an emerging literature within the constellation of tourism research.

Post-conflict destinations

As stated in the earlier section, post-conflict tourism has emerged recently as a new niche segment where tourists are mainly moved by the inspection of sites or areas which have been devastated by conflict and warfare (Séraphin et al., 2018; Currie, 2020). As some experts agree, a post-conflict destination fulfills a two-fold function. On the one hand, it helps a society or community to recover from a bloody conflict in the past (Gould, 2012). On the other, it provides to community and visitors a lesson to avoid a similar situation in the future (Séraphin, Korstanje & Gowreesunkar, 2020b). Unlike war-tourism which is defined as the segment that consumes active conflict zones (Lisle, 2000), post-conflict tourism alludes to the purpose of sightseeing former war zones. Richard Butler (2019) calls attention to war tourism which combines two opposing forces: satisfaction and the sense of adventure and risk.

Doubtless, tourists are moved with strong intention to visit zones devastated by war and conflict, probably like dark tourists to empathize with human suffering, but what is more important, we must distinguish between post-conflict tourism and war tourism. While the former signals to the quest for answers once the conflict has ended, the latter refers to the adrenaline of being there at the moment the conflict sparks. Complex in nature, as Butler acknowledges, the conflict period is divided into internal (characterized by the rivalries of internal agents) and external (marked by geopolitical tensions). Echoing this point, Timothy Dallen (2019) alerts us that even if there is substantial evidence which suggests that tourist destinations are negatively impacted by conflict and war, less is known about the emergence of new segments as religious or border tourism. These new forms of tourism seem to be less sensitive to conflict.

Under some conditions, the effort of one country to potentiate tourism wakes up discordant and hostile attitudes in a neighboring country if a climate of historical hostility prevails. In other cases, the tourism industry legitimates a vindication for much deeper historical and territorial claims while an international dispute arises. In this respect, Causevic and Lynch (2011) coin the term "phoenix tourism" to denote the growing context of recovery (renewal) where conflict is constructed as a new form of heritage. As they suggest, post-conflict tourism should not be seen as a new segment – mostly associated with dark tourism – but as a role that is a proper function of tourism. Centered on Yugoslavia as the main study case, they hold that the catharsis with the past of a warfare site is the main motivation of tourists. This curiosity is not only given by a dominant discourse that is previously articulated by the status quo but also each visitor internalizes, negotiates or even rejects such a narrative at his/her discretion. The concept of the double burial – created by Bloch – helps readers in expanding their understanding of this deep issue, as Causevic and Lynch put it. The term is observed by ethnographers in the indigenous Merina tribe community. While the first burial takes moment when the person dies, expressing the community's sorrow, a second one engages with a ritual where the body is exhumed and reburied in ancestral lands. The final preservation of the imagined body culminates with a sacralization process in which the final resting place is marked off as a site worthy of re-memoration. In this token, Reddy, Boyd and Nica (2020) state that the multiplication of post-disaster destinations was directly prone to the number of credited publications but no less true is that less attention was paid to post-conflict tourism. In perspective, the authors review more than 102 individual papers published in leading tourism journals. Reddy et al.'s data demonstrates that the literature not only situates tourism as a resilient activity but also credits the power of chaos to create an uncertain condition in which tourism moves today. Tourism has kept the capacity of self-organization even before global dangers (like war). If the destination protects successfully basic levels of service provision and attractions on offer, the probabilities of recovery are higher than those destinations which simply fail in their policies to deal with crises. Adaptation is a key concept to understand the reasons why some destinations perish or live. In consonance with this, Novelli, Morgan and Nibigira (2012) remind us of the importance of tourism in providing stability in fragile or failed nation states in developing economies. As a new source of wealth to assist post-conflict destinations, tourism offers a fertile ground for stimulating local development. However, the rule seems not to apply in all cases. Under some conditions, a strong tourism industry is not enough to develop the type of tourism the country needs:

> For instance, while tourism is included as a possible pathway to prosperity in over 80% of low-income countries poverty reduction strategies, there is an evident implementation gap, which has led to a world map of the poorest countries dotted with well-intentioned community-based tourism projects, delivering small benefits to people. (Novelli, Morgan & Nibigira, 2012: 1448)

Whatever the case may be, an additional problem lies in the fact there is no clear indicator that marks what a fragile state is. Post-conflict destination research aims to study new cases of dark or contested heritage which include internal turmoil, genocides and wars, acts of terrorism or political violence. A successful case in post-conflict recovery is given by the assistance of the government to reach the necessary investment associated with entrepreneur projects developed locally to achieve a climate of self-regulation that regulates internal social conflict (among stakeholders). Guasca, Vanneste and Van Broeck (2020) analyze the concrete contributions of tourism to the peace-building process in Colombia, Latin America. The post-conflict transition is torn between two antagonist forces. A much deeper process of reconciliation between rival groups is enacted by the introduction of the tourism industry, but at the same time community struggles against a neoliberal force that commoditizes the war-stricken region. Central to the thesis, tourism has a deeply rooted political nature, and the authors explore the real opportunities of dark heritage to revitalize areas devastated by conflict, blood and war.

Although tourism provides firm ground for the formation of durable political stability activating the necessary mechanisms of conflict-resolution proper of sustainable governance, in post-conflict areas tourism often fails to mitigate the devastating effects of a long-lasting war. Like many other Latin American countries, the history of Colombia is not only fraught with conflict and political violence but there is also an irreversible chasm between prosperous urban cities and the hinterland where peasants are debarred and occupy a peripheral position. Through agro-tourism, today peasants have greater opportunities to leave poverty behind but to some extent, these perspectives meet with economic and political barriers for them to access land. Tourism per se does not suffice to generate a climate of peace between the guerrilla and the security forces. As a peace-builder, tourism casts some doubts which remain open. With the benefit of hindsight, Comaroff and Comaroff (2009) discuss the problems of adopting tourism in communities marked by years of oppression, discrimination or segregation. Tourism gives opportunities for poverty relief but paradoxically it captivates the attention of central administration which imposes heavy taxes on the community. Historically pitted against the central authority, the community struggles to protect its economic interests. In the case of failed states, tourism engages directly in ethnic cleansing, war or extreme violent acts. This happens simply because there is a manifest rivalry between the segregated groups and the central administration. The imposition of taxes on these communities is simply repelled by violence.

In *Post Conflict Heritage and Postcolonial Tourism*, Tim Winter (2007) exerts a radical critique of post-conflict tourism as the continuation of center–periphery dependency, forged in the former colonial periods. Scholars should focus their attention on the critical and post-colonial theory more than they do today. Per his stance, post-conflict tourism activates some long-dormant stereotypes and narratives oriented to subordinate the "Non-Western Other" to European ideals. The material asymmetries between rich European economies and their former colonies aggravate because of post-conflict and post-colonial heritage. In other circumstances, post-conflict tourism should be commoditized as an ideological form of entertainment and political domestication, replicating a manifest sentiment of hostility for the "Other". Many tourists pay for the experience of being held in concentration camps alongside the territories of Palestine. Once there, they simulate training as IDF (Israeli Defense force) soldiers recruited in the struggle against terrorism. These morbid forms of consumption need not only form the human sense of adventure to obtain unique experiences but a gradual desensitization process to human suffering (Tzanelli & Korstanje, 2019).

A closer scan of the literature suggests that post-conflict consumption contributes directly to a peace-building process in those nations characterized by the following drivers: (a) strong democracies, where social institutions act as check-and-balance forces (Guerrón-Montero, 2004; Nicholls, 2013), (b) nations or cultures which have not been historically oppressed or segregated (Hazbun, 2012; Trogisch & Fletcher, 2022), (c) climate of durable political stability (Causevic & Lynch, 2011; Simone-Charteris & Boyd, 2010), (d) industries where local hosts are not subordinated to their guests by question of status or class (Higgins-Desbiolles & Blanchard, 2010; Korstanje, 2011), (e) the efficacy of local government to neutralize negative stereotypes resulting from previous conflicts (Korstanje, 2009), (f) countries with a prospering economy not exclusively dependent on the tourism industry (Honey, 2009; Var, Ap & Van Doren, 1998), and (g) efficient institutions that handle successfully local claims concerning abuses on the part of a central authority (Comaroff & Comaroff, 2009; Zhang, Lee & Xiong, 2019).

Last but not least, post-conflict tourism studies rest on the urgency to revitalize zones and areas destroyed by war and human conflict worldwide. In sharp opposition to other studies, which looked to prevent violence and conflict, post-conflict studies operate for adapting the community to future conflicts. In so doing, resilience occupies a central position in the configuration of post-conflict literature. However, neither peace tourism nor post-conflict studies are interested in deciphering the nature of war and its interconnection with tourism. The next section not only explores the importance of understanding the nature of war but also that, far from being affected, the tourism industry has resulted from two world wars.

Understanding the nature of war and tourism

One of the pioneering voices in describing the cycles of war, tourism and peace is Yoel Mansfeld. As per his viewpoint, there is a strong correlation between terrorist acts and the levels of economic production that delineate the future of the tourism industry in Israel (Mansfeld, 1999). As far-fetched as it sounds, tourism has resulted from the technological breakthroughs innovated just after the two world wars. Companies such as Ford, Mercedes Benz and Volkswagen have certainly played a leading role in constructing tanks, fighter aircraft and other components of the war machine. The peace process witnessed the recombination of new economic sources and these companies devoted efforts to introduce a radical revolution in transport systems. Faster cars and airplanes connected far-away cities in hours radically transforming the tourism and hospitality industries as never before. It is safe to say that tourism and war are inextricably intertwined (Bagwell, 1988; Pack, 2006). This moot point was brilliantly illustrated by Norbert Elias in his texts "On transformations of aggressiveness" and "Technization and civilization". The civilizing process, far from being stable or linear, comes from war and violence. In a closer look, German philosopher Norbert Elias argues that the civilizing process, which historically prospered in the West, comes from the war techniques successfully oriented to domesticate the lay-citizen in peacetime. As a gradual and cyclical process, the concept of civilization rested on two important axioms: on the one hand, self-consciousness in the so-called superiority over other cultures legitimated European cultural values as ideals to follow; on the other, the domestication of daily lifestyle which includes table manners, natural needs and, ultimately, the transformation of aggressiveness. The structure of society revolves around the capacity to regulate individual and collective violence into sublimated forms of coexistence. To put this bluntly, the West has successfully introduced radical changes that led individuals to self-control respecting violence. It does not authorize that war, conflict and violence disappear; rather, violence is exerted and of course administered rationally by the state to dominate citizens, limiting it to public spectacles only. Those citizens who are unable to control their aggressiveness are catalogued in insanity or as mentally unbalanced (Elias, 1978, 1995).

Starting from a similar premise, Miguel Angel Centeno holds the thesis that the two world wars accelerated a process of economic production where involved nations developed new skills and capacities to reduce (optimize) budget costs. War should be defined as a human construct where violence is organized and controlled according to functional (rational) goals. Unlike Latin American countries which share a similar ethnic background and language, European nations were historically struggling to impose their borderlands on their neighbors. Both wars sparked in Europe, not in Latin America, as Centeno states. Europe faced two total wars which led to a more efficient fiscal control; helpful, so to speak, in expanding its economies worldwide. Latin America never faced similar conflicts and has been also subject to asking for external loans as a remedy for fiscal imbalances. For Centeno, one of the problems of Latin American economies is the lack of fiscal control and the resulting inefficacy in planning a centralized means of production. What is more important, European economies developing a centralized authority which improved more efficient ways of production. To explain this with clarity, the longer the war, the more stable the state. A total war not only had incidence but also durable effects which have resonated in society over decades. These aftermaths include an efficient instrument to extract resources while centralizing power in national capitals, which led to the disappearance of regional loyalties (monopolies) (Centeno, 1997, 2002; Centeno & Enriquez, 2016). In sum:

> War is seen as destructive, cruel, brutal and useless. Such a view makes perfect sense, given the legacy of wars and their consequences. Nevertheless, wars throughout history have been the resources of fantastic social, technological, and political development. (Centeno & Enriquez, 2016: 118)

Wars give the capacity to build the institutional basis for modern states by imposing a degree of efficacy and self-organization while providing great stimulus to the economy and technological transformation. Since states are by-products of the rulers who make greater efforts to monopolize the means of war, the administrative machinery continues with the same plans in peacetimes. This means two important things. Firstly, wars pave the way for the rise of new organizational techniques oriented to improve economies. Secondly and most importantly, the technological inventions required for wars are recycled in modern (faster) transport means in peacetime (Centeno & Enriquez, 2016). This begs a more than the interesting question: what are the implications and contributions of Centeno's texts to the fields of tourism peace studies?

Spanish Emeritus economist Franjo Muñoz de Escalona provides a preliminary answer to this question. The cycles of production and consumption follow stages of disruption and temporal crises. Beyond the contentious tone of his texts, Escalona sheds light on the intersection of conflict and the formation of the necessary transport means to boost the tourism industry. Based on a historical sweep of the tourism economy, he holds that experts misjudged the nature of the industry as well as many other service sectors simply because they are obsessed with studying the demand (excluding the offer). The specialized literature focuses exclusively not only on the tourists´ motivations but also on their demographic assets; as a result of this, other all-encompassing macro-economic visions are systematically pushed to the periphery of knowledge production. This position has historically led to the moral sentiment that condemned the violence, acts of terrorism and, of course, warfare. Nevertheless, Escalona says that terrorism, in particular, and war, in general, contributed notably to the acceleration of the technological innovations that created the modern industry of tourism as we know it today.

Having said this, far from being affected by violence and conflict, the tourism industry appears to be the maiden of wars. The expansion of military forces (in former centuries) not only pacified overseas territories but also paved the way for the rise of a new epoch known as "European imperialism". At the same time, colonial voyages aligned with a wide range of European readership which was eager to consume stories of settlers in the new world. The colonization of the world ended with the rise of modern leisure activities, including tourism consumption (Muñoz de Escalona & Thirkettle, 2011). Last but not least, in earlier publications, Maximiliano Korstanje has alerted us to the methodological problems of studying peace tourism and ignoring the role of warfare. In fact, from its inception, the tourism industry was close to conflict and violence. In dialogue with Michelle Foucault, Korstanje explores the nature of the first anarchist movements that arrived from Europe in the Americas in the eighteenth century. Once in the new world, hundreds of anarchist activists witnessed the grim landscape of American workers, most of them exploited by long working hours and low pay. These radicalized groups struggled not only to reverse existing working conditions but also planned bombings and attacks against politicians and chief police officers. Not surprisingly, former president William McKinley was stabbed by an anarchist militant in 1901. The perpetrators of these violent actions were certainly arrested, sent to trial, exiled and even executed by the security forces to re-establish order. During these difficult days, a more moderate wing opted to train worker unions to introduce innovative policies that finally alleviated working conditions. These measures included the right to strike and working-hour reductions, as well as better salaries and wages for the workforce.

As a new movement, anarcho-syndicalism not only contributed directly to American economic expansion but also paved the way for the rise of the modern tourism industry. This suggests that tourism and terrorism are inevitably entwined. Based on Foucault's legacy, Korstanje explains that society remains united by the articulation of discipline instruments disposed to locate external dangers which threaten society. At a second stage, these dangers are stripped of their devastating effects to be incorporated in a mitigated (balanced) way. Like a vaccine should be understood as an inoculated virus, discipline mitigates (transforms) external dangers to take the part of an ideological core of society. As explained, terrorist groups were identified and exiled but the core of their ideology was incorporated as a mainstream cultural value of a new society based on progress and economic prosperity. This leads Korstanje to say that tourism is terrorism by other means. War, as an external conflict, optimizes necessary economic resources, adopting innovative technologies that improve the existing transport system. At the same time, internal violence (like terrorism) greases the rails for the workforce to accept (economic) policies that otherwise would be neglected (Korstanje & Clayton, 2012; Korstanje, 2016, 2018).

Future research agenda in peace and tourism

In the new century which is mainly marked by episodes of geopolitical tensions and rivalries, probably accelerated by the COVID-19 pandemic, it is important to redirect the discussion revolving around the connection between the tourism industry and peace. In so doing, scholars should adopt new paradigms which contemplate not only the industry as a peace builder but also as a generator of tensions and even warfare (Mostafanezhad, Cheer & Sin 2020; Korstanje & George, 2022). This raises a fundamental question: does the COVID-19 pandemic mark a new feudalization process or simply a new agenda for more open and sustainable tourism? An accurate answer seems to be far from easy. At the least, it probes the latest Russian invasion of Ukraine and the energy crisis that today whips Europe. A future agenda for the study of peace and tourism should include the following guidelines:

- Expressions of chauvinism, racism or anti-tourist sentiment expressed against foreigners.
- The correct use and application of incentive instruments to develop local economies while reducing inter-class or inter-ethnic conflict.
- A new research agenda that includes empirical indicators that explain the correlation between tourism and the peace process.
- New studies oriented to discuss economic de-acceleration and inflation as the main causes of conflict.
- New approaches directed to understand how tourism works in a warfare context.
- The understanding of those macro- and micro-economic factors that trigger a state of warfare.

Quite aside from the above-mentioned points, no less true is that the tourism industry, as well as our current travel behavior, directly results from the combination of wartime economic factors which assisted the movements of armed forces, re-utilized as a path for tourism in a time of peace. In this vein, the present chapter lays the foundation for a new understanding of the connections between war, peace and tourism.

Conclusion

As debated in this chapter, scholars have focused on the problem of war and violence in their effects on the tourism industry worldwide. Multiple studies and applied research suggest that tourism per se does not suffice to stimulate a climate of cooperation and durable peace. Peace tourism studies suggest that far from being a genuine peace-builder, tourism sometimes aggravates conflicts when host and guest relations are not given equal weight. What is more important, some countries marked by long-lasting ethnic wars or those colonized by other countries have fewer probabilities to adopt political stability. This opens the doors for the appearance of a second theory dubbed "post-conflict destination" which accepts conflict as a part of human behavior. As per post-conflict destinations studies, war not only is inevitable but also a human condition. Hence, scholars should devote efforts to calibrating models that help communities to instrumentalize tourism consumption to recover faster from the devastation of war. Ultimately, we proffer a different diagnosis (based on Norbert Elias' and Miguel Angel Centerno's works) showing a new light in peace tourism studies. Although the tourism industry is affected by warfare and conflict some historical approaches authorize us to say the modern tourism industry, as well as the transport system, derive directly from two world wars. This hypothesis, however, though illustrative, should be tested empirically in subsequent studies.

References

Bagwell, P. (1988). *The transport revolution 1770–1985*. London, Routledge.

Becken, S., & Carmignani, F. (2016). Does tourism lead to peace? *Annals of Tourism Research, 61*, 63–79.

Bramwell, B. (2011). Governance, the state and sustainable tourism: a political economy approach. *Journal of Sustainable Tourism, 19*(4–5), 459–77.

Bramwell, B., & Lane, B. (2011). Critical research on the governance of tourism and sustainability. *Journal of Sustainable Tourism, 19*(4–5), 411–21.

Butler, R. (2019). Tourism and conflict: a framework for examining risk versus satisfaction. In R. Isaac, E. Çakmak, & R. Butler (Eds.), *Tourism and hospitality in conflict-ridden destinations* (pp. 13–24). Abingdon: Routledge.

Çakmak, E., & Isaac, R. K. (2012). What destination marketers can learn from their visitors' blogs: an image analysis of Bethlehem, Palestine. *Journal of Destination Marketing & Management, 1*(1–2), 124–33.

Causevic, S., & Lynch, P. (2011). Phoenix tourism: post-conflict tourism role. *Annals of Tourism Research, 38*(3), 780–800.

Centeno, M. A. (1997). Blood and debt: war and taxation in nineteenth-century Latin America. *American Journal of Sociology, 102*(6), 1565–605.

Centeno, M. A. (2002). *Blood and debt: war and the nation-state in Latin America*. University Park, PA: Penn State Press.

Centeno, M. A. & Enriquez, E. (2016). *War and society*. Cambridge: Polity Press.

Cho, M. (2007). A re-examination of tourism and peace: the case of the Mt. Gumgang tourism development on the Korean Peninsula. *Tourism Management, 28*(2), 556–69.

Comaroff, J., & Comaroff, J. (2009). *Ethnicity Inc*. Chicago, IL: Chicago University Press.

Crouch, G. I., & Ritchie, J. B. (1999). Tourism, competitiveness, and societal prosperity. *Journal of Business Research, 44*(3), 137–52.

Currie, S. (2020). Measuring and improving the image of a post-conflict nation: the impact of destination branding. *Journal of Destination Marketing & Management, 18*, 100472.

D'Amore, L. (1988). Tourism: the world's peace industry. *Journal of Travel Research, 27*(1), 35–40.

Dallen, T. (2019). Tourism, border disputes and claims to territorial sovereignty. In R. Isaac, E. Çakmak, & R. Butler (Eds.), *Tourism and hospitality in conflict-ridden destinations* (pp. 25–38). Abingdon: Routledge.

Elias, N. (1978). On transformations of aggressiveness. *Theory and Society, 5*(2), 229–42.

Elias, N. (1995). Technization and civilization. *Theory, Culture & Society, 12*(3), 7–42.

Evans, N. H. (1976). Tourism and cross-cultural communication. *Annals of Tourism Research, 3*(4), 189–98.

Fallon, F. (2001). Conflict, power and tourism on Lombok. *Current Issues in Tourism, 4*(6), 481–502.

Farmaki, A. (2017). The tourism and peace nexus. *Tourism Management, 59*, 528–40.

Farmaki, A., & Stergiou, D. (2021). Peace and tourism: bridging the gap through justice. *Peace & Change.* https://doi.org/10.1111/pech.12472.

Gelbman, A. (2008). Border tourism in Israel: conflict, peace, fear and hope. *Tourism Geographies, 10*(2), 193–213.

Gelbman, A. (2010). Border tourism attractions as a space for presenting and symbolizing peace. In O. Moufakkir, & I. Kelly (Eds.), *Tourism, progress and peace* (pp. 83–98). Wallingford: CABI.

Gould, M. (2012). Branding a post-conflict destination: Northern Ireland. In N. Morgan, A. Pritchard, & R. Pride (Eds.), *Destination brands: managing place reputation* (pp. 321–33). London: Routledge.

Guasca, M., Vanneste, D., & Van Broeck, A. M. (2020). Peacebuilding and post-conflict tourism: addressing structural violence in Colombia. *Journal of Sustainable Tourism, 30*(2–3), 1–17.

Guerrón-Montero, C. (2004). Ethnic strategies, multicultural tourism, peace and democracy-building. In XXV International Congress of the Latin American Studies Association October 6–8, Las Vegas, Nevada, *Congress Proceedings* (p. 22).

Haessly, J. (2010). Tourism and a culture of peace. In O. Moufakkir, & I. Kelly (Eds.), *Tourism, progress and peace* (pp. 1–16). Wallingford: CABI.

Hazbun, W. (2012). Itineraries of peace through tourism: excavating territorial attachments across the Arab/Israeli frontier. *Peace & Change, 37*(1), 3–36.

Higgins-Desbiolles, F., & Blanchard, L. (2010). Challenging peace through tourism: placing tourism in the contexts of human rights, justice and peace. In O. Moufakkir, & I. Kelly (Eds.), *Tourism, progress and peace* (pp. 35–47). Walllingford: CABI.

Honey, M. (2009). Tourism in the developing world: promoting peace and reducing poverty. New York: United States Institute of Peace. https://www.usip.org/sites/default/files/tourism_developing_world_sr233_0.pdf.

Isaac, R. K. (2019). The attitude of Dutch market towards safety and security. In R. Isaac, E. Çakmak, & R. Butler (Eds.), *Tourism and hospitality in conflict-ridden destinations* (pp. 39–55). Abingdon: Routledge.

Isaac, R. K., Çakmak, E., & Butler, R. (Eds.) (2019). *Tourism and hospitality in conflict-ridden destinations.* Abingdon: Routledge.

Isaac, R. K., & Platenkamp, V. (2010). Volunteer tourism in Palestine. In O. Moufakkir, & I. Kelly (Eds.), *Tourism, progress and peace* (pp. 148–60). Wallingford: CABI.

Kim, S. S., Prideaux, B., & Prideaux, J. (2007). Using tourism to promote peace on the Korean Peninsula. *Annals of Tourism Research, 34*(2), 291–309.

Korstanje, M. E. (2009). Contributions of social psychology in the study of prejudice in tourism fields. *Journal of Travel and Tourism Research, 9*(1), 17–27.

Korstanje, M. E. (2011). Influence of history in the encounter of guests and hosts. *Anatolia, 22*(2), 282–85.

Korstanje, M. E. (2016). The spirit of terrorism: tourism, unionization and terrorism. *Pasos Revista de Turismo y Patrimonio Cultural, 14*(3), 239–50.

Korstanje, M. E. (2018). *Terrorism, tourism and the end of hospitality in the 'west'*. New York: Palgrave Macmillan.

Korstanje, M. E., & Clayton, A. (2012). Tourism and terrorism: conflicts and commonalities. *Worldwide Hospitality and Tourism Themes, 4*(1), 8–25.

Korstanje, M. E., & George, B. (2022). *The nature and future of tourism: a post-COVID-19 context*. Boca Raton, FL: CRC Press.

Leslie, D. (1996). Northern Ireland, tourism and peace. *Tourism Management, 17*(1), 51–5.

Levy, S. E., & Hawkins, D. E. (2009). Peace through tourism: commerce based principles and practices. *Journal of Business Ethics, 89*(4), 569–85.

Lisle, D. (2000). Consuming danger: reimagining the war/tourism divide. *Alternatives, 25*(1), 91–116.

Litvin, S. W. (1998). Tourism: the world's peace industry? *Journal of Travel Research, 37*(1), 63–6.

Mansfeld, Y. (1999). Cycles of war, terror, and peace: determinants and management of crisis and recovery of the Israeli tourism industry. *Journal of Travel Research, 38*(1), 30–36.

Mansfeld, Y., & Korman, T. (2015). Between war and peace: conflict heritage tourism along three Israeli border areas. *Tourism Geographies, 17*(3), 437–60.

Mansfield, C. (2017). Travel writing in place branding: a case study on Nantes. *Journal of Tourism, Heritage & Services Marketing, 3*(2), 1–7.

Maoz, D. (2010). Warming up peace: an encounter between Egyptian hosts and Israeli guests in Sinai. In O. Moufakkir, & I. Kelly (Eds.), *Tourism, progress and peace* (pp. 65–82). Wallingford: CABI.

Moscardo, G. (2011). Exploring social representations of tourism planning: issues for governance. *Journal of Sustainable Tourism, 19*(4–5), 423–36.

Mostafanezhad, M., Cheer, J. M., & Sin, H. L. (2020). Geopolitical anxieties of tourism: (im)mobilities of the COVID-19 pandemic. *Dialogues in Human Geography, 10*(2), 182–6.

Moufakkir, O., & Kelly, I. (2010). Introduction: peace and tourism: friends not foes. In O. Moufakkir, & I. Kelly (Eds.), *Tourism, progress and peace* (pp. xv–xxxii). Wallingford: Cabi.

Muñoz de Escalona, F. & Thirkettle, A. (2011). General theory of tourism: the case of war and terrorism. *International Journal of Tourism Anthropology, 1*(3–4): 208–25.

Nicholls, R. (2013). *Peace (tourism) as critical ecological democracy*. Abingdon: Routledge.

Novelli, M., Morgan, N., & Nibigira, C. (2012). Tourism in a post-conflict situation of fragility. *Annals of Tourism Research, 39*(3), 1446–69.

Pack, S. (2006). Tourism and dictatorship: Europe's peaceful invasion of Franco's Spain. New York: Springer.

Pennings, G. (2004). Legal harmonization and reproductive tourism in Europe. *Human reproduction, 19*(12), 2689–94.

Pinker, S. (2011). *The better angels of our nature: the decline of violence in history and its causes*. London: Penguin.

Pratt, S., & Liu, A. (2016). Does tourism really lead to peace? A global view. *International Journal of Tourism Research, 18*(1), 82–90.

Prayag, G. (2019). Building destination resilience through community, and organizational resilience. In R. Isaac, E. Çakmak, & R. Butler (Eds.), *Tourism and hospitality
in conflict-ridden destinations* (pp. 56–68). Abingdon: Routledge.

Reddy, M. V., Boyd, S. W., & Nica, M. (2020). Towards a post-conflict tourism recovery
framework. *Annals of Tourism Research, 84*, 102940.

Richter, L. K. (2007). Democracy and tourism: exploring the nature of an inconsistent
relationship. In *Tourism and politics* (pp. 25–36). Abingdon: Routledge.

Salazar, N. B. (2006). Building a 'culture of peace' through tourism: reflexive and analytical notes and queries. *Universitas Humanística, 62*, 319–36.

Séraphin, H., Butcher, J., & Korstanje, M. (2017). Challenging the negative images of
Haiti at a pre-visit stage using visual online learning materials. *Journal of Policy
Research in Tourism, Leisure and Events, 9*(2), 169–81.

Séraphin, H., Korstanje, M., & Gowreesunkar, V. (2020a). Diaspora and ambidextrous
management of tourism in post-colonial, post-conflict and post-disaster destinations. *Journal of Tourism and Cultural Change, 18*(2), 113–32.

Séraphin, H., Korstanje, M., & Gowreesunkar, V. G. (Eds.) (2020b). *Post-disaster and
post-conflict tourism: toward a new management approach.* New York: CRC Press.

Séraphin, H., Yallop, A. C., Capatina, A., & Gowreesunkar, V. G. (2018). Heritage in
tourism organisations' branding strategy: the case of a post-colonial, post-conflict
and post-disaster destination. *International Journal of Culture, Tourism and
Hospitality Research, 12*(1), 89–105.

Simone-Charteris, M. T., & Boyd, S. W. (2010). Northern Ireland re-emerges from
the ashes: the contribution of political tourism towards a more visited and peaceful environment. In O. Moufakkir, & I. Kelly (Eds.), *Tourism, progress and peace*
(pp. 179–98). Walllingford: CABI.

Tomljenovic, R. (2010). Tourism and intercultural understanding or contact hypothesis
revisited. In O. Moufakkir, & I. Kelly (Eds.), *Tourism, progress and peace* (pp. 17–34).
Wallingford: CABI.

Trogisch, L., & Fletcher, R. (2022). Fortress tourism: exploring dynamics of tourism,
security and peace around the Virunga transboundary conservation area. *Journal of
Sustainable Tourism, 30*(2–3), 352–71.

Tzanelli, R., & Korstanje, M. E. (2019). On killing the 'toured object': anti-terrorist
fantasy, touristic edgework and morbid consumption in the illegal settlements in
West Bank, Palestine. In R. Isaac, E. Çakmak, & R. Butler (Eds.), *Tourism and hospitality in conflict-ridden destinations* (pp. 71–83). Abingdon: Routledge.

Var, T., Ap, J., & Van Doren, C. (1998). Tourism and world peace. *Global tourism, 2*,
45–7.

Winter, T. (2007). *Post-conflict heritage, postcolonial tourism: tourism, politics and
development at Angkor.* Abingdon: Routledge.

Wohlmuther, C., & Wintersteiner, W. (Eds.) (2014). Peace sensitive tourism: how
tourism can contribute to peace. *International handbook on tourism and peace*
(pp. 31–61). Vienna: WTO & Klagen University Press.

Zhang, Y., Lee, T. J., & Xiong, Y. (2019). A conflict resolution model for sustainable
heritage tourism. *International Journal of Tourism Research, 21*(4), 478–92.

3 Media, animosity and peace through tourism

Anna Farmaki

Introduction

The importance of media in society is undoubted. Media plays a dual role as they both inform us and entertain us, exerting a great deal of impact on our daily life. Since the Second World War, when mass media emerged, they have become a dominant aspect of human life; even more so after the rise of social media platforms that allow people to interact and disseminate information by liking and sharing posts, thus partaking in the fast reproduction of information (Tandoc et al., 2020). Generally speaking, the effects of media include a range of positive and negative outcomes such as learning, news diffusion, socialising, influencing public opinion at times of voting as well as promoting inappropriate (e.g., violent, sexual) content (Perse & Lambe, 2016). Indeed, scholars from various fields such as education, sociology and politics have investigated the influence of the media, concluding that the effects are two-fold.

On the one hand, through the provision of information media allows individuals to add to their pool of knowledge and, accordingly, form opinions and develop attitudes towards people, countries and/or entities (Li & Tang, 2009; McCombs et al., 2011, McLeod et al., 2017). As such, the media plays a significant role in decision-making processes. In this context, the media has been acknowledged as a factor contributing to the function of democracies as they inform the public of governmental policies, trade treaties and environmental or social issues that require collective action (Bucy & Gregson, 2001; Sampei & Aoyagi-Usui, 2009). On the other hand, the media has been heavily criticised for misrepresenting information and for perpetuating inappropriate context of violent and sexual nature to audiences. According to Fog (2004: 1), media "frame stories in ways that hamper the ability of the democratic system to solve internal social problems as well as international conflicts in an optimal way". Social media, in particular, has often been condemned for eliminating people's ability to think independently as they easily believe messages posted online regardless of them being "fake news" (Di Domenico et al., 2021).

Indeed, the media have accumulated a large share of criticism with regard to how they portray a situation, often contributing to the formation of animosity and/or strengthening ethnocentrism (Kull et al., 2004). This may be due to political ideology, prejudice, governmental narrative or even national interests that shape how news is being presented (Chang et al., 1998; Pan et al., 1999; Yang, 2003). The ability of the media to present news as real has to do with how they frame the news. In other words, the media selects aspects of a perceived reality and highlights them as important (Zairis & Dimakakos, 2022). Likewise, in a crisis, content may be dramatized to influence public opinion about the importance of the crisis, how it started and who is responsible for it (Clark et al., 2004). In the context of conflict, the media was acknowledged as a contributing factor to animosity (Dai et al., 2022) with out-group animosity being identified as driving engagement in social media (Rathje et al., 2021).

Despite evidence of the effects of the media on animosity formation, the relationship between media and animosity has received scant attention within the tourism field. This is surprising because animosity against a country has been found to negatively impact travel intentions (Dai et al., 2022; Loureiro & Jesus, 2019; Stepchenkova et al., 2018). Hence, the aim of this chapter is to examine the role of media in forming animosity towards tourists and discuss associated effects in relation to peace through tourism. In so doing, the perceptions of people residing in Europe are drawn with regard to how the media affected their potential animosity against Russians following the Ukraine–Russia conflict, which culminated in February 2022 with the advance of the Russian military into Ukraine. As a response to this act that was condemned by global leaders, countries in the European Union and the West imposed a series of sanctions on the Russian Federation, making Russia the most sanctioned country in the world (Shapiro, 2022) with a tide of animosity rising against them worldwide (Farmaki, 2023).

Animosity, tourism and peace

A long-standing debate in tourism studies is the peace through tourism proposition. Peace through tourism essentially suggests that travel-induced contact improves people's perceptions and attitudes of an out-group; hence, contributing to the strengthening of country relations and global peace (D'Amore, 2009; Salazar, 2006). Although promising, this hypothesis is still to be confirmed due to the many studies yielding unfavourable findings (Farmaki, 2017). One factor identified as impairing the peace through tourism tenet is animosity among members of a society, which prevents them from visiting a hostile out-group (e.g., Alvarez & Campo, 2014; Farmaki et al., 2019; Khalilzadeh, 2018). Therefore, understanding how animosity is formed and maintained is important in order to more effectively consider the practicalities of peace through tourism.

In tourism, animosity was examined from a consumer perspective. In other words, scholars regarded destinations as products that tourists may choose or not depending on their perceptions and attitudes towards the country (Campo & Alvarez, 2019). In this context, animosity – conceptualised as the "anger related to previous or ongoing military, economic or diplomatic events" (Klein et al., 1998: 90) – was found to have a significant impact on travel behaviour as it worsens destination image negatively influencing visitation intentions (e.g., Abraham & Poria, 2020; Loureiro & Jesus, 2019). Animosity in tourism contexts was also found to have an enduring effect (Yu et al., 2020) yielding implications for reconciliation in destinations affected by conflict.

Animosity may arise from various sources including political, military, economic, socio-cultural and religious differences (Yu et al., 2020) that cause someone to feel hostility towards a member of an out-group. Factors like war, different political ideology, economic competition, dislike of social values of a societal group and cultural differences are among those that contribute to the development of animosity. Although animosity is often associated with cognitive aspects, studies acknowledge that it represents an affective construct as it is attitudinal and behavioural in nature (Brummett et al., 1998). Nonetheless, the presence of animosity does not necessarily mean that it can lead to a specific hostile behaviour. This may be the case where mutual benefits between two individuals are expected. Research on animosity also informs us that there are two types of animosity – personal which occurs at the individual level and national referring to antagonism felt at the national level (Jung et al., 2002). In relation to this point, studies highlight that animosity may be temporary, known as situational animosity, or stable arising from a historical background like war (Jung et al., 2002).

Within peace through tourism studies, what is noticeable is that animosity often exists due to political antagonism which not only fuels a conflict between two countries but can also be long-lasting given the duration of a conflict (Farmaki et al., 2019). In these cases, animosity is reinforced by various factors such as education, media representations and political tensions (Farmaki et al., 2019; Papadakis, 2008; Şahin, 2014). Media, in particular, seem to exert a great influence on animosity in a tourism context (Alvarez & Campo, 2020; Dai et al., 2022) as nowadays the increasing use of social media entails an immediate dissemination of information to a large audience, influencing tourist perceptions and travel intentions (Wong et al., 2020). Even so, the role of the media in animosity has not received extensive attention in tourism animosity studies. To this end, this study aims to fulfil this research gap and examine the role of media in animosity formation and its effects on travel intentions of people. In so doing, a sample of potential tourists residing in Europe were targeted and examined in terms of their animosity against Russians following the Ukraine–Russia conflict that climaxed in 2022. As a response, global leaders and the European Union member countries imposed a series of sanctions against Russia which became the most sanctioned country in the world over the course of a few weeks (Shapiro, 2022). Equally, a tide of animosity expressed against Russians has been on the rise since and during the time of writing this chapter.

Methodology

This study adopts a qualitative research approach. Specifically, interviews were conducted between March and October 2022 with a sample of potential tourists residing in various countries in Europe. Participants were selected using convenience sampling wherein the researcher targeted individuals that were easily accessible and willing to participate in the study. Convenience sampling is often used in studies wishing to explore a phenomenon although it may risk including people who don't fully represent the population (Cochran, 1997). In particular, the researcher used her network of friends and colleagues and contacted them on social media, asking them to participate whilst explaining that the data was confidential and to be used only for academic purposes. Data saturation was reached at 33 participants whereby no new information emerged from the data (Fusch & Ness, 2015). Participants came from various countries including Cyprus, Greece, the UK, Sweden, Germany, Spain, France, Bulgaria, Italy, Croatia and Hungary. Care was taken to ensure enough diversity was maintained in the sample in terms of gender, age and background (Ritchie et al., 2014). Out of the 33 participants, 19 were female and 14 were male of various ages and educational/occupational status.

The interviews took place on the Zoom platform at a day/time of convenience for the participants and lasted about 20–30 minutes. The researcher started each interview with a set of general questions to establish the background of the participants and help break the ice. Then, she moved to questions specific to the research aim which included perceptions of the media's effect on animosity and perceived impact on travel intentions. The following are examples of the questions asked:

- How do you feel about Russians after the recent events?
- Do you agree with the European Union's sanctions against Russia?
- Did your perceptions/feelings of Russians change with recent events?
- What role do you think the media played in regulating your perceptions/ feelings?
- Do you think the media influences our perceptions/attitudes/behaviours? If so, in what way?
- Would you say that the Western media is presenting the news in a skewed way?
- After what you've seen in the media, would you visit Russia for tourism purposes?
- Do you think people's travel intentions to Russia will be negatively impacted by what is presented in the media?

Data collected were analysed using thematic analysis (Braun & Clarke, 2006). Specifically, three rounds of coding were performed based on Gioia et al.'s (2013) suggestion where the researcher first read the transcripts numerous times and identified key themes. Then, she organised and categorised the themes into various sub-categories before sub-categories were combined to elaborate on key issues.

Findings

Both animosity and affiliation against Russians were detected with four categories of media effects being identified. The findings are presented according to these four categories of media effects on animosity/affinity, discussing in parallel their interrelationship with other factors and their impact on travel intentions.

Validating effect

Data analysis revealed that media can have a "validating effect" on animosity against Russians, especially in cases where negative perceptions and attitudes of Russia pre-exist. In other words, several participants expressed animosity against Russians but animosity arose as a validation of their previously held negative perceptions and attitudes of Russia. As a participant [male, 56, UK] stated, "... the Russians always did what they wanted without calculating consequences on the world ... they are a plague really ... this war proves how selfish they are!". Other participants agreed, citing political ideologies and government structures as the foundation of a so-called corrupted system dominating Russian politics. In relation to the Ukraine–Russian conflict, participants concurred with the EU's decision to impose sanctions. Such views are evident in the extracts below:

> Modern-day Russia is still the Soviet Union, it has that communist mentality, that hasn't changed. Just look at how Putin keeps being re-elected, so it is not surprising that they act the way they do ... no adherence to international law, nothing ... they are a corrupted nation and the world has begun to realise now the effects of this. [male, 47, Germany]

> Russia's politics reflect the inability of transition towards democracy, it is a totalitarian system that runs the show and the people can't even act against the regime. Thankfully, the EU does not accept such behaviour and they punished them (with sanctions) where it hurts, their economy. [female, 36, Bulgaria]

In this context, participants acknowledged the importance of media in spreading news and "uncovering the reality as the younger generations are unaware of the meaning of communism" [male, 66, UK]. When this group of participants were asked to state their intentions of travelling to Russia, they replied negatively not due to recent events but rather a general lack of interest in visiting Russia given a dislike of the political ideology of the country.

Steering effect

Findings also indicate that media has a "steering effect" on animosity whereby animosity arose due to media representations without any negative attitudes pre-existing. Many participants argued that they did not have any specific negative perceptions or attitudes towards Russia before the Ukraine–Russia conflict but developed negative thoughts and feelings after watching "the atrocities of the Russians as shown on television" [female, 28, France]. Some participants seem to have related themselves to the conflict due to similar past experiences. As a participant [female, 56, Cyprus] stated, "we (Cypriots) know what it means to be homeless because of war, watching the news was like a knife to the heart ... brings back memories of what we went through". Other participants appear to have been particularly moved by the media representations as a result of their interaction with Ukrainians who fled the country and sought refuge abroad. "You don't just see the mess in the news, you see it in the streets ... ever since (the conflict) there are Ukrainians in my city everywhere" said a participant [male, 38, Sweden].

In relation to this point, participants highlighted the role of social media in not only showing animosity against Russians but expressing affiliation with Ukrainians, "showing them that we care, we support them and condemn what is going on" [male, 24, Spain]. Indeed, while mass media tends to be one-sided in terms of providing information the rise of social media has given an opportunity to the audience to participate in the dissemination of news and express an opinion on events. When asked about their future travel intentions to Russia, this group of participants was more hesitant to answer negatively, suggesting that it is best "to wait how this (conflict) will turn out" [male, 33, Italy] with their travel intentions being largely framed by risk and safety perceptions rather than pre-existing animosity.

Defamating effect

There were participants who had neither positive nor negative opinions of Russians before the recent events, but who felt that the media was unfair in how they depicted the conflict with Ukraine. As a result, these participants expressed allegiance to Russia due to anger that was caused by the impartial representation of the conflict by the Western media. "It is very one-sided, we don't hear the other side so how can we form an unbiased opinion?" questioned a participant [male, 29, UK]. Indeed, participants commented on the ban of access to Russian media in Europe with some even accusing governments of breaching the right to freedom of speech. In the words of a participant [female, 36, Greece], "we have a right to hear the other side, if you restrict this right for me then I cannot hear the full story ... maybe this is what European leaders want to achieve?". In relation to this point, participants were critical of European governments and intergovernmental organisations suggesting that "they are not better than Russian government in this case" [female, 36, Greece].

Interestingly, there were participants who identified responsibility in the Ukrainian media fuelling stories to Western media in an attempt to create an impression. As a participant [male, 41, Italy] stated, "just look at the Eurovision song contest, the Ukrainian presenter sat in a room that looked like a basement clearly to create the impression of victimhood when he gave the points for Ukraine. I've been to the border of Ukraine recently, the Western part of the country is completely safe ... couldn't they tape this somewhere else? Do they really think we are that dumb?". Along the same lines, participants argued that national media channels frame news unethically to "dramatize and skew (situation) towards a specific narrative" [male, 51, Hungary]. As a participant [female, 31, Cyprus] explained, "a respected TV channel showed a video from Rome where there was chaos caused by faulty escalators after a football match but said it was from Ukraine ... complete lies!". In this case, it seems the media did not negatively impact people's perceptions and/or travel intentions as participants argued that they would potentially visit Russia when the conflict ended and sanctions were removed to facilitate travel.

Fortifying effect

Despite the fact that many of the participants depicted animosity against Russians, there were those who expressed affiliation with Russians with the media playing an enhancing role in their behaviour. Specifically, participants commented on how they had positive prior perceptions of Russia and that the media amplified these, causing at the same time animosity against Ukraine and the West. The following extracts illustrate such perceptions:

> The media is the West's pawn directed to show a drama for people to feel sorry for a group of fascists that are destroying their country [Ukraine], demanding more money and weapons! [male, 47, Greece]

> It [Ukrainian government] had the opportunity to end this fast but instead it is sacrificing its people … (who) have flooded Europe and will most likely stay even if it [conflict] ends causing further economic burden on Europe. [male, 45, UK]

In this context, participants argued that the media in the West has failed to be impartial and even showed faked news to create impressions as "people believe them and share them on their social media accounts" [female, 31, Cyprus]. Another participant [male, 32, Croatia] agreed, commenting that "people (in West) see a glimpse from a video and then if you manage to get access to Russian media like I had you see the continuation of that video where the 'dead body' scratches his ear … makes you wonder about all types of news really". Such comments not only illustrate the disbelief of people in the media but also raise issues of morality surrounding news framing and, most importantly in today's society, news sharing. In relation to their travel intentions, this group of participants said they would travel to Russia if the conflict ended and sanctions removed commenting that "it's hard to travel now as there are no direct flight from Europe and the credit cards are not working" [female, 38, Greece]. Thus, in the case of the Ukraine–Russia conflict the sanctions imposed on Russia seem to be a deterring factor for travel, albeit a temporary one.

Discussion and conclusions

Overall, this study's findings indicate that the media have an adverse effect on animosity-formation (steering effect) or in some cases strengthen pre-existing animosity (validating effect). In this regard, the study concurs with past research identifying media as an influencer on animosity especially in the context of conflict where news is often being dramatised (Clark et al., 2004; Dai et al., 2022). There were four categories of media effects that were acknowledged in the findings; these shape animosity, or in some cases, affiliation, accordingly. For example, there were participants who had stable animosity against Russians prior to the conflict due to a dislike of the political ideology or the political system of the country and the media validated this form of animosity, providing justification for such feelings. This effect of the media in this case was labelled "validating effect". Media has also been acknowledged as having a "steering effect" towards animosity as there were participants whose animosity perceptions arose after witnessing the representations of the conflict in the media. This situational form of animosity appears to be regulated by participants' past experience of conflict and interaction with Ukrainian displaced people and is most likely temporary.

On the contrary, findings also detect the potential for perceived "fake news" to exert affiliation towards an out-group provided that certain conditions (i.e., favourable pre-existing perceptions) are present. Indeed, affiliation towards Russians was expressed by participants who had rather neutral attitudes towards Russia prior to recent events. This form of situational affiliation arose due to a belief that Western media is impartially portraying the conflict. This group of participants seem to be critical of the representations in the media as well as the ban of access to Russian media in Europe. This media effect was labelled "defamating effect". A fourth category of media effect (fortifying effect) on affiliation was also recognised. Media seems to have a "fortifying effect" on participants' pre-existing affiliation to Russia. In other words, people with past positive attitudes towards Russia felt enhanced affiliation following media representations due to a dislike of Western politics and of the way Western media portray the situation. In this case, it can be argued that a stable form of affiliation is noted. Figure 3.1 displays these four types of media effects on animosity/affiliation in accordance to their nature (situational or stable).

Correspondingly, participants who expressed stable animosity stated they had no intentions of visiting Russia whilst those depicting a situational form of animosity suggested they might if conflict-related risk and restrictions were reduced. As such, this study confirms past findings: animosity has a direct impact on travel intentions (Abraham & Poria, 2020; Loureiro & Jesus, 2019). Likewise, participants demonstrating stable affiliation expressed a desire to visit the country whereas those with situational affiliation said they would like to visit after the conflict is over although both groups of participants highlighted the negative effect of the sanctions on travel intentions.

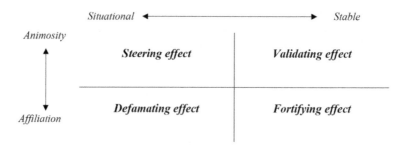

Situational ←————————————→ *Stable*

Animosity

Steering effect   **Validating effect**

Defamating effect   **Fortifying effect**

Affiliation

Figure 3.1   Types of media effect on animosity/affiliation

What the findings of this study tell us is that animosity or affiliation driven by media can have a temporary or a long-lasting effect, depending on previously held attitudes of an opposing group, political ideology, past experience of conflict and interaction with the victims of a conflict. In this sense, the study agrees with prior research which identified enduring effects of animosity due to political reasons (Yu et al., 2020) as well as the presence of a temporary form of animosity (Jung et al., 2002) arising from recent events that influence people's attitudes towards a nation. In this context, the role of media in framing news and shaping public opinion appears to be significant, carrying implications for peace through tourism. If travel intentions are negatively influenced due to the media effects on animosity formation and/or enhancement, then it is rather difficult for people to be motivated to visit an opposing or hostile community. Evidently, the media needs to be recognised as a catalyst factor in peace through tourism research as in many cases they may inhibit the desire to visit a country due to the way it is portrayed.

Indeed, the media represent a powerful source of information that shapes public opinion especially on matters that relate to politics and society. By presenting a specific narrative, the media can direct the success of peace projects and the duration of conflicts. Notwithstanding, such consideration remains under-researched in peace and tourism studies. In relation to this point, it is recommended that future research deepens examination of the influencing factors of the success of peace through tourism by taking into consideration the role of the media and especially of social media. Social media plays an integral role in today's information society (Tandoc et al., 2020) as it allows people to engage with (mis)information dissemination (Di Domenico et al., 2021). Researchers can, therefore, explore issues of morality and ethics in terms of the effect of media on perceptual and attitudinal dimensions of behaviour in a peace through tourism context. Considering that conflicts are unique to specific characteristics, with some being protracted (Farmaki, 2017), it is essential that future research compares the influence of media on animosity formation across a range of conflict types and contexts. Last, it may be worth investigating the role of media in success stories of peace through tourism where conflicts have been resolved to detect best practice examples in terms of information provision via various media channels, comparing in parallel the effectiveness of different media platforms (e.g., mass media, social media).

References

Abraham, V., & Poria, Y. (2020). Political identification, animosity, and consequences on tourist attitudes and behaviours. *Current Issues in Tourism, 23*(24), 3093–110.

Alvarez, M. D., & Campo, S. (2014). The influence of political conflicts on country image and intention to visit: a study of Israel's image. *Tourism Management, 40,* 70–78.

Braun, V., & Clarke, V. (2006). Using thematic analysis in psychology. *Qualitative Research in Psychology, 3*(2), 77–101.

Bucy, E. P., & Gregson, K. S. (2001). Media participation: a legitimizing mechanism of mass democracy. *New Media & Society, 3*(3), 357–80.

Brummett, B. H., Maynard, K. E., Babyak, M. A., Haney, T. L., Segler, I. C., Helms, M. J., et al. (1998). Measures of hostility as predictors of facial affect during social interaction: evidence for construct validity. *Annals of Behavioral Medicine, 20,* 168–73.

Campo, S., & Alvarez, M. D. (2019). Animosity toward a country in the context of destinations as tourism products. *Journal of Hospitality & Tourism Research, 43*(7), 1002–24.

Chang, T. K., Wang, J., & Chen, C. (1998). The social construction of international imagery in the post-cold war era: a comparative analysis of U.S. and Chinese national TV news. *Journal of Broadcasting and Electronic Media, 42*(3), 277–96.

Clark, G., Thrift, N., & Tickell, A. (2004). Performing finance: the industry, the media and its image. *Review of International Political Economy, 11*(2), 289–310.

Cochran, W. H. (1997). *Sampling techniques.* New York: Wiley.

Dai, X., Stepchenkova, S., & Kirilenko, A. P. (2022). The effect of media on tourists' perceptions of a country-target of animosity in the China–US context. *Journal of China Tourism Research,* 1–24. https://doi.org/10.1080/19388160.2022.2150349.

D'Amore, L. (2009). Peace through tourism: the birthing of a new socio-economic order. *Journal of Business Ethics, 89*(4), 559–68.

Di Domenico, G., Sit, J., Ishizaka, A., & Nunan, D. (2021). Fake news, social media and marketing: a systematic review. *Journal of Business Research, 124,* 329–41.

Farmaki, A. (2017). The tourism and peace nexus. *Tourism Management, 59,* 528–40.

Farmaki, A. (2023). Animosity and tourism: resident perspectives. *Journal of Travel Research.* https://doi.org/00472875221146784.

Farmaki, A., Antoniou, K., & Christou, P. (2019). Visiting the "enemy": visitation in politically unstable destinations. *Tourism Review, 74*(3), 293–309.

Fog, A. (2004). The supposed and the real role of mass media in modern democracy. https://www.researchgate.net/publication/250629133_The_Supposed_and_the_Real_Role_of_Mass_Media_in_Modern_Democracy_-_an_Evolutionary_Model.

Fusch, P. I., & Ness, L. R. (2015). Are we there yet? Data saturation in qualitative research. *The Qualitative Report, 20*(9), 1408–16.

Gioia, D. A., Corley, K. G., & Hamilton, A. L. (2013). Seeking qualitative rigor in inductive research: notes on the Gioia methodology. *Organizational Research Methods, 16*(1), 15–31.

Jung, K., Ang, S. H., Leong, S. M., Tan, S. J., Pornpitakpan, C., & Kau, A. K. (2002). A typology of animosity and its cross-national validation. *Journal of Cross-Cultural Psychology, 33*(6), 525–39.

Khalilzadeh, J. (2018). Demonstration of exponential random graph models in tourism studies: is tourism a means of global peace or the bottom line? *Annals of Tourism Research, 69*, 31–41.

Klein, J. G., Ettenson, R., & Morris, M. D. (1998). The animosity model of foreign product purchase: an empirical test in the People's Republic of China. *Journal of Marketing, 62*(1), 89–100.

Kull, S., Ramsay, C., & Lewis, E. (2004). Misperceptions, the media and the Iraqi war. *Political Science Quarterly, 118*(4), 569–98.

Li, H., & Tang, L. (2009). The representation of the Chinese product crisis in national and local newspapers in the United States. *Public Relations Review, 35*(3), 219–25.

Loureiro, S. M. C., & Jesus, S. (2019). How perceived risk and animosity towards a destination may influence destination image and intention to revisit: the case of Rio de Janeiro. *Anatolia, 30*(4), 497–512.

McCombs, M., Holbert, L., Kiousis, S., & Wanta, W. (2011). *The news and public opinion: media effects on civic life.* Oxford: Polity Press.

McLeod, D. M., Wise, D., & Perryman, M. (2017). Thinking about the media: a review of theory and research on media perceptions, media effects perceptions, and their consequences. *Review of Communication Research, 5*, 35–83.

Pan, Z., Lee, C., Chan, J., & So, C. Y. K. (1999). One event, three stories: media narratives from cultural China of the handover of Hong Kong. *International Communication Gazette, 61*(2), 99–112.

Papadakis, Y. (2008). Narrative, memory and history education in divided Cyprus: a comparison of schoolbooks on the "History of Cyprus". *History & Memory, 20*(2), 128–48.

Perse, E. M., & Lambe, J. (2016). *Media effects and society.* London: Routledge.

Rathje, S., Van Bavel, J. J., & Van Der Linden, S. (2021). Out-group animosity drives engagement on social media. *Proceedings of the National Academy of Sciences, 118*(26), e2024292118.

Ritchie, J., Lewis, J., Nicholls, C. M., & Ormston, R. (2014). *Qualitative research practice.* Los Angeles, CA: Sage.

Şahin, S. (2014). Diverse media, uniform reports: an analysis of news coverage of the Cyprus problem by the Turkish Cypriot press. *Journalism, 15*(4), 446–62.

Salazar, N. B. (2006). Building a 'culture of peace' through tourism: reflexive and analytical notes and queries. *Universitas Humanística, 62*, 319–36.

Sampei, Y., & Aoyagi-Usui, M. (2009). Mass media coverage, its influence on public awareness of climate-change issues, and implications for Japan's national campaign to reduce greenhouse gas emissions. *Global Environmental Change, 19*(2), 203–12.

Shapiro, J. (2022). Russia surpasses Iran to become world's most sanctioned country. *Axios*. Available at https://www.axios.com/russia-most-sanctioned-country-0de10d02 -51aa-46c4-9711-bb45303fdfb8.html (accessed 11 March 2022).

Stepchenkova, S., Shichkova, E., Kim, M., & Rykhtik, M. I. (2018). Do strained bilateral relations affect tourists' desire to visit a country that is a target of animosity? *Journal of Travel & Tourism Marketing*, *35*(5), 553–66.

Tandoc Jr, E. C., Lim, D., & Ling, R. (2020). Diffusion of disinformation: how social media users respond to fake news and why. *Journalism*, *21*(3), 381–98.

Wong, J. W. C., Lai, I. K. W., & Tao, Z. (2020). Sharing memorable tourism experiences on mobile social media and how it influences further travel decisions. *Current Issues in Tourism*, *23*(14), 1773–87.

Yang, J. (2003). Framing the NATO air strikes on Kosovo across countries: comparison of Chinese and US newspaper coverage. *International Communication Gazette*, *65*(3), 231–49.

Yu, Q., McManus, R., Yen, D. A., & Li, X. R. (2020). Tourism boycotts and animosity: a study of seven events. *Annals of Tourism Research*, *80*, 102792.

Zairis, A., & Dimakakos, D. (2013). Consumer ethnocentrism, economic animosity and the role of media: the case of Greek products. *EDITORIAL*, *22*, 21–43.

4 Peace, social justice and the preservation of cultural heritage in tourism

Craig Webster

Introduction: social justice, George Floyd, and public outrage

"Social justice" is a concept that has been discussed increasingly in recent years and is frequently attached to social and political movements that seek social, economic, and political outcomes that seem to be fair. While the concept of social justice was not mentioned by the great philosophers such as Plato, Aristotle, Rousseau, or Kant, among others (United Nations, 2006), some of it descends from the philosophical work of John Rawls (Kechen, 2013). In his seminal work, Rawls (1971) expounded upon the concept that justice includes the notion of the distribution of social goods in society, something that highlights fairness in the distribution of goods in a society. As a descendant of the philosophy of Rawls and some other cultural and historical forces (United Nations, 2006: 2), it seems that the phrase "social justice" reflects a distain for the unpleasant distributive practices of the past.

Specifically, the language of "social justice" has been championed by neo-Marxists (those Marxists influenced by the Frankfurt School and Critical Theory) who have been influential in terms of inculcating their philosophy via various institutions in Western societies by encouraging a focus upon the unequal outcomes based upon the sex, religion, sexuality, and race of people in a society (Pluckrose & Lindsay, 2020). The Frankfurt School and Critical Theory mindset has become a mainstay in many universities in the West and stresses the importance of sex, religion, sexuality, and race/ethnicity to inform adherents to the ways that the characteristics of individuals shape unequal outcomes in society and undermine social harmony. The movement, as a descendant of Marxist thinking is aimed at transforming the social, economic, and political order, using various cleavages apart from class as proxies for class, in ways that will sow discontent to undermine the Western constitutional order.

By the summer of 2020, the phrase "social justice" had become mainstream and many understood its power since large numbers of people throughout the world went to the streets to protest the status quo and call for changes, since many viewed the death of George Floyd as an event caused by racism inherent in U.S. society in particular and the West in general. The organization Black Lives Matter (BLM) played an active role in the riots and protests and was rewarded with an avalanche of 90 million dollars in donations in 2020 alone (Kulish, 2022). While the organization was created in 2013 ostensibly to combat police brutality against black Americans (Black Lives Matter, n.d.), it is a radical Marxist organization that has broader interests beyond merely safeguarding the rights of black Americans (Gonzales, 2021; Lindsay, 2022).

In the summer of 2020, street mobs in the USA threatened, vandalized, and destroyed monuments that seemed to portray parts of history that would be considered offensive, specifically those things associated with racism, following the death of George Floyd in police custody. There were also political forces that were receptive to the mobs, using legitimate and accepted political processes to discuss the destruction, removal, or relocation of monuments that seemed to offend the mobs. At any rate, the social justice movement seems to play a role in terms of forcing society to rethink its monuments. Political actors and mobs have played a role in terms of reassessing how history should be portrayed. This chapter explores how the death of George Floyd and subsequent aftershocks have caused many to rethink the preservation and nurturing of cultural heritage, which according to the European Union's Foreign Affairs Council is imperative for long-lasting peace and security. This chapter discusses the events of the summer of 2020 and how monuments became targets of political figures, rioters, and mobs. It also explains intelligent ways of dealing with sensitive parts of history and the possible policy choices that can be used to deal with such issues. Finally, the conclusion discusses the future of the preservation of historical monuments and how this may impact the cultural landscape and the tourism industry, illustrating that internal turmoil in a society can have a deleterious impact upon a destination and undermine the qualities of destinations for visitors. So, while a movement on its face purports to concentrate upon the creation of a society with more equitable outcomes, it has the potential to cause a great deal of destruction, undermine the quality of life, and ultimately subvert the uniqueness of destinations, while also attempting to use cultural heritage as a vehicle for reconciliation, peace, mutual understanding and intercultural dialogue.

The spark(s) leading to attacks on public monuments

The death of George Floyd on May 25 instigated a global movement for social justice that flared up violently during the summer of 2020. The global movement for global justice did not just include peaceful and benign actions but also included a great deal of violence, rioting, and the destruction of property (public and private). In the USA alone, the material damage done by riots, arson, and looting was massive with around two billion dollars in damage done (Justice, 2021). There was also a great deal of bloodshed. Between May 25 and June 8, 2020, in the USA, 19 people died from the unrest attributed to the chaos following the death of George Floyd (McEvoy, 2020).

The destruction did not end at the USA's border, since social justice is a widespread ethos in the Western world. The United Kingdom experienced a large number of extensive and active protests and they were noted to be the largest protests outside of the USA (Mallinson & Ackerman, 2020). In Canada, as well, there were a large number of protests throughout the country; while there are no deaths in Canada attributed to the results of George Floyd riots, there is an indication of substantial property damage (Laframboise & Olivier, 2020). While the most violent and expensive reactions to the incident were in the USA there were significant and noteworthy reactions in many other countries throughout the world.

In terms of the event that instigated a global movement and global reaction, it seems some background is needed. The George Floyd protests began following an unprecedented period in which the world suffered from a terrible pandemic and the political fallout that resulted following the pandemic. In December 2019 the SARS-CoV-2 that causes COVID-19 was identified in China (Buckley, 2020). Following that, governments instituted some drastic restrictions on human movement to contain the spread of the virus to the world's populations (Pew Research Center, 2020). From about mid-March 2020, much of the USA and many people in the world were largely forced into a new lifestyle in which people were forced to remain home, telecommute for their jobs, and were permitted to leave the house only for necessities. This was the social background in which the George Floyd protests came about, with many citizens having been contained in their homes for several months.

Footage of the George Floyd incident was broadcast on televisions and through the internet on May 25, 2020. George Floyd, an African American ex-convict who had moved to Minneapolis, was arrested on suspicion of using counterfeit cash. He was detained by the police and had a great deal of fentanyl and methamphetamine in his system. While there was some contention about what the cause of death was, video footage showed an arresting officer placing his knee on the suspect's neck. The video footage and racial sensitivities in the USA worked in ways that led many to conclude that the death was caused by the arresting officer and that the actions of the arresting officer were symbolic of a large-scale problem of police victimizing black Americans systematically. In that way, the death of one person fed into a commonly accepted narrative about racism in the USA and instigated a massive reaction.

It would be easy to draw some parallels between the George Floyd riots and the events that transpired in Canada about a year later. In Canada during the summer of 2021, mobs toppled several statues, including a statue of Queen Victoria and Queen Elizabeth in reaction to the discovery of the remains of indigenous children (Sharma, 2021). In addition to the toppling of these statues, there was damage (ranging from desecration, vandalizing, or simply the burning down) to 68 churches in Canada (Dzsurdzsa, 2021). About 25 churches were burned, many of them destroyed (Dzsurdzsa, 2021). While the protests and damage that occurred in Canada during 2021 were not caused by the death of George Floyd a year earlier, there were some similarities, since there was a racial component in both North American cases. While the George Floyd incident seemed to have been caused by perceptions of police treatment of black Americans, in Canada it was the treatment of indigenous peoples by colonizers/Christians of European descent. At any rate, the same social justice instinct seems to have influenced the reactions of many people; that is, that racial minorities had been systematically discriminated against in the past and that the discrimination continues to this day.

What is interesting is that the concept "social justice" seems rather benign since it suggests that outcomes should be relatively equitable and fair. In fact, the language used from the philosophical movement has permeated institutions and has been very influential in terms of policy. For example, Sustainable Development Goal (SDG) 16 in the United Nations' Agenda 2030 utilizes language from the social justice paradigm. SDG 16 states that a goal is to "Promote just, peaceful and inclusive societies for sustainable development, provide access to justice for all and build effective, accountable and inclusive institutions at all levels." The language used is indicative that the goals are aimed at a specific social outcome. The curiosity is that peace is also mentioned as a particular desired outcome, as well as the promotion of a different type of society, meaning that much of the goals of SDG 16 encapsulates a major transformation of society, as per the basic Marxist goals of Critical Theory and the Frankfurt School. There is a great deal of literature specifically in the tourism field that is also supportive of sensitivities towards local communities that are generally disadvantaged (see, for example, Jamal and Camargo, 2014) or even considers that tourism can be a vehicle for a more peaceful world (Farmaki & Stergiou, 2021). The paradox is that the social justice movement, a movement that many perceive as a positive thing to make the world more just and equitable worked in ways to instigate violence and destruction, leading to outcomes that would damage and destroy cultural heritage. As such, the movement worked in ways to promote violence and destruction and undermine tourism potential in destinations.

The destruction of monuments

Because the death of George Floyd was interpreted as an incident that reflected inherent racism in American society, many of the protesters turned their ire upon all sorts of monuments that had perceived connections with racism in the USA. Table 4.1 illustrates a small fraction of the public monuments that have been damaged or destroyed by the protesters in the USA. In all the examples in the table, it seems that the protesters were most attracted to public monuments that were associated with the Confederacy (and thus associated with racism/slavery), the mistreatment of indigenous peoples, and opposition to civil rights for non-whites.

Table 4.1   Examples of USA monuments and destruction by protesters

Location/name	Action and reason
Charles Didier Dreux bust (New Orleans, Louisiana)	Toppled by protesters. Bust commemorating Confederate officer Charles Didier Dreux. The nose had been chiseled off the statue by protesters.
Sampson County Confederate Monument (Clinton, North Carolina)	Damaged by protesters after the city council passed a resolution asking the county to remove it. Confederate monument.
Robert E. Lee memorial (Roanoke, Virginia)	Toppled and damaged by protesters, city removed monument afterwards. Confederate monument.
Williams Carter Wickham statue (Richmond, Virginia)	Toppled by protesters. Bust commemorating a Confederate officer. Pulled from its base and tumbled to the ground.

Location/name	Action and reason
Civil War monument (Denver, Colorado)	Toppled by protesters. Monument honors Colorado citizens who served in the Union Army. It listed battles against Native Americans in addition to battles against the Confederacy. It listed the Sand Creek massacre (a mass killing of Cheyenne and Arapaho Native Americans) as a battle.
Junípero Serra statue (San Francisco, California)	Toppled by protesters. Monument associated with conversion of indigenous people to Catholicism.
Theodore Roosevelt, Rough Rider statue (Portland, Oregon)	Toppled by protesters. Roosevelt is recorded as having had a hostile attitude toward Native Americans.
Abraham Lincoln statue (Portland, Oregon)	Toppled by protesters. "Dakota 38" was spray-painted on the pedestal, a reference to Lincoln's approving the execution of 38 Dakota men after the Dakota War of 1862.
Christopher Columbus monument (Baltimore, Maryland)	After the statue was toppled from its base, it was dumped into Baltimore's Inner Harbor. He was associated with poor treatment of indigenous populations and colonization.
Edward W. Carmack statue (Nashville, Tennessee)	Toppled by protesters. Senator Carmack was an opponent of Ida B. Wells (an NAACP founder) and encouraged retaliation for her support of the civil rights movement.

However, the destruction and vandalization of statues and other monuments were not just isolated to the United States. Table 4.2 illustrates that there was also a great deal of damage done to various monuments outside of the USA. One thing that differentiates the damage done to monuments outside of the USA is the lack of monuments that celebrate the heroes of the Confederacy. However, many monuments were damaged because of links with slavery and imperialism. Table 4.2 is not an exhaustive list and many other examples could be found throughout the world to illustrate that many monuments that could be associated with racism, imperialism, or the poor treatment of indigenous peoples would be considered legitimate targets for the protesters.

Table 4.2   Examples of monuments and destruction by protesters outside the USA

Location/name	Action and reason
Leopold II bust (Brussels, Belgium)	Toppled during the night. Bust associated with imperialism in Africa. The bust was pulled down, red paint was splashed on it, and a photograph of Patrice Lumumba, the independent Congo's first prime minister, was placed on the pedestal.
Cecil Rhodes bust, at the Rhodes Memorial (Cape Town, South Africa)	Removed after being decapitated by protesters. Cecil Rhodes is associated with imperialism in Africa. The head was repaired and reattached in September 2020.
Edward Colston statue (Bristol, UK)	Toppled by protesters and thrown into the harbor. Edward Colston was a slave trader. The defaced statue was put on display at the city's M Shed museum.
Victor Schœlcher bust (Basse-Terre, Guadeloupe)	Decapitated, stolen overnight, and discovered more than 40 kilometers away the following morning. Victor Schœlcher was associated with French imperialism.
Empress Joséphine statue (Fort-de-France, Martinique)	Toppled by protesters. Joséphine, the first wife of Napoleon, was born on Martinique to a family that owned a sugar plantation.
Sir John A. Macdonald monument (Montreal, Canada)	Statue was toppled and decapitated by protesters. John Macdonald was the first Prime Minister of Canada.
Sebastián de Belalcázar equestrian statue (Popayán, Colombia)	Toppled and decapitated by members of the Misak indigenous community. Belalcázar was a Spanish conquistador credited with the foundation of important cities in modern-day Colombia and Ecuador. The monument was located on top of Morro del Tulcán, an indigenous archaeological site.

While monuments to Confederate war heroes and those associated with brutalities towards indigenous peoples seem like obvious and rather unsurprising targets for the anger of the mobs on the street, there were also some other figures that were surprising targets of the mobs. For example, a statue of famed black American abolitionist Frederick Douglass in Rochester, New York was removed from its pedestal by unknown people, damaged, and left at a gorge some distance from the site (Schwartz, 2020). What is especially interesting about this issue is that for many years, Frederick Douglass was revered for his escape from slavery and his outspoken opposition to slavery in his oration and writings. He was also the first black American to run for president of the USA.

Another surprising monument that fell victim to the protesters' ire was a statue of Mohandas Gandhi in London, a statue defaced with "racist" spray-painted onto it (Canton, 2020). The mobs unleased by the death of George Floyd throughout the world went beyond the most obvious targets and seem to have also damaged monuments to those considered heroes by mainstream citizens. On the other hand, the targeting of churches in Canada in 2021 seemed to be a generalized anti-Christian campaign, whether coordinated or not.

The destruction of cultural heritage is nothing new since a great deal of cultural history has been destroyed for various reasons. For example, of all the ancient wonders of the world, only the Great Pyramids of Giza still exist. However, in recent years, the destruction of cultural heritage has been quite deliberate and increasingly a topic for public discussion. In the West, for example, the substantial destruction of ancient sites by ISIS (Curry, 2015) became a major concern, as was the destruction of cultural heritage in Afghanistan (Atai, 2019). What is most noteworthy is that while there was so much interest and concern for the preservation of cultural heritage in the non-Western world (see, for example, Gibson, 2015; Vrdoljak, 2015), there seems to be little organized or vocal opposition to the destruction of cultural heritage that may be controversial in the West.

The monuments that were damaged or destroyed during the 2020 protests/riots and since were not necessarily top-tier tourism magnets to various destinations. However, they were part of the urban landscapes in which they were found and added to the unique qualities of the destinations, enriching the cultural landscape. Sustained attacks by mobs and political authorities to destroy tangible elements of history risk undermining historical memory and rob populations of visible reminders of history. The individuals and mobs that attacked such cultural monuments undermined a good opportunity for the development of tourism, not just because of the potential of dark tourism and interpretive benefits, but something that has potential for developing a more harmonious environment (Carbone, 2022). Inadvertently, destructive mobs may have a negative impact upon tourism, since there is substantial evidence that tourists typically avoid places of unrest, risk, or violence (Llorca-Vivero, 2008; Neumayer, 2004). The actions of the mobs may not only lead to a situation in which a useful tool for interpreting the past is lost but also a situation in which tourism potential is undermined because tourists have less to see of interest and also because they may associate the destination with violence and mayhem. Indeed, as has been argued, the relationship between tourism and peace can be more complicated than one would expect (Farmaki, 2017).

The issues at hand and solutions

It is understandable that current sensitivities may be offended by a prior regime's monuments and symbols. This is an important issue, since individuals interpret aspects of their cultural environment and relate it to themselves at visitor sites (Poria, Reichel, & Biran, 2006), meaning that the cultural monuments are noticed and interpreted not necessarily in their historical context but in relation to the individual viewing the monument. As such, it would be understandable for some historical reminders to be considered impolite or unpleasant in public settings and there are some precedents for how these have been dealt with in the past.

Poria, Ivanov, and Webster (2013) explored how communist heritage was treated or could be treated and explained four prevailing strategies for dealing with a past that many would deem embarrassing or offensive. In their work, they outlined that the policy choices included preserving and protecting the cultural history in place; allowing the cultural history to rot in situ; removing the cultural history to a place that is out of sight and where it could be protected and interpreted consistent with the prevailing modern mores; and the destruction of the cultural history. Table 4.3 illustrates the four major strategies for dealing with embarrassing or offensive monuments or sites and how they can be dealt with, based upon the policy choices discussed by Poria, Ivanov, and Webster (2013).

Table 4.3   Policy choices, values, and examples

Policy	Value implied	Cost	Example(s)
Preserve, protect, and maintain as is in situ	History has value and some is worth investing in	High	Lenin's mausoleum; Auschwitz-Birkenau concentration camp
Leave in situ and do not maintain	History has value but some history is worthy of preservation and other history is not	Low	German pillboxes and bunkers on Danish coast; generic small-scale communist monuments throughout Eastern Europe

Policy	Value implied	Cost	Example(s)
Remove from broad public view and protect and preserve (likely a museum)	History has value but some should be shielded from public view, as it may be controversial or offensive to some	High	Szoborpark/Statue park in Hungary; Theodore Roosevelt statue in New York City moved to storage
Destroy	Some historical remnants must be destroyed, since they offend or embarrass	Low, or one-time expenditure	Charlottesville's Robert E. Lee statue melted down; Königsberg Royal Castle dynamited in 1968; Hitler's bunker in Berlin; destruction of Buddhas in Afghanistan

The first policy choice is the decision to protect and preserve something of historical value. For example, Lenin's mausoleum has been kept as a historical and national monument. While the mausoleum seems to be dedicated to a totalitarian ideology that claimed millions of victims in Russia (and many other countries), it has been preserved and is utilized for tourism. What is interesting about the mausoleum is that it is enjoyed as a memory of a dark and interesting part of Russian history but can also be a point for those who venerate the socialist period of Russian history. Auschwitz-Birkenau is similarly preserved to retain the memory and at great cost (Doerry, 2019), with a great deal of concern with preserving even the most minute details (Miszczyk, Szocinski, & Darowicki, 2016). While the purpose of the preservation of the concentration camp is not for revering those who took part in the genocide, the purpose is to keep a tangible historical venue for tourists to help them reflect upon the genocide to prevent any further genocides in the future.

A second policy is to essentially allow for monuments to rot in place. In some cases, such as with many small-scale monuments to the dominance of communism, many are left to decay where they are. Small towns and big cities have several monuments that are often overlooked or ignored with little or no funds used to preserve them. Similarly, the West coast of Denmark is littered with bunkers that are relatively untouched, a reminder of the German occupation of the country during the World War II. They are likely left in place because the cost of destroying and removing them would be very high and require a massive investment of funds. In Italy, there are many sites left to decay with little or no effort exerted to protect and preserve them (Tondo, 2019). In addition, there are also some examples of the intentional retaining of destruction from conflict to serve as a reminder, such as the Broken Bells of St. Mary's in

Lübeck, Germany, the rubble of Dresden's Frauenkirche until 1996, and rubble in Belgrade.

A third (and rarer) policy is to remove monuments to a location where they do not offend and can be protected. The most interesting and innovative is probably Szoborpark in Hungary. It is a place outside of Budapest where massive monuments to the socialist regime have been placed so that those interested in the socialist period and its art can visit those monuments. At the same time, the monuments are preserved from vandalism as well as removed from the daily view of citizens who do not want to see physical embodiments of a detested political ideology that dominated the country for many decades. Similarly, the removal of the Theodore Roosevelt statue from public view in New York City will preserve it as a piece of artwork and not offend those citizens who disapprove of the 26th President of the United States.

A final policy is simply the destruction of historical monuments. While Auschwitz-Birkenau has been preserved at great expense – including the barracks of the prisoners, as shown in Figure 4.1 – Hitler's bunker in Berlin is noteworthy since there is no attempt to even mark the spot where it was. Instead of utilizing the bunker as an interesting historical site, it was intentionally converted into a parking lot with nothing to denote anything special about the spot. The Soviets destroyed the Königsberg Royal Castle since it was falling into disrepair, meaning that it was easier to declare it a fascist monument and simply erase the German cultural monument from the landscape. In a similar way, the Robert E. Lee statue in Charlottesville will be melted down into something else (Shivaram, 2021).

There is a gamut of opportunities for how to deal with the various forms of cultural heritage. We see that it is not just those types of monuments that are sensitive to those offended by monuments that seemed to reflect something about racial relations but they are also quite international and cross cultural boundaries. For example, the destruction of the massive Buddha statues in Afghanistan (Atai, 2019) can be viewed as either a religious issue or a political one. Likewise, we see that the views of the destruction of the Buddhas may have been different depending upon if a person is from Afghanistan or elsewhere (Chiovenda, 2014). There is also an interesting discussion on the preservation of the much-detested Berlin Wall, a political barrier designed to separate Berliners who were under Soviet tutelage and those in a free-market economy (see, for example, Camia, Menzel, & Bohn, 2019; Harrison, 2011).

These political choices could also be conceptualized as consisting of two dichotomies. The first dichotomy is the issue of cost and whether the public

Figure 4.1   Auschwitz prisoners' brick barracks today

should invest in the preservation of historical monuments. Those monuments that political authorities may see value in preserving may be high on the list for the allocation of funds. For example, the preservation of Auschwitz-Birkenau is costly but authorities (in Poland and elsewhere) see the value in preserving it, have invested in it, and will likely continue to do so. There are other monuments that many would not see as useful in terms of investment, such as the many small-scale communist monuments in central Europe.

However, an additional question is whether a particular monument should be preserved. The preservation of cultural heritage that may offer opportunities to explore the darker parts of history and such elements in the cultural landscape provide opportunities for discussion and reflection, as has been noted (Friedrich, Stone, & Rukesha, 2018; Sharpley, 2020). This is a critical, interesting, and ethical/normative question since it has something to do with how societies view some parts of history and to what extent there are sectors of the society that would like to eliminate or minimize remnants of some parts of history people would like to forget. Table 4.4 illustrates how these two different questions (fund/not fund) and (preserve/not preserve) and the likely policies that such resources, values, and perspectives suggest that a monument should be treated.

Table 4.4   Fund or not fund

	Historical monument should be preserved	Historical monument should not be preserved
Fund preservation	Preserve, protect, and maintain in situ; preserve in museum or other area	–
Not fund preservation	Leave in situ and do not maintain	Leave in situ and do not maintain; destroy (one-off expenditure)

The two choices, fund/not fund and preserve/not preserve, are based not just upon the financial capabilities of the society to maintain the monuments but are also something to think about with regard to the historical monuments and their value to modern culture. While some ugly parts of history (for example, the genocide of Jewish populations during World War II in Europe) may be deemed to be worthy of protecting and preserving since their intended lesson is to prevent future genocides, some other ugly parts of history seem to be worthy of destruction. One interesting theme that seems to illustrate which history seems to be worthy of preservation seems to be the interests behind preservation. While international Jewry and the enemies of fascism may have substantial resources, there are no substantial and organized interests that would want to preserve monuments to the Confederacy or glorify the enslavement of black people in the USA.

Finally, the preservation of historical monuments seems to be an issue not just concerning the availability of public funds but also the interplay between the prevailing political and social ideology in society and the prevailing attitudes towards the past. In the case of Lenin's mausoleum, it seems that while the prevailing modern nationalist ideology of the current regime in Russia is clearly in conflict with Soviet ideology, attitudes towards what otherwise would be a national disgrace and visible reminder of a disgraced ideology are interpreted as something that has historical value (and is also venerated by those who cling to their communist ideology and past). Auschwitz-Birkenau, on the other hand, is preserved to serve as a reminder to future generations. It should be noted that these two preserved large monuments are not particularly mobile, meaning that it would be hard to remove them to place them in a more appropriate spot. At any rate, it must be seen that there seems to be substantial interest in preserving these two historical reminders.

Those monuments that are left in place to rot seem to largely be understood as unfortunate small-scale objects that are reminders of unpleasant historical times but either inconvenient to remove or inoffensive enough that they can just be ignored. Thus, the ideological element seems to be present but, for some reason, it does not reach a threshold that brings enough ire to locals to destroy on their own accord or political forces to look into their destruction.

The most radical solution seems to be based upon the inconsistency of the prevailing ideology in society and the historical ideology. The examples dealt with here seem to suggest that those in political power may want to destroy history to either reclaim something or prevent the return of ideological foes. In the case of Königsberg Royal Castle, the Soviets not only wanted to illustrate dominance over their ideological enemies, the fascists (even though the castle predated fascism by many centuries), as well as erase a visible reminder that Königsberg was a German city and not a Russian one, historically. The destruction and paving over of Hitler's bunker was ideological, to prevent it from being venerated by National Socialists and to prevent the ideology and its adherents from returning. In addition, the destruction of the Buddhas in Afghanistan seems to be influenced primarily by religious ideology, done to illustrate the dominance of Islam and also to prevent a resurgence of Buddhism, even if such a resurgence is highly unlikely. What is most outlandish, in this case, is that the Robert E. Lee statue was sentenced to destruction by the political authorities, since there is no realistic threat of a Confederacy resurgence nor of a revival of race-based slavery in the USA. However, in the case of the Robert E. Lee statue, the existence of the statue itself did attract controversy, protests, and violence at the place where it was displayed, meaning it risked being a magnet for continuing unrest; its removal alleviated potential future problems for city authorities.

Conclusion: peace, social justice, and the commodification of history

In conclusion, the question of the destruction of historical monuments is a major question that could result in a more sterile historical landscape in many destinations (Sanni, 2021). If all public monuments are removed from the cultural landscape, it would have a noteworthy impact on the built environment, subtracting from the charm of destinations and largely undermining tourism potential. However, we are living in a time in which there is a stress on the removal of cultural monuments and this could have implications for travel and tourism since the cultural monuments of a location are what makes the location distinctive. The potential sterility of destinations becomes a possibility in the future. Indeed, there are distinct tensions between history and tourism, as has been noted (Nuryanti, 1996), illustrating the potential for history to attract visitors, although some monuments may also repel them.

By removing aspects of the built environment that make destinations unique, there is a risk that there will be increased sterility of destinations. In terms of research, one possible avenue to explore is the value of the built and cultural environments to visitors. While destinations attract travelers because of their cultural environments, an exploration of the value that people put into the preservation of cultural history at specific sites is worthy of study. It would also be beneficial to see how some controversial aspects of cultural heritage can be leveraged for a greater sense of peace and reconciliation, since it is possible that dark tourism and controversial heritage preservation may actually impede reconciliation and peace-building.

In addition, future research should investigate further the different visions of the value of cultural history viewed from the outside and the inside of a culture, as done by Chiovenda (2014). We are living in a time in which Westerners are quite adamant about the preservation of cultural monuments outside of the Western world but there is less concern with the preservation of such monuments in the West. Why Westerners seem to value non-Western cultural heritage more than Western cultural heritage is somewhat enigmatic and leads to a question of ideologies and self-perception that seems to be specific to Westerners.

One likely topic for research is political ideologies and their perceptions on the preservation of history. The social justice movement and its direct antecedents of the Frankfurt School and Critical Theory tend to have a very negative approach towards Western societies, societies that they wish to change forever into Marxist utopias. Marcuse (1969) is mainstream in his writing on the topic, citing that tolerance should be extended to movements on the left to revolutionize society, while such tolerance should not be extended to the right. Also typical of the Frankfurt School is Althusser's (1972) contention that there is an ideological and repressive state apparatus. The Frankfurt School and Critical Theory have central beliefs that include the use of power to fundamentally transform society by using power to destroy institutions that are reflective of capitalist values. As such, the movements that exploded violently in the summer of 2020 and since can largely be seen as movements that follow the thought systems of the Frankfurt School and Critical Theory, seeking to destroy the culture and institutions of the West with the use of power without a detailed plan for setting up what would supplant them.

Future research should not just look into the cultural monuments that exist all over the world but also look into the motivations of those forces that seek to destroy said cultural monuments. While the Frankfurt School and Critical Theory have successfully infiltrated cultural institutions in the West, there is still some resistance to their ideological takeover of schools, universities, law, and other institutions. Part of the resistance is likely from the lack of pragmatic institutions that would successfully replace Western institutions. For example, while there was a great deal of pressure to defund police departments in the USA following the George Floyd protests and riots, there were no viable institutions to replace them. Similarly, Critical Theory does not have viable cultural monuments that would be inspirational nor accepted by large swaths of society, although they have slogans that seem to inspire and are accepted by many.

Future research should also examine if the social justice movement has damaged tourism and undermined opportunities for peace and reconciliation. While the social justice movement, in its most superficial understanding, should lead to greater understanding between peoples and create an environment in which people feel safer, with the removal of anything controversial in the environment, it may be that it creates a sterile landscape that undermines tourism potential and does little or nothing to promote mutual understanding. In a deeper way, it would be good for future researchers to investigate more thoroughly how the social justice movement identifies targets for its ire, so that proactive moves can be taken to protect cultural heritage monuments. There may also be potential to utilize the adherents of the social justice movement in ways that would allow them to limit the damage to cultural heritage so that it can be used for the promotion of peace and tourism. Finding a pathway to exploit social justice instincts in ways that are positive, leading to peace-building, an increase in the quality of life, and the development of the economy would be a very fruitful research path.

In the end, sterile landscapes void of cultural monuments will lead to a dull and uninspired ecosystem for tourism. The George Floyd protests/riots resulted in a re-evaluation of such monuments but did not offer anything inspiring to replace them. These movements are reminders that there have been historical movements that have destroyed a great deal of cultural history and that there will likely always be movements to destroy cultural monuments and history. The continued path of these movements suggests a bleak future for tourism and social harmony, since they are ideological movements that see many physical manifestations of history as threatening and offensive and as such a target for destruction. Continued internal strife leading to violence and the destruction of cultural monuments creates an environment in which few successful tourism enterprises could flourish. In addition, the continual erosion of socially agreed-upon values and mores undermines social cohesion and peace in Western societies, illustrating that few or no central characters are accepted and revered by the broader public. While the Frankfurt School and Critical Theory seem to have a penchant for the destruction of cultural monuments, it is questionable as to whether they have anything with staying power to replace the West's current monuments.

References

Althusser, L. (1972), Ideology and ideological state apparatuses: notes towards an investigation, in L. Althusser (ed.), *Lenin and Philosophy and Other Essays* (pp. 85–126), New York: Monthly Review Press.

Atai, J. (2019), The destruction of Buddhas: dissonant heritage, religious or political iconoclasm? *Tourism Culture & Communication*, 19(4), 303–12. https://doi.org/10.3727/194341419X15554157596173.

Black Lives Matter (n.d.), Herstory, https://blacklivesmatter.com/herstory/ (accessed May 9, 2022).

Buckley, C. (2020), Chinese doctor, silenced after warning of outbreak, dies from coronavirus. *New York Times*, https://www.nytimes.com/2020/02/06/world/asia/chinese-doctor-Li-Wenliang-coronavirus.html (accessed May 9, 2022).

Camia, C., Menzel, C., & Bohn, A. (2019), A positive living-in-history effect: the case of the fall of the Berlin Wall, *Memory*, 27(10), 1381–9, https://doi.org/10.1080/09658211.2019.1661494.

Canton, N. (2020), 35 cops injured in further London violence as Gandhi statue defaced, *Times of India*, https://timesofindia.indiatimes.com/world/uk/35-cops-injured-in-further-london-violence-as-gandhi-statue-defaced/articleshow/76269593.cms (accessed May 9, 2022).

Carbone, F. (2022), "Don't look back in anger": war museums' role in the post conflict tourism-peace nexus, *Journal of Sustainable Tourism*, 30(2–3), 565–83, https://doi.org/10.1080/09669582.2021.1901909.

Chiovenda, M. K. (2014), Sacred blasphemy: global and local views of the destruction of the Bamyan Buddha statues in Afghanistan, *Journal of Muslim Minority Affairs*, 34(4), 410–24, https://doi.org/10.1080/13602004.2014.984904.

Curry, A. (2015), Here are the ancient sites ISIS has damaged, *National Geographic*, https://www.nationalgeographic.com/history/article/150901-isis-destruction-looting -ancient-sites-iraq-syria-archaeology (accessed May 9, 2022).

Doerry, M. (2019), The immense challenge of preserving Auschwitz, *Spiegel International*, https://www.spiegel.de/international/the-immense-challenge-of-preserving -auschwitz-a-1248007.html (accessed May 9, 2022).

Dzsurdzsa, C. (2021), UPDATE: a map of the 68 churches that have been vandalized or burned since the residential schools announcement, *True North*, https://tnc.news/ 2021/08/23/a-map-of-every-church-burnt-or-vandalized-since-the-residential-school -announcements/ (accessed May 9, 2022).

Farmaki, A. (2017), The tourism and peace nexus, *Tourism Management*, 59, 528–40, https://doi.org/10.1016/j.tourman.2016.09.012.

Farmaki, A., & Stergiou, D. (2021), Peace and tourism: bridging the gap through justice, *Peace and Change*, https://doi.org/10.1111/pech.12472.

Friedrich, M., Stone, P. R., & Rukesha, P. (2018), Dark tourism, difficult heritage, and memorialisation: a case of the Rwandan genocide, in R. Stone, P. Hartmann, R. Seaton, T. Sharpley, & L. White (eds.), *The Palgrave Handbook of Dark Tourism Studies*, London: Palgrave Macmillan, https://doi.org/10.1057/978-1-137-47566-4_11.

Gibson, E. (2015), The destruction of historical monuments should be a war crime, *The Wall Street Journal*, https://www.wsj.com/articles/the-destruction-of-cultural -heritage-should-be-a-war-crime-1425073230 (accessed May 9, 2022).

Gonzalez, M. (2021), Black Lives Matter leader resigns, but this radical Marxist agenda will continue, *Heritage*, https://www.heritage.org/progressivism/commentary/black -lives-matter-leader-resigns-radical-marxist-agenda-will-continue (accessed May 9, 2022).

Harrison, H. M. (2011), The Berlin Wall and its resurrection as a site of memory, *German Politics & Society*, 29(2), 78–106, https://doi.org/10.3167/gps.2011.290206.

Jamal, T., & Camargo, B. A. (2014), Sustainable tourism, justice and an ethic of care: toward the Just Destination, *Journal of Sustainable Tourism*, 22(1), 11–30, https://doi .org/10.1080/09669582.2013.786084.

Justice, T. (2021), Estimates: George Floyd riots to cost 66 times more than Capitol damage, *The Federalist*, https://thefederalist.com/2021/02/26/estimates-george-floyd -riots-to-cost-66-times-more-than-capitol-damage/ (accessed May 9, 2022).

Kechen, M. (2013), Social justice: concepts, principles, tools, and challenges, https:// www.unescwa.org/sites/default/files/pubs/pdf/social-justice-concepts-principles-tools -challenges-english.pdf (accessed May 9, 2022).

Kulish, N. (2022), After raising $90 million in 2020, Black Lives Matter has $42 million in assets, *New York Times*, https://www.nytimes.com/2022/05/17/business/blm-black -lives-matter-finances.html (accessed August 8, 2022).

Laframboise, K., & Olivier, A. (2020), Legault supports anti-racism protesters but says there is no systemic discrimination in province, *Global News*, https://globalnews.ca/ news/7010714/montreal-george-floyd-protest-arrests (accessed May 9, 2022).

Lindsay, J. (2022), *Race Marxism: The Truth about Critical Race Theory and Praxis*, Orlando, FL: New Discourses.

Llorca-Vivero, R. (2008), Terrorism and international tourism: new evidence, *Defence and Peace Economics*, 19(2), 169–88.

Mallinson, N., & Ackerman, M. (2020), London Black Lives Matter team says next pro-tests will be largest yet, *The Evening Standard*, https://www.standard.co.uk/evening -standard/news/uk/london-black-lives-matter-george-floyd-protest-a4457621.html (accessed May 9, 2022).

Marcuse, H. (1969), Repressive tolerance, in R. P. Wolff, B. Moore, Jr., & H. Marcuse (eds.), *A Critique of Pure Tolerance* (pp. 95–137), Boston, MA: Beacon Press.

McEvoy, J. (2020), 14 Days of Protests, 19 Dead, *Forbes*, https://www.forbes.com/sites/jemimamcevoy/2020/06/08/14-days-of-protests-19-dead/?sh=49e4fb044de4 (accessed May 9, 2022).

Miszczyk, A., Szocinski, M., & Darowicki, K. (2016), Restoration and preservation of the reinforced concrete poles of fence at the former Auschwitz concentration and extermination camp', *Case Studies in Construction Materials*, 4, 42–8, https://doi.org/10.1016/j.cscm.2015.12.002.

Neumayer, E. (2004), The impact of political violence on tourism: dynamic cross-national estimation, *The Journal of Conflict Resolution*, 48(2), 259–81.

Nuryanti, W. (1996), Heritage and postmodern tourism, *Annals of Tourism Research*, 23(2), 249–60.

Pew Research Center (2020), More than nine-in-ten people worldwide live in countries with travel restrictions amid COVID-19, https://www.pewresearch.org/fact-tank/2020/04/01/more-than-nine-in-ten-people-worldwide-live-in-countries-with-travel-restrictions-amid-covid (accessed May 9, 2022).

Pluckrose, H., & Lindsay, J. (2020), *Cynical Theories: How Activist Scholarship Made Everything about Race, Gender, and Identity and Why This Harms Everyone*, Durham, NC: Pitchstone.

Poria, Y., Ivanov, S., & Webster, C. (2013), Attitudes and willingness to donate towards heritage restoration: an exploratory study about Bulgarian socialist monuments, *Journal of Heritage Tourism*, 9(1), 68–74, https://doi.org/10.1080/1743873X.2013.778266.

Poria, Y., Reichel, A., & Biran, A. (2006), Heritage site management: motivations and expectations, *Annals of Tourism Research*, 33(1), 1172–88.

Rawls, J. (1971), *A Theory of Justice*, Cambridge, MA: Harvard University Press.

Sanni, J. S. (2021), The destruction of historical monuments and the danger of sanitising history, *Philosophia*, 49, 1187–200, https://doi-org.proxy.bsu.edu/10.1007/s11406-020-00275-6.

Schwartz, M. S. (2020), Frederick Douglass statue torn down on anniversary of famous speech, NPR, https://www.npr.org/sections/live-updates-protests-for-racial-justice/2020/07/06/887618102/frederick-douglass-statue-vandalized-on-anniversary-of-famous-speech (accessed May 9, 2022).

Sharma, S. (2021), Statue of queen pulled down by protesters in Canada, *The Independent*, https://www.independent.co.uk/news/world/americas/queen-victoria-statue-canada-indigenous-graves-b1876803.html (accessed May 9, 2022).

Sharpley, R. (2020), 'Kamikaze' heritage tourism in Japan: a pathway to peace and understanding? *Journal of Heritage Tourism*, 15(6), 709–26, https://doi.org/10.1080/1743873X.2020.1758117.

Shivaram, D. (2021), Charlottesville's statue of Robert E. Lee will soon be melted down into public art, National Public Radio, https://www.npr.org/2021/12/07/1062106020/charlottesvilles-confederate-statue-robert-e-lee-public-art (accessed May 9, 2022).

Tondo, L. (2019), Italy's new ruins: heritage sites being lost to neglect and looting, *The Guardian*, https://www.theguardian.com/world/2019/may/28/italys-new-ruins-heritage-sites-being-lost-to-neglect-and-looting (accessed May 9, 2022).

United Nations (2006), The International Forum for Social Development: social justice in an open world: the role of the United Nations, United Nations, https://www.un.org/esa/socdev/documents/ifsd/SocialJustice.pdf (accessed May 9, 2022).

Vrdoljak, A. F. (2015), The criminalisation of the intentional destruction of cultural heritage, in M. Orlando & T. Bergin (eds.), *Forging a Socio-Legal Approach to Environmental Harm: Global Perspectives* (chapter 12), London: Routledge.

5 Dark tourism acceptance and peacebuilding in troubled destinations

Vasilis Papavasiliou, Elena Malkawi and Maria Hadjielia Drotarova

Introduction

Odd or normal, disgusting, perhaps interesting to see people taking photos next to dead bodies or at places where others lost their lives. Dark tourism has a long story. Its theoretical origins date back to 1993 when Rojek introduced the concept of "Black Spots". This concept is related to "the commercial developments of sites in which celebrities or a large number of people met a sudden or violent death" (Stone, 2006, p. 148). In 1996, Seaton suggested that dark tourism is mostly associated with events, monuments and sites from the Middle Ages and the Romantic period of the eighteenth and nineteenth centuries. These specific periods were known for their contemplation of death. Seaton (1996) refers to this form of tourism as "thanatopic traditions" where touristic sites take the form of graves and cemeteries, prisons and places of public executions. Dark tourism, as a concept, was introduced in 1996 by Foley and Lennon (1996) who defined the term as tourism "associated with sites of death, disaster and depravity" (Lennon & Foley, 1999, p. 46).

Miles (2002) came to argue that dark does not always represent the same dark, and he questioned what is real and what is visual in the context of "what is a museum". A museum where an actual death took place is not the same as the one which symbolizes death only, and Miles (2002) introduced the "dark-darker framework of dark tourism" where a product of dark tourism is, in this specific case, a tourist's experience. For instance, Auschwitz-Birkenau Museum in Poland represents "darker tourism", whereas the U.S. Holocaust Memorial Museum in Washington is a lighter form of dark tourism. An essential development in dark tourism research is Stone's (2006) "typological foundation of dark tourism supply", also referred to as the "seven dark suppliers". Within this, Stone conceptualized seven different suppliers of dark tourism: (1) a dark fun factory, (2) dark exhibitions, (3) dark dungeons, (4) dark resting places, (5) dark shrines, (6) dark conflict sites, and (7) dark camps of genocides. Within this typology identified he gave characteristics, examples and descriptions of what each dark tourism supplier entailed (Stone, 2006).

As years passed, researchers called for more research studies on "dark tourism" to shed light on its emergence, content and nuances (Sharpley & Stone, 2008). The tourism research community responded effectively and, today, dark tourism represents an established area of research (Podoshen, 2018; White & Frew, 2013). Despite the growing number of studies, there is still shortage of academic attention on how dark tourism can help people in destinations with troubled pasts to accept violent events and how such acceptance can eventually lead to reconciliation and peacebuilding. This is surprising as dark tourism was recognized as contributing to the acknowledgement and acceptance of past violent and negative events, leading to greater understanding between people and potentially moving towards peace (Honey, 2008). To this end, this chapter focuses on the island of Cyprus – a destination tormented by conflict for decades – and discusses the issues presented in the guided tour narratives from the de facto Turkish Republic of Northern Cyprus and the Republic of Cyprus. This chapter discloses that various (troubled past) countries have different, perhaps personal approaches when acknowledging their dark pasts, as some actively commemorate and educate while others choose to reframe their culture. The chapter concludes with a discussion of related implications to peacebuilding and a recommendation for further research.

Literature review

Accepting places of violence and death

In their study devoted to genocide, Friedrich and Johnston (2013) employed the term thanatourism rather than dark tourism, because of thanatourism's lesser media popularity. Lee et al. (2012) position thanatourism as helping to understand better peace tourist sites such as Mt Kumgang resort in North Korea instead of war tourism or dark tourism. Further, it seems that slavery heritage seems to be studied more under the concept of thanatourism rather than dark tourism (Buzinde & Santos, 2008; Seaton, 2001). On the other hand, Yankholmes and McKercher (2015) argue that slavery heritage sites such as those connected to the transatlantic slave trade cannot be placed and studied under the concept of either thanatourism or dark tourism. The issue still remains debatable concerning the exact distinction between thanatourism and dark tourism. Having said this, it is evident that a destination's acknowledgement and acceptance of places with negative pasts and associations with death is pivotal in moving forward.

Germany, for example, has actively acknowledged its difficult past and has set up monuments and tours to educate the public about the atrocities of the Second World War (Cohen, 1995; Grüning, 2010; Rivera, 2008), although there has been a great debate on how much of Nazi history and Nazi-erected monuments/buildings should be displayed, preserved and converted into alternate used spaces, since it is argued that there should be a balance "about how to recognise the place of National Socialism as an unavoidable part of Germany identity but at the same time try to prevent it taking on too central and sacred role" (Macdonald, 2006, p. 22). On the other hand, countries like Croatia have actively erased their "difficult" and unwanted pasts. Croatia is reframing the culture rather than acknowledging the war with Yugoslavia and the Balkan regions (Beirman, 2003; Hall, 2002; Rivera, 2008).

In a recent article published by Beerda (2022) for the Dutch Research Council, it is highlighted that heritage tourism sites around the Amsterdam canals bring back traces of past slavery. "Black Heritage Tours in Amsterdam are an example of how tourism can compress time and space. It shows that slavery was not just a faraway matter. It was also here" (Beerda, 2022). Consequently, it is understood that through the participation of tourists engaging in dark tourism, places are kept alive by ticket sales, the revenue used for restoration and maintenance. In this sense, it can be argued that history that was deliberately made absent becomes visible through the activities of tourism.

Destinations focus on tourism marketing tactics in order to distinguish themselves from other places. Doing so creates issues in the long run of stereotyping and difficulty in escaping the general perceived image of a destination (Olick, 1998). For example, people from across globe visit the Nazi Nuremburg rally site due to the fact that they recognize Germany and Germans in relation to it. Thus, Nazi relics and Holocaust history generally have a more global tourist pull (Macdonald, 2006). However, there still seems to be a debate on the issue of how many dark heritage sites should be promoted and to what end should places where death took place be marketed, remembered or forgotten. Careful consideration needs to be placed on what and how these places and spaces of death are selected and interpreted. Whatever the case, troubled destinations where death, war, slavery and execution existed need to acknowledge their pasts. Dark tourism can help distinguish destinations from other places and even foster reconciliation with their pasts and bring peace.

Memory representation of troubled pasts

Memory is a process, not a thing (Zelizer, 1995); neither is it a static vessel that carries the past into the present. Following Olick and Robbins (1998), memory is approached through four key concepts: identity, contestation, malleability and persistence. Social identities are constituted mainly through memory processes. Where troubled pasts are concerned, national, ethnic and civic identities need to be taken into consideration. The construction process involves the selection and interpretation of past historical events. Hence, identity is almost always situated within cultural struggles (Sturken, 1997). Thus, "different stories vie for a place in history" (Sturken, 1997, p. 1) while at the same time collective groups of people fight for their stories (Olick & Robbins, 1998). Contestation is at the centre of the study of the past. Passerini (2003) remarks that the twentieth century has been, for the most part, a time of cancellation of memory. This has been attempted by totalitarian regimes but it can also happen in democratic or transitional regimes. Since the mid-1990s, public interest in memory has grown considerably. "Troubled" pasts are a common scholarly topic among humanists, and social and political scientists. A key concept in the study of the past is collective memory.

According to Halbwachs (1992), memory is clearly situated not in the subjective minds of individuals but in social arrangements: "it is in society that people normally acquire their memories (p. 38). It is also in society that they recall, recognize and localize their memories. Collective memory, the active past that forms our identities (Bell, 2006; Roudometof, 2002), refers less to the past and the way the past is remembered than to the present, denominating itself through actions and statements of people (Kansteiner, 2002) – what Assmann (1998) calls "mnemohistory". Consequently, the management of difficult pasts is especially challenging due to the fact that it can prove to be (i) embarrassing to those sponsoring the remembrance of specific events, (ii) sensitive and emotionally charged due to the association to casualties and destruction or people displacement and (iii) a contested interpretation of events (Fine & Beim, 2007; Schudson, 1984). The acknowledgement of controversial pasts is, however, necessary for the construction of identity but also peacebuilding (Kuus, 2002; Shapira, 1996; Tindemans, 1996).

Interpretation of controversial historical events in Europe

The fall of communism brought a cataclysmic reinterpretation of the past in the East and the West (Irwin-Zarecka, 1995). The Holocaust, as an integral part of European experience and European identity, contributed to a radical re-evaluation of the Second World War as a shared European fight against fascism (Mälksoo, 2009). Lastly, within the rubric of postmodernity, postmodernists (France & Reynolds, 1996; Huyssen, 2012) deconstructed the conceptual underpinnings of linear historicity, truth and identity, raising interest in the links between history, memory and power. The politics of memory highlight issues of popular memory, memory contestation and instrumentalization of the past. Public debates on historical issues such as the Holocaust, civil wars, authoritarian regimes and dictatorships, communism or colonial past are less about historiography than about contemporary political identities. The Second World War (the dark years of Europe) became – through its central role in European memory – a dominant site of victimhood and atrocity in Europe that triggered the need for European integration. Habermas and Derrida (2003) claim that contemporary Europe is the result of the experience of the totalitarian regimes of the twentieth century and through the Holocaust.

Beyond monuments and public celebrations, representations of the past in genres such as cinema, oral tradition, theatrical plays, textbooks, art, comics, memoirs, photography and online spaces show the "democratization" of the flow of memories, creating a truly novel commemorative universe, where new categories of memory makers, mediators and consumers emerge. Collective memories brought new perspectives into the public sphere and provided new narrative paths to deal with the past. At the same time, however, the emergence of alternate stories in recent decades deconstructed some myths that for a long time constituted the cornerstones of post-war European societies (i.e., about unity against the Axis and the mass character of civil or armed resistance). As these myths are increasingly being contested, so is the idea of European integration (Spohn, 2005; Verovšek, 2016).

Trauma, post-memory and the third-generation phenomenon

The habit of violence, speechlessness and helplessness are transmitted on a genetic level. There is a whole field of study on post-memory research (Frost, 2010; Hirsch, 2008; Wolf, 2019) about how trauma is passed on to the next generations. The interesting aspect about this is that it works exactly like memory. Victims' children can't physically remember it, but the knowledge they get about it isn't just information. It is exactly something in between knowledge and memory; it is knowledge that lives on at a very emotional level, found subconsciously. Just like memory, this knowledge shapes a person's reactions in the present (Wolf, 2019).

Post-war generations have knowledge about what the aggressor can do. For them, this knowledge is the undisputed truth that lives at a very deep psychological level. This knowledge and interpretations are not laid down by personal experiences, but by the experiences of their ancestors. This is known as the third-generation phenomenon (Winship & Knowles, 1996). Countries that have dealt with aggression illustrate that it is impossible to simply forget large-scale violence against fellow citizens (Assmann & Clift, 2016; Novick, 2000). It is postulated that cultural trauma is "a discursive response to a tear in the social fabric, occurring when the foundations of established collective identity are shaken by one or a series of seemingly interrelated occurrences" (Eyerman, Madigan, & Ring, 2017, p. 13).

Moving forward without talking about the past increases trauma within a destination. It is displaced into the subconscious of the local citizens, which, one way or another, will at some point in time surface and will need to be addressed (Bohleber, 2007; Neal, 1998). As such collective memories are "subject to transformation by the present when they are retrieved" (Bohleber, 2007, p. 329). Thus, the past can be reinterpreted due to trauma and reinterpreting the past allows you to change the present (Siegert, 2016). Consequently, it is important to emphasize the importance of dark tourism sites within troubled destinations and highlight their contributions to peacebuilding since elements of narrative selectivity by tourist guides can actually foster nationalist discourses rather than reconciliation with past traumatic events.

Cyprus: the study context

Cyprus is an island located in the Eastern Mediterranean Sea. It is a crossroads between vital pathways that link North Africa and the Middle East to Europe. The island has had a long and vibrant history due to its rich trade links, and conquests by colonialists such as the Franks, Romans, Venetians, Ottomans and, last but not least, the British (Catling, 1980; Karageorghis, Peltenburg & Swiny, 1979). Consequently, Cyprus is a beacon of culture and beauty in this region, featuring a diverse range of languages and customs. Due to its rich history as well as beautiful landscape, the island quickly became a popular tourist destination with tourism representing an important pillar of the Cyprus economy.

Cyprus has also become known for its troubled past owing to the conflict that arose between its two main communities, the Greek Cypriots and Turkish Cypriots. Tensions between the two communities arose in the late 1950s when Greek Cypriots expressed a desire to unify with Greece. Being under British rule at the time, the Greek Cypriot military organization – National Organization of Cypriot Fighters (EOKA) – revolted against the British in an effort to achieve the goal of unification with the motherland (Enosis), much to the displeasure of the Turkish Cypriots. In the end, Cyprus was given its independence by the British and became a republic in 1960. However, throughout the decade, intercommunal violence climaxed leading to a buffer zone being established in 1963, known as the Green Line, which divided the island into two. The line became impassable in 1974 when Turkey invaded Cyprus and occupied the northern part of the island, which became the self-declared Turkish Republic of Northern Cyprus that is only recognized by Turkey (Bryant & Papadakis, 2012; Cyprus Friendship Programme, 2017; Stavrinides, 1975).

As a result, around 160,000 Greek Cypriots were displaced to the southern part of the island while 40,000 Turkish Cypriots moved to the northern part. The two communities lived in complete isolation from each other until 2003, when the Turkish Cypriot administration allowed access to the north, setting up checkpoints at various parts along the Green Line, since members of both communities cross the Green Line, albeit for different reasons. According to Farmaki et al. (2019), most of the Greek Cypriots visited the north out of curiosity and nostalgia while the Turkish Cypriots visited the south for shopping and entertainment.

Cyprus' European Union (EU) accession in 2004 has made the "Cyprus problem" a European one, a constant source of tension in EU–Turkey relations that hampers political stability in the region. Despite ongoing negotiations and the EU endorsement of a final settlement, there is a real risk that the existing division will be permanent. Thus, the de facto Turkish Republic of Northern Cyprus will either become recognized and Cyprus will officially have two recognized states, or a resolution to the conflict will be found (e.g., the formation of a federal state). Within this context, it is interesting to examine the representation of the island's contested dark tourism sites that present contradicting narratives of the history and conflict.

Dark tourism readiness in Cyprus: "attractions" or "memorials"

Cyprus resonates in an ambiguous historical pool that leads to a kaleidoscope of destination identity opinions (Bryant & Papadakis, 2012). Both the southern and the northern areas of the island have had a powerful position to encompass and promote official and trusted narratives (Attalides, 2003; Mavratsas, 1997; Morag, 2004; Nevzat & Hatay, 2009; Pollis, 1996; Vural & Özuyanık, 2008). Reflecting on the timeline of historical past events, the Greek Cypriot and Turkish Cypriot tourism authorities have different representations of collective memories. Each tries to attempt to shape their own communities based on their individual objectives and political agendas to stress and/or distinguish who they are. Hence, emphasis on selected monuments of dark associations has been "used" by each side to project their own narratives and purposes. Consequently, it can be argued that the island is stuck in a "liminal state" (Higgott & Nossal, 2008; Rumelili, 2012) in which it has never really identified one unique narrative to the world of what it really means to be a Cypriot islander.

Herewith, tourism has the possibility of assuming the role of a catalyst for positive changes in behaviour. Therefore, "peace must be more than an absence of conflict, and tourism must be worked on in a way that truly benefits the local communities and the environment" (Honey, 2008, p. 1). However, it is noted that dark heritage interpretation in troubled destinations like Cyprus is often the product of political direction, commemorating the past and to a great extent influencing the future of a society (Farmaki & Antoniou, 2017). In this context, arguably, dark heritage is assumed to serve a political purpose directed towards the local communities. The selective narratives on particular sites are not geared mainly towards tourism purposes. They essentially create a dichotomy between the two communities (Turkish Cypriot and Greek Cypriot) since each selects and represents their own narratives based on their own interpretations of past events.

According to Papadakis (1998), in societies where there are polarizing disparities along ethno-national lines, political party ideologies infiltrate historical and educational narratives. Collective groups distinguish themselves from other collective groups by emphasizing the differences between the two rather than the similarities. Consequently, this selectivity of narratives and historical interpretations creates a "self–other" relationship (Kuus, 2002). Cyprus' historical narrative stresses the nation's suffering at the hands of the "other" in order to justify its political objectives. In this sense, it is impossible to define oneself without also identifying what one is not. In doing so, troubled destinations cause conflicts between themselves and others (Brown, 2000; Kuus, 2002). Both Turkey and Greece, for example, exclude from their own historical consciousness the past and culture of the "others" and any similarities are not acknowledged and are sometimes even degraded (Millas, 2005). These ethno-nationalistic sentiments are ideological instruments that stipulate and infiltrate popular loyalty to the nationalist interpretations of history and, in the case of Cyprus, justify and typify nationalistic projects such as "Enosis" (Cyprus union with Greece) and "Taksim" (Cyprus union with Turkey) (Morag, 2004).

In the Republic of Cyprus, dark tourism sites make no direct reference to 1974, but rather emphasize the struggles and victimization of the Cypriots under British colonial rule, making indirect inferences on how Cypriots are victims (Farmaki & Antoniou, 2017). The de facto Turkish Republic of Northern Cyprus, however, makes strong emphasis of the 1974 atrocities using artefacts and photos of Turkish Cypriots killed by Greek Cypriots. Farmaki and Antoniou (2017) have attempted to demonstrate how conflicting heritage interpretation in a post-conflict context is frequently the result of political direction and selective commemoration. Through the presentation and discussion of the cases of two opposing dark sites such as the national museums on the divided island of Cyprus, the authors have identified that the management of such sites is in opposition to peacebuilding efforts taking place in a post-conflict context (Farmaki & Antoniou, 2017). The national struggle museum in northern Cyprus opened in 1989. Its purpose is to remember and teach generations to come about the struggles undertaken by Turkish Cypriots from 1878 to the present day. It focuses on a narrative in which Greek Cypriots cannot be trusted, giving evidence of their atrocities as proof (i.e., Turkish Cypriot blood stains on artefacts caused by Greek Cypriot nationalist aggression). The national struggle museum in southern Cyprus exhibits records, photographs, heroes' personal objects and other artefacts related to the Greek Cypriots' resistance to British rule. The museum uses references to British occupation and Greek Cypriot victimhood rather than references to Turkish Cypriots and the atrocities of the 1974 Turkish invasion of Cyprus. Farmaki and Antoniou (2017) conclude that visitation to dark heritage sites in Cyprus is culturally motivated rather than death-related, which suggests that efforts should be combined to target particular visitor demographics if the potential for reconciliation offered by dark tourism is to be fully realized. Similarly, Bounia and Stylianou-Lambert (2011) argue that national museums in both parts of Cyprus "construct, reinforce and project specific dominant values and national narratives. [With national museums] run exclusively by various ministries and the vertical bureaucratic systems of decision-making that [this] entails, these museums project a cultural policy that is unavoidably influenced by political situations" (p. 190).

Disputes over the border/demarcation line in Cyprus echo basic disagreements over how history should be presented in public. In the southern part of the island, the claims on land are supported by archaeology. "The emphasis placed on archaeology by the Greek Cypriot government and other organizations (the majority of South Cyprus' state museums) is justified within the context of Hellenism and its two main tenets, antiquity and Christianity" (Bounia and Stylianou-Lambert, 2011, p. 190). However, the de facto Turkish Cypriot administration places more emphasis on historical aspects rather than archaeological claims. "Its main museums focus on aspects of the Ottoman past of the island – claiming, in this sense, their share of it. There is an attempt to justify the separation, by placing emphasis on the impossibility of co-existence between the two communities ..." (Bounia and Stylianou-Lambert, 2011, p. 190).

The Greek Cypriots themselves are polarized over certain events – one example is the infamous EOKA-B coup. During 1963–64 and 1967, tensions between the two communities escalated within the island. This had led to major political confrontations between Greece and Turkey for resolution of the matters in Cyprus since they were guarantors for peacekeeping as per the Treaty of Guarantee signed in 1960. Because of this dispute during the 1960s the Turkish Cypriots suffered the majority of losses (Papadakis, 1998). Notably after 1967, confrontations between the communities eased but new inter-conflicts between the Greek Cypriots began. The so called "ultra-nationalists" (a small group of right-wing extremists that still aimed for union with Greece) formed the EOKA-B and staged a coup on 15 July 1974 against the island's president, Archbishop Makarios. These events gave Turkey the pretext for a military offensive to protect Turkish Cypriots and establish peacekeeping on the island (as guarantor). However, this resulted in the division of the island on 20 July 1974 and an exchange of population. The EOKA-B coup is a controversial and a polarizing event among the Greek Cypriot community. For example, the right wing democratic political party does not recognize the EOKA-B coup that occurred on 15 July 1974; however, it commemorates 20 July 1974, the day the Turks invaded Cyprus (Bryant & Papadakis, 2012; Dodd, 2010). On the other hand, the left-wing communist party chooses to organize a joint commemoration of the events emphasizing the coup events of 15 July. They blame nationalism and the constant persistence of joining with Greece as being the cause of the division of the island (Morag, 2004). Consequently, there is significant evidence that points to the fact that left-wing political parties construct a different story of the past from right-wing political parties.

With such contradicting narratives, one wonders how in places of conflict like Cyprus reconciliation may evolve. Papavasiliou (2022) argues that one way to foster peace through tourism in Cyprus is to firstly highlight the importance of narratives in such dark spaces where death had taken place. The author demonstrated in his research that in Cyprus the official tourist guides, which are the cultural brokers (Bryon, 2012) of a destination, in the northern and in the southern areas of the island narrate different stories based on specific dark tourism sites. Doing so, these stories create different contrasting narratives of the destination. Hence, dark places become a means of national identity formation mainly aimed at reminding locals of selective narratives of past events, thus boosting a national identity that is different from the "opposing" collective group. Papavasiliou (2022) indicated that the stories the tourist guides narrate are influenced by the respective destination management organizations (DMOs). However, they are also influenced by the tour guides' collective memories that are reflective of their respective communities, namely the Turkish Cypriot and Greek Cypriot communities. Consequently, in this sense, it can be argued that dark sites in Cyprus are mainly memorials used for political purposes serving the reinforcement of identity construction for the locals, rather than dark tourism spaces for inbound tourist consumption.

Shedding "light" on the darkness: discussion and conclusions

In light of the above, efforts should be made to discuss and debate how tourism can support peacebuilding activities through the acknowledgement of all dark sites within the island of Cyprus and possibly include them in specialized tours or routes of points of interests, where the tourists can make up their own mind concerning the island's dark and turbulent past. Locals – Greek Cypriots and Turkish Cypriots – can also benefit through the visitation of dark attractions that are made accessible both in the north and the south geographic areas of the island. These dark attractions should comprise spaces of dark sites where both communities suffered, hence providing a holistic rather than one-sided view of narratives. Even though the histories and the sites of death that took place in Cyprus bring back traumatic memories, it is deemed essential that collaboration between the two communities is created. Acknowledgement rather than dismissiveness can pave the path towards peacebuilding.

It is postulated that the tourism industry fabricates a destination image that seems to reflect the established demand status quo (Baudrillard, 1994). Research has pinpointed that DMOs frequently use romanticized storytelling with references to a nostalgic past (Smith, 1989); this is said to be systematically "echoed" through publicized adverts and products (Goulding, 2001). Consequently, DMOs aim to produce positive feelings. In this sense, Cyprus has systematically utilized the "Sun and Sea" destination image (Farmaki, 2012; KPMG, 2017) and a romanticized narrative. It has also toned down the politicized dark sites narratives and interpretation of the aforementioned controversial events in Cyprus (Avgousti, 2012; Bryant, 2004; Christou, 2006; Dodd, 2010; Jansen, 2005; Papadakis, Peristianis & Welz, 2006; Scott, 2002; *The Cyprus Mail*, 2015). Focusing on dark sites and fostering a collaboration between the two communities within the island can create an environment of mutual understanding and reconciliation. For example, there are specialized tours that promote a neutral narrative in Israel and Palestine. These tours are conducted by both Palestinian tourist guides and Israeli tourist guides where tourists are taken to dark sites that are commemorated by both Israelis and Palestinians. Guided tours offered by Hands for Peace (2023), Mejdi Tours (2023) and Political Tours (2023) provide such opportunities for tourists and locals. During such specialized tours, interested individuals (locals and tourists) are accompanied by Palestinian and Israeli tour guides. Both of the tourist guides provide narratives in which they explore the region's complex political realities while at the same time they explain the rich cultural and religious heritage of both Palestine and Israel. Anyone interested in the various (occasionally opposing) storylines that run throughout the two regions can attend these specialized tours. In contrast to other excursions, such tours foster peace as they also provide opportunities for the tourists and locals to meet other individuals from Palestinian and the Israeli sides as well as their families. Doing so, such tours provide a personal connection to explore common ideals and forge long-lasting partnerships between the two communities but they also help tourists understand the issues presented by both communities' point of view. Consequently, there are opportunities to be gained through the projection of dark tourism sites within the tourism industry rather than isolating these dark places.

In order for Cyprus to truly move forward from its "liminal state" (Higgott & Nossal, 2008; Rumelili, 2012), dark specialized tourism can be developed with the collaboration of trained licenced tour guides of the two communities. Through this specialized collaborative tours by the two communities, the inbound tourists as "outsiders" can also add their insights and their interpretations through their own lived experiences. Tourists as actors hold a potential subjectivity to transcend meanings in space. Being a tourist, a total stranger to a situation and a place, can mean that one's perception and understanding of things can be different. Tourist behaviours may dissolve boundaries (Foucault, 1997). The tourists' encounter with the locals may result in a more lasting alteration of the environment that lessens the conflict's history, military supremacy and pervasive surveillance. Tourists can act as transgressive actors in between two distinct stories, two contested parties, and two separated conditions in Cyprus.

Furthermore, it is recommended that the DMOs in the northern and southern parts of the island move away from what authors within the tourism field state as political "heritagization" (Bessière, 2013; Busby, Korstanje & Mansfield, 2011; Franklin, 2001). In Cyprus, particular dark heritage sites are left out of promotional material or sightseeing tours (Papavasiliou, 2022). This can be due to the fact that they might be perceived to have limited significant visual opportunities, any real memorable relevance for the tourists (Albano, 2016; Rubin, 1986) or an undesired and best forgotten historical past (Wong, 2013). This has often been associated with the notion of the Disneyfication of society (Bryman, 2004) which infers to the cleansing of controversial narratives. It describes how things or environments are made simpler, more controlled and safer for commercial purposes. In this case, destinations such as Cyprus are presented in a fun and entertaining manner. Cyprus has strived to rebuild its tourism industry post-1974. It can be postulated that no references to the past's controversial events have been incorporated due to the fact that right after 1974 Cyprus needed to quickly regain tourism popularity and tourism income hence the "Cyprus Economic Miracle" (*The Economist* – Levant Correspondent, 1977).

Specific undesired narratives and heritage sites that don't follow the predetermined official narratives set out by the respective DMOs are left out of tourism guided tours (Papavasiliou, 2022). Currently, the Deputy Ministry of Tourism of the Republic of Cyprus is increasingly looking for ways to revitalize the image of the destination and introduce specialized interest attractions and routes. It has recently launched the special interest tourism webpage "Heartlands of Legends" (2022) focusing on authentic Cypriot rural villages and activities. Through the official DMO webpage, Cyprus has also predominantly focused on tourism forms such as religious tourism, food tourism and heritage tourism; hence the introduction of destination labels such as (i) Nature Trails, (ii) Taste of Cyprus and (iii) Wine Routes. Likewise, the North Cyprus Ministry of Tourism, Culture, Youth and Environment is seeking to move away from the typical "sun and sea" image of the island. The Turkish Cypriot DMO webpage offers experiential activities in relation to, for example, (i) History and Religion, (ii) Gastronomy and (iii) Culture (Visit North Cyprus, 2023). Dark tourism attractions and dark places of historical significance are absent from the process of heritagization on both sides of the island. Hence, it is proposed that residents and experts within the fields of archaeology and history in Cyprus collaborate to identify dark places and create a coherent narrative that is also open to dialogue and interpretations. The process of heritagization can, thus, identify "new heritage" that was not previously recognized by the authorities, such as abandoned Turkish Cypriot and Greek Cypriot villages. Furthermore, already designated heritage can be reaffirmed, reinterpreted or even rejected to make way for new narratives.

New narratives can foster dialogue and pave the path for peacebuilding. In order to bypass the established inconsistent narratives told by the tour guides on both sides of Cyprus (Papavasiliou, 2022), it is recommended that a space of interaction is created for the official tour guides where they can learn from each other as well as from scholars and experts, and foster discussions between them. Thus, differences between the narratives can be highlighted. Setting up a special programme for dark tourism sightseeing in the north and in the south of the island with one Turkish Cypriot tourist guide and one Greek Cypriot tourist guide can pave a path of dialogue between the two communities but also provide an objective narrative that is open to interpretation by the inbound tourists within these tours.

Moreover, a pilot project can be implemented between the two communities where one specialized route concerning dark spaces and places is offered to the tourists – both domestic and inbound. According to the authors' knowledge, there is no platform or any specialized tours dedicated to dark tourism in Cyprus where the two communities can contribute to it. As such, it is recommended that online platforms be set up to further expand the dialogue and impressions between the locals and the tourists that have attended these tours. Indeed, official government support with EU economic collaboration (e.g., through various funding schemes) is an essential way forward. As a result, dark tourism should not be feared or utilized as a means of selective narratives to project one's own constructed collective identity; it can rather be used as a tool to foster peacebuilding, bringing communities together and slowly overcoming past traumas – especially in destinations with troubled pasts such as Cyprus.

References

Albano, C. (2016). *Memory, forgetting and the moving image*. Palgrave Macmillan.

Assmann, A., & Clift, S. (2016). *Shadows of trauma: memory and the politics of postwar identity*. Fordham University Press.

Assmann, J. (1998). *Moses the Egyptian*. Harvard University Press.

Attalides, M. A. (2003). *Cyprus: nationalism and international politics*. Cyprus Bibliopolis.

Avgousti, K. (2012). The use of events in the development of the tourism industry: the case of Cyprus. *Event Management*, *16*, 203–21.

Baudrillard, J. (1994). *Simulacra and simulation*. University of Michigan Press.

Beerda, E. (2022). Tourism brings a dark past closer by 2022. Available at https://www.nwo.nl/en/cases/tourism-brings-dark-past-closer (accessed 3 January 2022).

Beirman, D. (2020). *Restoring tourism destinations in crisis: a strategic marketing approach*. Routledge.

Bell, D. (2006). Introduction: memory, trauma and world politics. In D. Bell (Ed.), *Memory, trauma and world politics: reflections on the relationship between past and present* (pp. 1–29). Palgrave Macmillan.

Bessière, J. (2013). 'Heritagisation', a challenge for tourism promotion and regional development: an example of food heritage. *Journal of Heritage Tourism, 8*(4), 275–91.

Bohleber, W. (2007). Remembrance, trauma and collective memory: the battle for memory in psychoanalysis. *The International Journal of Psychoanalysis, 88*(2), 329–52.

Bounia, A., & Stylianou-Lambert, T. (2011). *National museums in Cyprus: a story of heritage and conflict.* In P. Aronsson & G. Elgenius (Eds.), *EuNaMus Report No 1* (published by Linköping University). Available at https:// ep .liu .se/ ecp/ 064/ 009/ ecp64009.pdf (accessed 15 December 2022).

Brown, D. (2000). *Contemporary nationalism: civic, ethnocultural, and multicultural politics.* Psychology Press.

Bryant, R. (2004). *Imagining the modern: the cultures of nationalism in Cyprus.* IB Tauris.

Bryant, R., & Papadakis, Y. (2012). *Cyprus and the politics of memory: history, community and conflict.* Bloomsbury.

Bryman, A. (2004). *The Disneyization of society.* Sage.

Bryon, J. (2012). Tour guides as storytellers – from selling to sharing. *Scandinavian Journal of Hospitality and Tourism, 12*(1), 27–43.

Busby, G., Korstanje, M. E., & Mansfield, C. (2011). Madrid: literary fiction and the imaginary urban destination. *Journal of Tourism Consumption and Practice, 3*(2), 20–37.

Buzinde, C. N., & Santos, C. A. (2008). Representations of slavery. *Annals of Tourism Research, 35*(2), 469–88.

Catling, H. W. (1980). *Cyprus and the West 1600–1050 BC.* Department of Prehistory and Archaeology, University of Sheffield.

Christou, M. (2006). A double imagination: memory and education in Cyprus. *Journal of Modern Greek Studies, 24*(2), 285–306.

Cohen, S. (1995). State crimes of previous regimes: knowledge, accountability, and the policing of the past. *Law & Social Inquiry, 20*(1), 7–50.

Cyprus Friendship Programme (2017). Cyprus population exchange. Available at http://cyprusfriendship.org/?page_id=3035 (accessed 10 January 2023).

Dodd, C. (2010). *The history and politics of the Cyprus conflict.* Springer.

Eyerman, R., Madigan, T., & Ring, M. (2017). Cultural trauma, collective memory and the Vietnam War. *Politička misao: časopis za politologiju, 54*(1–2), 11–31.

Farmaki, A. (2012). A comparison of the projected and the perceived image of Cyprus. *Tourismos, 7*(2), 95–119.

Farmaki, A., & Antoniou, K. (2017). Politicising dark tourism sites: evidence from Cyprus. *Worldwide Hospitality and Tourism Themes, 9*(2), 175–86.

Farmaki, A., Antoniou, K., & Christou, P. (2019). Visiting the "enemy": visitation in politically unstable destinations. *Tourism Review, 74*(3), 293–309.

Fine, G. A., & Beim, A. (2007). Introduction: interactionist approaches to collective memory. *Symbolic Interaction, 30*(1), 1–5.

Foley, M., & Lennon, J. J. (1996). JFK and dark tourism: a fascination with assassination. *International Journal of Heritage Studies, 2*(4), 198–211.

Foucault, M. (1980). *Language, counter-memory, practice: selected essays and interviews.* Cornell University Press.

France, P., & Reynolds, S. (1996). A post-modern cathedral? Lieux de mémoire, the topology and topography of France. *Modern & Contemporary France, 4*(2), 227–30.

Franklin, A. (2001). The tourist gaze and beyond: an interview with John Urry. *Tourist Studies, 1*(2), 115–31.

Friedrich, M., & Johnston, T. (2013). Beauty versus tragedy: thanatourism and the memorialisation of the 1994 Rwandan Genocide. *Journal of Tourism and Cultural Change*, *11*(4), 302–20.

Frost, H. D. (2010). Recent literatures of the holocaust: negotiations with (post) memory and the archive (PhD thesis, University of the Witwatersrand). https://core .ac.uk/download/pdf/39667822.pdf.

Goulding, C. (2001). Romancing the past: heritage visiting and the nostalgic consumer. *Psychology & Marketing*, *18*(6), 565–92.

Grüning, B. (2010). The art of narrating and the question of cultural acknowledgment: the case of Die Kinder von Golzow and a reunified Germany. *The Sociological Review*, *58*(2), 44–59.

Habermas, J., & Derrida, J. (2003). February 15, or what binds Europeans together: a plea for a common foreign policy, beginning in the core of Europe. *Constellations*, *10*(3), 291–7.

Halbwachs, M. (1992). *On Collective Memory*, ed. and trans. L. A. Coser. University of Chicago Press.

Hall, D. (2002). Brand development, tourism and national identity: the re-imaging of former Yugoslavia. *Journal of Brand Management*, *9*(4), 323–34.

Heartland of Legends (2022). *Heartland of Legends of Cyprus*. Available at https:// heartlandoflegends.com/route/ (accessed 10 January 2023).

Higgott, R. A., & Nossal, K. R. (2008). Odd man in, odd man out: Australia's liminal position in Asia revisited – a reply to Ann Capling. *The Pacific Review*, *21*(5), 623–34.

Hirsch, M. (2008). The generation of postmemory. *Poetics Today*, *29*(1), 103–28.

Honey, M. (2008). Tourism: preventing conflict, promoting peace. Available at https:// africanphilanthropy.issuelab.org/ resources/ 20316/ 20316 .pdf (accessed 15 January 2023).

Huyssen, A. (2012). *Twilight memories: marking time in a culture of amnesia*. Routledge.

Irwin-Zarecka, I. (1995). Frames of remembrance: the dynamics of collective memory. *History and Theory*, *34*(3), 245–61.

Jansen, M. E. (2005). *War and cultural heritage: Cyprus after the 1974 Turkish invasion*. University of Minnesota Press.

Kansteiner, W. (2002). Finding meaning in memory: a methodological critique of collective memory studies. *History and Theory*, *41*(2), 179–97.

Karageorghis, V., Peltenburg, E., & Swiny, S. (1979). *Cyprus BC: 7000 years of history*. British Museum Publications for the Trustees of the British Museum.

KPMG (2017). *Cyprus Tourism Market Report*. Available at https://assets.kpmg.com/ content/ dam/ kpmg/ cy/ pdf/ cyprus -tourism -market -report -fourth -edition .pdf (accessed 3 December 2022).

Kuus, M. (2002). European integration in identity narratives in Estonia: a quest for security. *Journal of Peace Research*, *39*(1), 91–108.

Lee, C. K., Bendle, L. J., Yoon, Y. S., & Kim, M. J. (2012). Thanatourism or peace tourism: perceived value at a North Korean resort from an indigenous perspective. *International Journal of Tourism Research*, *14*(1), 71–90.

Lennon, J. J., & Foley, M. (1999). Interpretation of the unimaginable: the US Holocaust Memorial Museum, Washington, DC, and "dark tourism". *Journal of Travel Research*, *38*(1), 46–50.

Macdonald, S. (2006). Undesirable heritage: fascist material culture and historical consciousness in Nuremberg. *International Journal of Heritage Studies*, *12*(1), 9–28.

Mälksoo, M. (2009). The memory politics of becoming European: the East European subalterns and the collective memory of Europe. *European Journal of International Relations*, 15(4), 653–80.

Mavratsas, C. V. (1997). The ideological contest between Greek-Cypriot nationalism and Cypriotism 1974–1995: politics, social memory and identity. *Ethnic and Racial Studies*, 20(4), 717–37.

Mejdi Tours (2023). Mejdi Tours overview. Available at https://mejditours.com/home -mejdi/ (accessed 4 January 2023).

Miles, W. F. (2002). Auschwitz: museum interpretation and darker tourism. *Annals of Tourism Research*, 29(4), 1175–8.

Millas, H. (2005). *The imagined 'other' as national identity*. Turkish-Greek Civic Dialogue Project.

Morag, N. (2004). Cyprus and the clash of Greek and Turkish nationalisms. *Nationalism and Ethnic Politics*, 10(4), 595–624.

Neal, A. G. (1998). *National trauma and collective memory: major events in the American century*. M. E. Sharpe.

Nevzat, A., & Hatay, M. (2009). Politics, society and the decline of Islam in Cyprus: from the Ottoman era to the twenty-first century. *Middle Eastern Studies*, 45(6), 911–33.

Novick, P. (2000). *The Holocaust and collective memory: the American experience*. Bloomsbury.

Olick, J. K. (1998). What does it mean to normalize the past? Official memory in German politics since 1989. *Social Science History*, 22(4), 547–71.

Olick, J. K., & Robbins, J. (1998). Social memory studies: from "collective memory" to the historical sociology of mnemonic practices. *Annual Review of Sociology*, 24(1), 105–40.

Papadakis, Y. (1998). Greek Cypriot narratives of history and collective identity: nationalism as a contested process. *American Ethnologist*, 25(2), 149–65.

Papadakis, Y., Peristianis, N., & Welz, G. (2006). *Divided Cyprus: modernity, history, and an island in conflict*. Indiana University Press.

Papavasiliou, V. (2022). Collective memory and narrated destination image: interpreting the tour guides narratives in guided tours (PhD thesis, Hong Kong Polytechnic University). https://theses.lib.polyu.edu.hk/handle/200/11952.

Passerini, L. (2003). *Memories between silence and oblivion contested pasts*. Routledge.

Hands for Peace (2023). *Hands for Peace – guided tours*. Available at https://handsofpeace.org/tours-of-the-region/ (accessed 11 December 2022).

Podoshen, J. S. (2018). Dark tourism in an increasingly violent world. In R. Stone, P. Hartmann, R. Seaton, T. Sharpley, & L. White (Eds), *The Palgrave handbook of dark tourism studies*. Palgrave Macmillan.

Political Tours (2023). Political Tours – travel beyond the headlines. Available at https://www.politicaltours.com/tours/israel-and-palestine-tours-2020/ (accessed 4 January 2023).

Pollis, A. (1996). The social construction of ethnicity and nationality: the case of Cyprus. *Nationalism and Ethnic Politics*, 2(1), 67–90.

Rivera, L. A. (2008). Managing "spoiled" national identity: war, tourism, and memory in Croatia. *American Sociological Review*, 73(4), 613–34.

Roudometof, V. (2002). *Collective memory, national identity, and ethnic conflict: Greece, Bulgaria, and the Macedonian question*. Greenwood Publishing Group.

Rubin, D. (1986). Autobiographical memory. In *Encyclopedia of Cognitive Science*. John Wiley.

Rumelili, B. (2012). Liminal identities and processes of domestication and subversion in international relations. *Review of International Studies*, *38*(2), 495–508.

Schudson, M. (1984). Embarrassment and Erving Goffman's idea of human nature. *Theory and Society*, *13*(5), 633–48.

Scott, J. (2002). World heritage as a model for citizenship: the case of Cyprus. *International Journal of Heritage Studies*, *8*(2), 99–115.

Seaton, A. V. (1996). Guided by the dark: from thanatopsis to thanatourism. *International Journal of Heritage Studies*, *2*(4), 234–44.

Seaton, A. V. (2001). Sources of slavery-destinations of slavery: the silences and disclosures of slavery heritage in the UK and US. *International Journal of Hospitality & Tourism Administration*, *2*(3–4), 107–29.

Shapira, A. (1996). Historiography and memory: Latrun, 1948. *Jewish Social Studies*, *3*(1), 20–61.

Sharpley, R., & Stone, P. (2008). Consuming dark tourism: a thanatological perspective. *Annals of Tourism Research*, *35*(2), 574–95.

Siegert, N. (2016). The archive as construction site: collective memory and trauma in contemporary art from Angola. *World Art*, *6*(1), 103–23.

Smith, A. D. (1989). The origins of nations. *Ethnic and Racial Studies*, *12*(3), 340–67.

Spohn, W. (2005). National identities and collective memory in an enlarged Europe. In W. Spohn & K. Eder (Eds), *Collective memory and European identity: the effects of integration and enlargement* (pp. 1–14). Routledge. Available at https://citeseerx.ist.psu.edu/document?repid=rep1&type=pdf&doi=9b4911fb23147836d040f074e448adc0194c26d9 (accessed 3 December 2022).

Stavrinides, Z. (1975). *The Cyprus conflict: national identity and statehood*. Z. Stavrinides.

Stone, P. R. (2006). A dark tourism spectrum: towards a typology of death and macabre related tourist sites, attractions and exhibitions. *Tourism: An International Interdisciplinary Journal*, *54*(2), 145–60.

Sturken, M. (1997). *Tangled memories: the Vietnam War, the AIDS epidemic, and the politics of remembering*. University of California Press.

The Cyprus Mail (2015). History as dogma. Available at http://cyprus-mail.com/2015/12/06/history-as-dogma/ (accessed 9 December 2022).

The Economist – Levant Correspondent (1977). Cyprus: miracle in half an island. Available at https://www.reddit.com/r/cyprus/comments/x3xwhl/a_1977_the_economist_article_regarding_the/ (accessed 10 January 2023).

Tindemans, L. (1996). *Unfinished peace: report of the International Commission on the Balkans*. Aspen Institute Press.

Verovšek, P. J. (2016). Collective memory, politics, and the influence of the past: the politics of memory as a research paradigm. *Politics, Groups, and Identities*, *4*(3), 529–43.

Visit North Cyprus (2023). North Cyprus. Available at https://www.visitncy.com/ (accessed 5 January 2023).

Vural, Y., & Özuyanık, E. (2008). Redefining identity in the Turkish-Cypriot school history textbooks: a step towards a united federal Cyprus. *South European Society and Politics*, *13*(2), 133–54.

White, L., & Frew, E. (2013). *Dark tourism and place identity: managing and interpreting dark places*. Routledge.

Winship, G., & Knowles, J. (1996). The transgenerational impact of cultural trauma: linking phenomena in treatment of third generation survivors of the Holocaust. *British Journal of Psychotherapy*, *13*(2), 259–66.

Wolf, D. L. (2019). Postmemories of joy? Children of Holocaust survivors and alternative family memories. *Memory Studies, 12*(1), 74–87.

Wong, C. U. I. (2013). The sanitization of colonial history: authenticity, heritage interpretation and the case of Macau's tour guides. *Journal of Sustainable Tourism, 21*(6), 915–31.

Yankholmes, A., & McKercher, B. (2015). Rethinking slavery heritage tourism. *Journal of Heritage Tourism, 10*(3), 233–47.

Zelizer, B. (1995). Reading the past against the grain: the shape of memory studies. *Critical Studies in Mass Communication, 12*, 214–39.

6 The ecclesial cultural parks in Italy as places of inner peace: an investigation of the perceptions of stakeholders

Filippo Grasso and Marco Platania

Introduction

Tourism is a key force for peace and a primary component of sustainable development, as clarified by United Nations (UN) and European Union (EU) reports, which recognize the social and human dimension of tourism and its ability to promote and support world peace. Over the years, scholars have tried to better quantify and qualify this form of tourism known as peace tourism. D'Amore (2009) talks about an emerging market of "peace tourism," which includes traveling to places that are significant for national or global peace, peace with others or nature, peace with one's past and future generations as well as inner peace. Sánchez Sánchez and Fernández Herreira (1996) in speaking of the three dimensions of peace (personal, social and environmental) highlight the importance of man's peaceful and harmonious relationship with himself (inner peace). In particular, this last aspect linked to well-being, greatly depends on the characteristics of the place visited, on the values it expresses and also on some elements related to heritage tourism. In this context, ecclesial cultural parks become relevant as places promoting inner peace and wider peace at large.

The ecclesial cultural parks have established themselves in Italy in recent years as a territorial system of management of the vast museum heritage of sacred art which promotes, recovers, and enhances, through a coordinated and integrated strategy, the rich liturgical, historical, artistic, architectural, receptive, playful heritage of one or more dioceses. They represent an institution that belongs to the Italian ecclesiastical order and that can be led, more generally, to the "sacred natural sites" (Tigano, 2020). These can be understood as natural areas (of land or water) where specific cultural and spiritual values are established, as well as material goods of historical importance, to be protected and enhanced, so that the very protection of the sacredness of the place is functional to the conservation of biodiversity. The Church walks a man through the art and offers him images, furnishings, environments (architectural and natural), musical and literary productions, traditions, meaningful spaces, opportunities for prayer and praise, paths of research, of living memory, of conveyance of values. The ecclesial cultural parks are, therefore, places that the traveler chooses for their natural and architectural beauties and for their religious value and that allow the achievement of peace in the minds of men.

The purpose of this chapter is to know the stakeholder perception in order to understand the strengths and weaknesses of this type of tourist attraction and, subsequently, define the potential of the ecclesial cultural park with respect to its suitability as a place for gaining inner peace. To achieve its aim, a qualitative study was undertaken using semi-structured direct interviews with the directors of the parks in Italy as well as with local stakeholders. As such, this chapter contributes to the knowledge on the relationship between peace tourism and heritage tourism by highlighting the importance of heritage attractions in promoting inner peace and the latter's role in fostering world peace.

Theoretical background

Tourism, peace, and development

Tourism is seen as a force for peace and a primary component of sustainable development, as exemplified by UN and EU reports, which recognize the social dimension of tourism and its ability to promote and sustain world peace (Wintersteiner & Wohlmuther, 2014; Farmaki, 2017). Discussion on the relationship between peace and tourism is not new. In fact, the peace through tourism relationship has been discussed since the 1920s, with "Travel for Peace" as the theme of the British Travel and Holidays Association's inaugural conference of 1929 (Wintersteiner & Wohlmuther, 2014). Further milestones in the debate on tourism's role as a peacemaker include the United Nations "Tourism: Passport to Peace" in 1967, the 1980 declaration of the World Tourism Organization in Manila (tourism as a force for global peace) and in 1986, the International Institute for Peace through Tourism. These events were based on the aspiration that tourism becomes the largest "peace industry" in the world and that every tourist is an "Ambassador for Peace" (Salazar, 2006). Over time, several conferences have been organized, including one in Jordan in 2000 which produced the "Amman Declaration on Peace Through Tourism," formally adopted by the United Nations.

Faced with this evolutionary path, the academic debate on the relationship between peace and tourism has also advanced, presenting different inter-pretations. We have gone from an approach in which tourism is seen as an instrument of peace on the basis of contact theory (i.e., peace arises from the cultural exchange for a positive guest–host encounter) to a conceptualization of "peace sensitive tourism" (Wintersteiner & Wohlmuther, 2014) which suggests that tourism can extend beyond visitation to cultural or heritage sites to more specialized forms of tourism related to peace such as peace museums. Beyond the chosen interpretation, the difficulties in demonstrating a causal relationship for tourism as a contributor to peace remain (Salazar, 2006). On the one hand, there is some positive evidence that travel can improve visitors' perceptions and attitudes towards a hostile community (e.g., Causevic & Lynch, 2011; Durko & Petrick, 2016). On the other hand, tourism is perceived as a profit-oriented industry with capitalistic tendencies whereas the nature of mass tourism implies socio-economic inequalities between hosts and guests (Farmaki, 2017). As Wintersteiner and Wohlmuther (2014, p. 52) posit, "in the tourism and peace literature, we sometimes find confusion between normative goals and empirical facts."

Notwithstanding, according to D'Amore (2009), there is an emerging market for peace tourism that has arisen in recent years as a form of responsible tourism and which includes travel to places that are significant for the peace of one's own country or of several countries, peace with others or nature, peace with past and future generations and peace with oneself. Here, it would be necessary to resume Hansen's subdivision of peace (2016, p. 212) according to which "… peace could be thought of as three interrelated branches of peace: peace within (inner peace), peace between (relational peace), and peace among (structural/environmental peace)." In particular, there are several contribu-tions that have highlighted the importance of inner peace and how this then contributes to proactive behavior in favor of peace. For example, Schwartz (1992) found significant associations between having inner harmony (at peace with oneself) and the desire to live in a world at peace (free from war and conflict).

Visiting different countries and cultures is seen as an exercise to broaden the mind (Kim et al., 2007; WTTC, 2016). The places where symbols of a con-cluded conflict are found (e.g., war memorials) play an important role in man-aging post-conflict emotions (Novelli et al., 2012) and for sharing history and cultural heritage. In this sense, tourist guides who facilitate the achievement of positive exchanges and educational outcomes in postwar regions play a critical role in peace tourism promotion (Friedl, 2014). It is, therefore, clear that the overall context in which tourist consumption takes place can represent an element that facilitates the exercise of peace. Among the various tourist attractions, that of heritage plays a very important role. According to UNESCO, heritage tourism in addition to allowing economic development can be used for a much more ambitious goal – to produce peace in the minds of men.

This is not an easy task since the enhancement processes must acknowledge, as Di Giovine (2010, p. 8) states that "... people's identities are problematically based on traditional territorial conceptions that are constructed and diffused through [these] emotionally charged monuments." The discovery of the cultural richness of each country allows the achievement of peace in the minds of men. Heritage includes multiple categories of attractors according to Boyd (2000) who identified historical, industrial, cultural, natural and educational attractions of heritage tourism (Table 6.1).

Table 6.1   Categories of heritage attractions

Historical	Elements within the built landscape (e.g., houses, castles, monuments, cathedrals)
Industrial	Links to products indicative of the region's past (e.g., linen, pottery, whiskey, crystal)
Cultural	Links to past societies, lifestyles, customs (e.g., early settlement, early British presence)
Natural	Elements of the natural landscape (e.g., causeways, country and forest parks, caves)
Educational	Links to attractions where the ultimate purpose is the dissemination of information for the purposes of learning (e.g., museums, visitor centers, libraries, planetariums)

Source: Our elaboration from Boyd (2000).

In some cases, there are attractors that bring together different categories. Think, for example, of a temple or a church, which brings together both the cultural and the historical element. In Italy, a nation famous throughout the world for its cultural heritage, there are some types of cultural parks recently created by the Italian Church known as ecclesial cultural parks. These parks, which are the subject of our study, bring together multiple elements of the categories of heritage and due to their particular characteristics could represent tourist attractions that associate the cultural experience with that of peace of mind (inner peace).

The ecclesial cultural parks

In May 2018 the CEI (Italian Bishops' Conference) published the volume *Beauty and Hope for All*, dedicated to the project of "ecclesial parks" or "ecclesial cultural networks." By ecclesial cultural park (ECP) we mean a "territorial system that promotes, recovers and enhances, through a coordinated and integrated strategy, the liturgical, historical, artistic, architectural, museum, receptive, playful heritage of one or more Dioceses" (the diocese, from the Latin dioecesis and from the Greek διοίκησις meaning "administration," is a type of administrative subdivision used in the organization of Catholic churches) (CEI, 2018). It is a new proposal which offers considerable opportunities for involving local communities in heritage tourism.

The reasons that led the CEI to design a cultural management system like this arise from the need to rethink tourism in the places where faith and religious culture exist, enhancing material and intangible heritage to offer it to travelers, pilgrims and visitors. The tasks include promoting, announcing, transmitting the faith, enhancing and networking the vast heritage of ecclesiastical cultural heritage together with the Dioceses. Therefore, ecclesial cultural parks are a response to the need for protection and enhancement according to the different peculiarities, promoting the organization of a system, rooted in the territory, capable not only of coordinating (parishes, sanctuaries, monasteries, pilgrimage routes, brotherhoods, religious institutions, and so on) but also putting the religious, social, and economic actors in relationship for a greater use and safeguarding of their function and identity (Ferrari & Nicotera, 2021).

It remains clear that *parco* is clearly an act of the Church in pastoral concern for the local community and in contributing to the good of the territory in which it is located. This does not take away, but rather favors the fact that the ECP can also become a place where the pilgrim finds peace with himself, regardless of whether his approach is religious or devotional. At the time of writing, there were about 30 Italian dioceses where the ecclesial cultural park is developing or has already been built. In many territories it is, therefore, a novelty and the possible results are not well known.

Methods

To achieve its aim of understanding the relationship between ECP and peace tourism, we conducted 48 semi-structured interviews with stakeholders. As suggested for analyses of this type (Reed et al., 2009), we identified the stakeholders using a snowball approach (Noy, 2008; Allen, 2017). The 48 participants listed in Table 6.2 belong to different institutions and sectors, have very different positions and skills in the tourism sector and come from geographic areas close to ECP (Table 6.3). We interviewed representatives of local institutions, university professors, entrepreneurs in the tourism sector, representatives of cooperatives and associations that deal with tourism, professionals of recognized competence and religious personalities. We have tried to diversify as much as possible and not focus on a single type of competence and sector, thus collecting opinions on several fronts.

The final list of interested parties can be aggregated into six categories (Reed et al., 2009): tourism sector, other economics sector, public sector, research and education, associations/cooperatives, and Church, as can be seen in Table 6.2.

Table 6.2   Characteristics of interviewees

Sector	n	%
Tourism sector	13	27.1
Other economics sector	9	18.7
Public sector	6	12.5
Research and education	10	20.8
Associations/cooperatives	5	10.4
Church	2	4.2
n.r.	3	6.3
Total	48	100

Table 6.3   Geographical origin of the stakeholders interviewed

Italian regions	Number of ecclesial cultural parks	Number of stakeholders interviewed
Sicilia	4	38
Lazio	1	3
Toscana	1	1
Campania	1	1
n.r.	–	5

The interviews were based on a structured outline on two macro themes: (1) characteristics of the ECPs and (2) the relationship between ECP and peace. We have, specifically, foreseen two overall macro questions: (1) In your opinion, what is an ecclesial cultural park? What is its mission? And (2) In your opinion, what relationship is there between (interior) peace and an ecclesial cultural park? A preliminary version of the question protocol was tested with some stakeholders and corrections were made where appropriate. The final version was then administered to 48 stakeholders between July 2022 and August 2022. The interviews were conducted in Italian and translated into English for the purposes of this study.

The qualitative data collected (interview transcripts) were subsequently analyzed through a thematic analysis (Braun & Clarke, 2006; Nowell et al., 2017). Thematic analysis is one of the basic techniques used by researchers dealing with qualitative data in applied research (Braun & Clarke, 2006). It aims to identify, analyze and report patterns (themes) within the data (Braun & Clarke, 2006). The identification of the relevant key issues depends on the judgment of the researcher, and therefore, is not associated with any quantifiable measure. We followed the thematic analysis steps (phases) established by Braun and Clarke (2006). On the basis of an inductive "data-driven" and semantic approach to the research of the themes, we first transcribed all the direct interviews conducted with the stakeholders and encoded the data. Then, we sorted and aggregated the encoded data at a larger level, identifying key themes. Finally, we examined the themes using direct citations (extracted from interview transcripts) in the text to provide clear evidence of the essence of a theme, as suggested by Braun and Clarke (2006, p. 23) and based on how it was done in other studies using thematic analysis (see, e.g., Ellis & Kitzinger, 2002; Kitzinger & Wilmott, 2002).

Results

Definition, mission, and organizational model of the ecclesial cultural park

The first topics discussed with the stakeholders concern the meaning of the ecclesial cultural park. We considered it necessary to start with this as a first topic in order to give the interviewees the opportunity to express their thoughts on the role of the ECP in the territory, also considering the novelty of this tool for the promotion and care of the heritage. According to some interviewees, the presence of the word "park" means an area linked not only to the geographical territory but also to culture, traditions, lifestyles, religious experiences as a response to the need for protection, enhancement in its specific peculiarity historical, cultural, environmental, economic, spiritual. One interviewee from the public sector, for example, said: "Ecclesial cultural park means a territorial system that promotes, recovers, enhances, through a coordinated and integrated strategy, the liturgical, historical, artistic, architectural, museum, hospitality and recreational heritage of one or more particular Churches." Another interviewee from the research and education field commented that ECP is a "project that enhances, promotes and recovers the liturgical, historical, artistic, architectural, museum and hospitality heritage of a territory." Stakeholders argued that the ECP would make it possible to create a system rooted in a territory, in relationship with parish communities, monasteries, sanctuaries, creating a connective tissue capable of enhancing the ancient pilgrimage routes. An interviewee from another economic sector denoted an ECP as "a place where cultural paths linked to religious art and architecture take place" whereas an interviewee from the public sector argued that "it is a connective tissue capable of enhancing aggregative and receptive spaces, ancient pilgrimage routes, the most diverse cultural initiatives, traditions rooted in popular culture and religiosity."

Some of the stakeholders also refer to the possibility of ECPs to contribute to the sustainable economic and social development of the area through the generation of a local economy but also by offering concrete job opportunities to young people. According to an interview belonging to the Church, ECPs are "giving value to the cultural and landscape resources of the territory, creating jobs." An interviewee from associations and cooperatives agreed, saying that ECP carry "the knowledge and enhancement of the same, as well as economic development generated by an intelligent vision of tourism." According to the stakeholders, the opportunity for growth for the life of ecclesial communities which are urged to welcome pilgrims with different history, sensitivities and experiences, is not secondary, albeit for limited periods of time. An interviewee from associations and cooperatives noted that "an ecclesial cultural park is the work of the Church in pastoral concern for the Christian community and in contributing to the good of the territory in which it is located," while another from the tourism industry said ECPs represent "a community in which we talk about culture, especially the religious one."

During the interviews, stakeholders were also asked to specify the mission that the ecclesial cultural park should have. In the opinion of the interviewees, the ECP should enhance the assets through an approach that highlights the spiritual aspect. According to an interviewee from the public sector, "its usefulness is current, that is, the desire for spirituality in order to come out of increasingly homologated communities." Stakeholders from the tourism sector commented that ECPs are "recovering the dimension of the sacred and the transcendent, with guided tours, thematic readings and conversations and performances of sacred music" and that their mission "is to provide a place for everyone in which to connect man with nature, spirituality, culture. Its usefulness is to lead people to find inner peace and sharing between people and spirituality."

A very important issue concerning the governance of the parks came up in the interviews. In fact, the interviewees were asked to express their thoughts on the ways in which an ecclesial cultural park should be managed. The purpose of this question is not connected only to organizational and managerial aspects, but rather to the need to understand whether governance should be secular or professional. Some interviewees stated that governance could also be entrusted to secular subjects, albeit with specific knowledge. For example, interviewees from the public sector said that "certainly not politicians but associations of people who believe in it" should manage ECPs, identifying "an expert person with clear managerial skills and specific skills in the area of ecclesial culture." Likewise, interviewees from associations and cooperatives highlighted the need for "competent and passionate people" while stakeholders from research and education noted that an ECP "should be managed by a person who is educated and prepared both in the naturalistic field than in the religious field." For others, involvement with the administrative structure of the Church (the dioceses), the local bishops, or with the religious orders present in the territory is necessary and these should be "in agreement with the local authority." As a stakeholder clarified, "[it is necessary to involve] the bishops with the participation of the various ecclesial communities."

The relationship between the ecclesial cultural park and peace

Moving on to the next question, it is important to highlight that almost all the interviewees stated that the relationship between ECPs and peace exists and is a strong positive one. Only five respondents stated that they did not know how to answer this question while three considered that there is no relationship.

As for those who supported the existence of the relationship, some interviewees believe that the Ecclesial Cultural Park has the task of contributing to inner peace. As an interviewee from Associations/Cooperatives puts it,

> Inner peace is a state of great serenity that persists in everyday life, in every action you make, in the choices you make keeping in mind that the decisions you make you feel good. Furthermore, it is a feeling of great peace in which, free from fear, stress,

suffering, you can enjoy a state of well-being. An ecclesial cultural park should help to achieve inner and social peace.

The reference to social peace almost seems to echo the thought of Galtung (1996) that peace should represent a "nonviolent and creative conflict transformation," which would mean working toward the presence of social justice (Hansen, 2016). So, according to the interviewees, the ECP represents a physical place that allows you to reach a state of mind of "peace with yourself." Some capture a particular aspect of inner peace and refer more to meditation and relaxation. Thus, inner peace was conceptualized as a state of mind in which to confront oneself and meditate. "The relationship is absolutely there, the ecclesial cultural park should give you inner peace. The purpose of an ecclesial park should really be able to create an elite tourism that can make you reflect, meditate on many topics and relax," said an interviewee from the research and education field.

An interesting point was raised in the response of this interviewee, who seems to grasp the existence of a niche tourist segment in the relationship between peace and tourism. Indeed, as McKercher et al. (2002, p. 26) argued, "the cultural tourism market is not homogeneous and that different types of attractions will appeal to different types of cultural tourist." This segment could possibly be related to the reasons that lead a tourist to visit an ECP, which could be religious. In this regard, one of the objectives we set ourselves was also to investigate the relationship between religious aspects and peace tourism. According to a public sector stakeholder, the relationship between ECP and peace would be directly linked to the Christian nature of the park, its intrinsic characteristic:

> It is necessary to remain attentive to the Christian nature of the activity generated by the Park, since it is inspired and continuously nourished by the light of Christ, the new man, a man redeemed and reintegrated in his original dignity. This is why the Christian community he can regenerate himself through this broadening of his breath to the totality of social experience, without dualisms and separations between faith and life, between culture and the Gospel.

This opinion is present in many interviewee responses who believe that the religious aspect is indissoluble with that of inner peace. For example, an interviewee said that "[Peace and the ECP] are intimately connected, ecclesiastical cultural assets are not only works of art but also signs of the relationship between man and God." Another agreed that "the park can be a place for meditation, inner peace and prayer."

It is very interesting to note how, in the opinion of some stakeholders, there is this indissoluble relationship between a work of art and a sign of the divine presence. In this sense, the work of art is contemplated because it refers to the transcendent and this contemplation leads to a state of mind of peace and serenity. The peace to which the interviewees refer seems to be a state of communion with the human race; we are faced with "shalom," the biblical term that is commonly translated as peace but which has a very broad meaning, namely "completeness, integrity" which is the condition of a man, of a community that is in harmony with nature, with himself, with God, with other men.

The relationship between the ECP and peace also passes through the context in which the tourist experience is lived. In other words, we refer to naturalistic and architectural attractions. In this case, the stakeholders believe that the context in which the visit takes place naturally leads the visitor to live an experience of inner peace. As an interviewee said, "Nature inspires spirituality, not necessarily religious or Christian." Another stakeholder agreed, stating that "the context itself, especially if surrounded by Nature, instills Peace." In the words of a tourism sector stakeholder: "The relationship is the result of the serenity that comes from a more niche tourism experience, and from the beauty of the places of worship that will make up this reality." In the case of this niche tourism type, the reduced number of tourists seems to be more of an aspiration, a necessary requirement for the meditative experience that promotes peace of mind.

Discussion and conclusion

The study carried out made it possible to know the perceptions of stakeholders in ecclesial cultural parks and understand how this type of heritage attraction can contribute to inner peace and subsequently world peace. The study first highlighted the interest in this form of promotion, albeit still to be discovered, together with the need to identify a more reliable and responsible governance model for management over time. The ECPs seem to be still at the beginning of their development path. Many stakeholders do not fully understand their functionality. In some cases, the parks' promotion is confined to the religious aspects.

The relationship between the ECP and peace remains complex to decipher, but some elements identified during our investigation make us think that this relationship may be strong and lasting, even though at an early stage. Visiting these places seems to contribute to "peace of mind," that is, to a positive form of peace which Hansen (2016, p. 212) argued "… consists of direct actions of kindness, fostering the well-being of the body, mind, and spirit for oneself (inner peace) and others, meeting everyone's basic needs (including love and identity)." The possibility of meditation and listening to oneself, in contexts characterized by evocative beauty, leads to that capacity for active listening, referred to by Redekop (2014) as a capacity that then helps to identify the symptoms of internal conflict and to better manage the dynamics of emotions.

On the other hand, the possibility identified by some interviewees of enhancing the pilgrimage routes and routes that are connected to the ECPs is very interesting. This form of tourism has some characteristics that can easily associate it with forms of "peace with oneself" tourism (i.e., wellness tourism). Another aspect is the relationship between the ECP and spirituality. According to stakeholders such places, because they are sacred, should foster "inner peace" and spirituality. The sacredness seems to allow us to get out of homologated contexts to find ourselves. In this sense, the aspects connected to the Christian religion (Gopin, 1997) – as indeed with religions in general – certainly contribute to fostering a climate of reconciliation and peace.

In the analysis of stakeholder perceptions, some interesting aspects also emerge relating to the characteristics of the tourist demand that the ECPs will be able to visit. The concern that this takes the form of elite tourism, and therefore of niche tourism, must push the governance of the parks to identify the most suitable tools in order to avoid the presence of niche tourism forms which would be sustainable for the territory, yet may reduce the potential of the park.

The relationship between this form of protection of the local religious and historical heritage and peace, therefore, seems to have room for growth. However, we believe that the approach will greatly depend on the origin of the tourists. In fact, if these will be local, and probably excursionists, the search for peace will also be linked to aspects of identity; that is, finding oneself will be greatly influenced by the fact that the ECP still represents a strongly identifying place for the local community. On the contrary, tourists who come from distant regions and international tourists will have a different attitude. The heritage that characterizes the ECPs invites beauty and contemplation. Peace with oneself and in one's mind will represent a natural consequence of a tourist experience in these places. This can obviously happen if there are forms of governance shared with the local community and managed with managerial criteria, which can favor the growth of the tourist services necessary to make these places real tourist destinations.

In fact, from the findings elaborated above, the need to start a management process of ecclesial cultural parks that makes them visible in the territory emerges including the stakeholder network, the strategic choices eco-compatible with the environment and with the protection of creation, the usability of experiential journeys made by cultural and religious travelers. This makes it possible to place ecclesial cultural parks among the tools for promoting the area. The next step will have to materialize, in full sharing between the local community, park governance, and public administration, in the recovery of the tangible and intangible heritage of the territories to return it to the usability of the community. In this sense, the concept of tourism as a resource of peace finds its full meaning not intended as individual tranquility but as social and economic well-being for a healthy and shared life.

Finally, the future lines of research that this study suggests are related to the knowledge of demand and the role of ECPs within tourist destinations. As regards the first aspect, studies and empirical researches that analyze the characteristics of visitors to these parks will be very important in order to understand the role of inner peace among the different motivations of tourists. The knowledge of the reasons for the demand (i.e., why an ECP is chosen) combined with the knowledge of its economic characteristics (price sensitivity, characteristics of no price factors, country of origin, income, etc.) will therefore be decisive for setting market strategies to enhance the ecclesial cultural parks. The other aspect to be explored is to analyze the ECPs with respect to the tourist destination. It is, hence, necessary to evaluate whether ECPs can be considered tourist attractions within a more general tourism system, or whether they are capable of being a tourist destination on their own. This will obviously depend greatly on the territorial characteristics and the governance capacity of the park, aspects widely highlighted by the stakeholders in our research.

References

Allen, M. (2017). *Snowball Subject Recruitment*. Sage Publications.

Boyd, S. W. (2000). 'Heritage' Tourism in Northern Ireland: Opportunity Under Peace. *Current Issues in Tourism*, 3(2), 150–74.

Braun, V., & Clarke, V. (2006). Using thematic analysis in psychology. *Qualitative Research in Psychology*, 3(2), 77–101.

CEI (2018). *Bellezza e speranza per tutti, Parchi e Reti Culturali Ecclesiali: quando il Turismo diventa via di vita buona e speranza concreta*. Rome: Ufficio nazionale per la pastorale del tempo libero, turismo e sport.

Causevic, S., & Lynch, P. (2011). Phoenix tourism: post-conflict tourism role. *Annals of Tourism Research, 38*(3), 780–800.

D'Amore, L. (2009). Peace through tourism: the birthing of a new socio-economic order. *Journal of Business Ethics, 89*(4), 559–68.

Di Giovine, M. A. (2010). World Heritage Tourism: UNESCO's vehicle for peace? *Anthropology News, 51*(8), 8–9.

Durko, A., & Petrick, J. (2016). The Nutella project: an education initiative to suggest tourism as a means to peace between the United States and Afghanistan. *Journal of Travel Research, 55*(8), 1081–93.

Ellis, S. J., & Kitzinger, C. (2002). Denying equality: an analysis of arguments against lowering the age of consent for sex between men. *Journal of Community & Applied Social Psychology, 12*, 167–80.

Farmaki, A. (2017). The tourism and peace nexus. *Tourism Management, 59*, 528–40.

Ferrari, S., & Nicotera T. (2021). *Primo rapporto sul turismo delle radici in Italia.* Padova: Egea.

Friedl, H. (2014). "I Had a Good Fight with my Buddy!" Systemic conflict training in tourism education as a paradigmatic. Approach to stimulating peace competence. In C. Wohlmuther & W. Wintersteiner (Eds.), *International Handbook on Tourism and Peace* (pp. 335–54). Klagenfurt: Drava.

Galtung, J. (1996). *Peace by Peaceful Means: Peace and Conflict, Development and Civilization.* Thousand Oaks, CA: Sage.

Gopin, M. (1997). Religion, violence, and conflict resolution. *Peace & Change, 22*(1), 1–31.

Hansen, T. (2016). Holistic peace. *Peace Review, 28*(2), 212–19.

Kim, S. S., Prideaux, B., & Prideaux, J. (2007). Using tourism to promote peace on the Korean Peninsula. *Annals of Tourism Research, 34*(2), 291–309.

Kitzinger, C., & Willmott, J. (2002). The thief of womanhood: women's experience of polycystic ovarian syndrome. *Social Science & Medicine, 54*, 349–61.

McKercher, B., Ho, P. S., Cros, H. D., & So-Ming, B. C. (2002). Activities-based segmentation of the cultural tourism market. *Journal of Travel & Tourism Marketing, 12*(1), 23–46.

Novelli, M., Morgan, N., & Nibigira, C. (2012). Tourism in a post-conflict situation of fragility. *Annals of Tourism Research, 39*(3), 1446–69.

Nowell, L. S., Norris, J. M., White, D. E., & Moules, N. J. (2017). Thematic analysis: striving to meet the trustworthiness criteria. *International Journal of Qualitative Methods, 16*(1), 1–13.

Noy, C. (2008). Sampling knowledge: the hermeneutics of snowball sampling in qualitative research. *International Journal of Social Research Methodology, 11*(4), 327–44.

Redekop, P. (2014). Inner peace and conflict transformation. *Peace Research, 46*(2), 31–49.

Reed, M. S., Graves, A., Dandy, N., Posthumus, H., Hubacek, K., Morris, J., & Stringer, L. C. (2009). Who's in and why? A typology of stakeholder analysis methods for natural resource management. *Journal of Environmental Management, 90*(5), 1933–49.

Salazar, N. B. (2006). Building a 'culture of peace' through tourism: reflexive and analytical notes and queries. *Universitas Humanística, 62*, 319–33.

Sánchez Sánchez, A., & Fernández Herreira, A. (1996). *Dimensiones de la educación para la paz. Teoría y experiencia.* Granada: Eirene.

Schwartz, S. H. (1992). Universals in the content and structure of values: theoretical advances and empirical tests in 20 countries. *Advances in Experimental Social Psychology*, *25*, 1–65.

Tigano, M. (2020). The encyclical letter "LaudatoSi" between sustainable development and integral ecology. In *Sustainability in Transforming Societies*, Budapest: 26th annual conference of international sustainable development research society.

Wintersteiner, W., & Wohlmuther, C. (2014). Peace sensitive tourism: how tourism can contribute to peace. In C. Wohlmuther & W. Wintersteiner (Eds.), *International Handbook on Tourism and Peace* (pp. 31–61). Klagenfurt: Drava.

WTTC [World Travel and Tourism Council] (2016). Tourism as a driver of peace. Available at http://www.wttc.org (accessed May 12, 2016).

7 The peace and conflict duet: a complex systems perspective

Jalayer Khalilzadeh

Introduction

Tourism and peace relationship is a specific form of the general relationship between international trade and peace rooted in the Kantian notion of peace (Dorussen & Ward, 2010; Khalilzadeh, 2018). According to the literature, tourism is correlated with some of the types of peace. Peace can be categorized into two concepts of negative peace and positive peace. Positive peace is the institutionalization of peace in society concerning healthy business environments, well-functioning governance, lack of corruption, human rights and capital, freedom of information, and so on. Negative peace, on the other hand, is the absence of violence and divides into two types of internal (within boundaries) and external (bilateral state level) peace (WTTC, 2016). Tourism has shown meaningful correlations with external negative peace and overall positive peace but has not shown any significant correlations with internal negative peace (WTTC, 2016). These statements, however, must not be taken as definite relationships as there are many contradictory findings in the literature as to whether tourism is a peacemaking or peacekeeping agent (Khalilzadeh, 2018).

Theoretically speaking, trade reduces conflict's expected utility (Dorussen & Ward, 2010). However, it is important to note that a positive or negative association between tourism/trade and conflict does not necessarily indicate a causal relationship between them (Jackson, 2019) and that the reality is more complex than a simple interaction between the two. Therefore, similar to the research findings on the relationship between trade and conflict (Cranmer et al., 2012; Dorussen & Ward, 2010; Hafner-Burton & Montgomery, 2012), there is a mix of supporting and opposing findings regarding the relationship between tourism and conflict/peace (Khalilzadeh, 2018).

Furthermore, due to features and mechanisms such as feedback loops, large number of components and interactions, emergence, self-organization, and so on, efforts to discover and/or explain causality chains in complex systems (such as tourism) are a fruitless endeavor (Kramer, 2017). Moreover, predicting the behavior of complex systems, in most cases, is inaccurate due to their nonlinear nature (Kramer, 2017). Therefore, this chapter aims to shed light on some of the shortcomings of tourism–peace studies' existing approaches. Most of the studies that investigate tourism's role in the global peace–conflict interactions belong to the reductionist camp. While the reductionist approach and Newtonian mechanics are highly effective in producing knowledge about linear, simple, and complicated systems, their employment in studying complex adaptive systems can lead to serious epistemological deficiencies. Complex systems should be approached holistically, meaning that all system components should be taken into account simultaneously. The outcome of a complex system is more than the sum of its parts, and its synergic-emergent behavior cannot be reduced to its components (de Domenico et al., 2019).

To study and model systems including complex adaptive systems, network science is arguably the best approach (Barabási & Albert, 1999). In its simplest notion, a network or a graph is a set of vertices and edges $G = \{V, E\}$. There are different terms for each graph element. For example, node, actor, player, or agent are other terms for vertex; and link, arc, line, or connection are standard terms for edge. Networks can be directed or undirected (i.e., edges with or without direction), unipartite with only one type of vertices or multipartite (the most common multipartite is bipartite or two-mode network), nested within each other (i.e., each node can be a network itself), hypergraphs in which edges are enclosed shapes containing connected nodes, multigraph (having multiple edges between the same dyads), and multilayer or multitype (having the same vertices in different layers with regular connections within each layer and interconnected nodes between layers). It is worth mentioning that a combination of the above configurations can also be used to model more complex systems. For example, a multi-hypergraph complex network is formed by intersecting communities or subgraphs (Hammoud & Kramer, 2020).

Despite the development of a large set of network science techniques over the past 30 years, their applications in solving real-world issues were restricted due to the limitations of computational power and the unorthodox nature of these techniques to the traditionally trained social science scholars. More recently, the concepts, methods, and approaches developed in social physics made it possible to investigate social dynamics as large as the global tourism system, trade network, mass migration, and so on. Various contributors to social physics such as thermodynamics, statistical physics and mechanics, as well as mathematical branches such as graph theory and game theory, have provided us with such a powerful toolbox to study complex adaptive systems the likes of which have never been seen before (Jusup et al., 2022). By adding the exceptional computational power that we have in social science nowadays (Khalilzadeh, 2022) to the mix above, we can employ network science to study tourism and peace/conflict systems and overcome most of the limitations with which we have dealt for more than 50 years.

Despite the long history of academicians' interest in the impact of trade on peace in general and tourism on peace in particular, the question of whether trade networks reduce the interstate conflicts was asked only about two decades ago (Dorussen & Ward, 2010). While the use of network science in peace/conflict general studies has increased (Dorussen & Ward, 2010), its use in studies that examine the relationship of tourism with peace/conflict remains scant. In fact, to the best of the author's knowledge, up to now, only three studies have employed network science to study the role of tourism in relation to peace/conflict (Farmaki et al., 2019; Khalilzadeh, 2018; Su et al., 2020).

Complexity: globalization

Now that the necessity, reasons, and utility of using network science and complex systems approach in studying tourism and trade relations with peace and conflicts have been explained, we need to establish the complexity of the concepts discussed above. The complexity of the tourism–peace relationship is mainly because of the complexity of tourism as a player in global trade and the complexity of peace–conflict components. The complexity of tourism at destination level and as an entire system has been adequately discussed in tourism literature (Baggio, 2013; Khalilzadeh, 2022). Here, instead, I will take a step back and will focus on the process and history of globalization as the main mechanism driving the exponential growth of international trade and tourism complex systems.

Globalization is rooted in various technological advancements that can be broken down into commute and communication evolutions. Early changes in commuting technology emerged with the construction of 37,000 United States interstate expressway systems between the 1950s and 1980s, which transformed the ancient road system in a revolutionary fashion. In the same vein, the advent of jet airliners in the late 1950s and the airline deregulation act in the 1970s contributed to making the world smaller and more accessible than ever (Rainie & Wellman, 2012). The three initial waves of change in communication technology were made by automation of local telephone systems in the 1930s and direct distance dialing within the country in the 1960s and between countries in the 1970s. Similarly, mobile lines revolutionized communication technologies; in the U.S.A., by 2006, there were more mobile lines than landlines (Rainie & Wellman, 2012). However, despite everything said above, the main revolution in communication technologies was public access to the internet in the late 1980s and early 1990s which later on was integrated with other technologies, such as mobile phones, the internet of things, smart technologies, and virtual reality, making globalization what it is today.

Globalization and advances in technology in general and information and communication technologies in particular, have facilitated the creation and preservation of relationships, especially distant ones (Jackson, 2019). In fact, todays' extensive and dense travel and tourism and trade networks are the direct outcome of globalization (Rainie & Wellman, 2012). Connectivity and its density improve the equilibrium of the system and significantly impacts the economy by easing international trade, which in turn makes the world more peaceful (Jackson, 2019). Also, countries with higher economic interdependence have a lower propensity to involve in conflictual interactions. For instance, Europe has been experiencing the most peaceful time ever since the establishment of European Union (not considering the recent Russia–Ukraine war) (Jackson, 2019). Furthermore, over the past half century, the likelihood of interstate war has declined to one-tenth (Jackson, 2019) not only because of economic interdependence but also because of military alliances (e.g., The North Atlantic Treaty Organization (NATO)). Accordingly, over the past 30 years, the density of military alliance networks has increased significantly as well (Jackson, 2019).

It is too naïve to think that globalization and its processes have only been contributing to the global peace landscape as they have also played a part in conflicts (e.g., impact of internet on Arab Awakening (Kramer, 2017)). In fact, globalization has changed the structure and function of the peace/conflict firmament. To be specific, an investigation of global conflicts from the 1950s onward shows that while both extrastate (almost nonexistent nowadays) and interstate conflicts have had a downward trend, intrastate conflicts have had a steep upward trend for the most part (the peak was in the 1990s and is on a decline since then) (Rainie & Wellman, 2012). Moreover, globalization has made the concept of borders less meaningful for both international trade and conflicts. The cross-border nature of today's conflicts has weakened the role of central authorities (e.g., governments) in controlling these conflicts. Rebellion groups and extremists can recruit in one country, reside in a different country, and conduct operations in yet another country. The prolonged and numerous conflicts of North and West Africa are a witness to the above claim (OECD/SWAC, 2021). Due to their adaptive nature, the configuration of local extremists and rebellion groups drastically changes when military interventions take place. In North and West Africa, these drastic changes in composition have made these organizations more resilient, violent, and efficient, and have made the military interventions less effective (OECD/SWAC, 2021). More than 100,000 civilian lives have been lost over the past ten years (Walther et al., 2021), and conflicts in this region have become more widespread and violent. Unfortunately, due to an increase in the complexity of the conflict system (the interactions among the extremists and rebellions), finding a solution seems farther away than ever (OECD/SWAC, 2021; Walther et al., 2021).

The common belief that also drives most of the tourism studies (Khalilzadeh, 2018) is that higher density of global network results in better communication, mutual understanding, and exchange of ideas and opinions, which should lead to hostility and violence decline (Kramer, 2017). This assumption/belief, however, has already been challenged empirically (Khalilzadeh, 2018) and it is now known that globalization plays a pivotal role in the global violence and conflict firmament (Kramer, 2017). The continuous globalization process leads to an increase in size of the network, therefore creating more capacity for structural entropy which makes the system more complex (Cai et al., 2017). Complex systems show sensitive dependence on initial conditions, meaning that any negligible alteration might result in major, dramatic, and amplified effects on the system and its components because of positive feedback loops. As a result, in growing globalized networks, while we cannot expect higher levels of order and stability, it is reasonable to expect more disorder and conflictual responses to the stimuli in the system (Kramer, 2017). Therefore, the globalization process is a double-edged sword that causes the oxymoron of peace and conflict to simultaneously emerge from the systems' behavior.

Complexity: violence and conflict

Now that globalization's process is explained and globalization's simultaneous contribution to peace and conflict is demystified, I examine concepts such as power and violence on a deeper level to better conceive the complexity of violence and conflict systems. Power in its relational capacity is the ability to exert dominance on the subject (Kramer, 2017). An example of visible power is violence, and the most prevailing impression of violence is war. Violence, in spite of being destructive and having the capacity to create suffering, is an innate characteristic of human communication, behavior, identity, and meaning (Kramer, 2017). Due to limited resources, unlimited wishes, and the desire to maximize the return on relationships, internal and external conflicts have always been and will always be an integral part of most networked systems (Kramer, 2017). However, these external and internal conflicts are not serious issues unless accompanied by violence (e.g., war). Here, it is important to note that unlike violence, war is not a universal experience (unless it is a situation like world war) and cannot be fully comprehended by external observers who are not involved in the conflict (Kramer, 2017). Therefore, the complexity of conflict is not entirely due to its existence in a system's structure, nor is it solely dependent on the complexity of its components such as violence but is also entangled with the complexity of observer/observee relations.

As discussed before, globalization and its underlying processes contribute to the distribution of violence within and between networks. We can recognize the role of information and communication technologies in the development of violence and global conflicts firmament only if we understand that violence is just another form of communication in the network (Kramer, 2017). In a society where the threat of violence is absent, actors have multiple identities and are part of several networks. However, when violence becomes apparent, networks start the adaptation process by restructuring, and actors start reducing their identities and networks to minimize the threat (Kramer, 2017). Stated differently, in order to control the homeostasis of the system, the complex system promotes and demotes violence by using positive and negative feedback loops, respectively. It is important to note, however, that the effects of violence are not all immediate and that they disrupt the supply chain in the long run by feeding insecurity and conflict over scarce resources (Kramer, 2017). All these events can push the system towards disintegration without proper intervention.

In our global community network and its subsystems, violence not only exists but also persists. Violence is harsh and infectious; in the context of international relations, violence can create large-scale disasters such as mass migrations, organized crime, religious extremism, and infrastructure destruction (Kramer, 2017). Each year, in addition to the direct impact of violence on global society, its (i.e., violence) containment imposes a significant economic burden on the global economy. In 2014, about 13.4 percent of global GDP or roughly $14.3 trillion was spent on violence containment (WTTC, 2016). Part of the resilience we observe in violence is ingrained in its transmission mechanisms as the contagiousness of violence makes it a dynamic phenomenon without borders (Kramer, 2017). Similar to conflicts (as discussed previously under globalization), violent conducts are not bounded by geographic boundaries; spillovers of troubles between Turkey and Kurds to Iraq, the influence of ISIS in both Iraq and Syria, the impact of Syria's civil war on many countries in Europe, Turkey, and especially Lebanon, and Pakistan's border communities' extremisms spillover to Afghanistan and vice versa, are all examples of how violence spreads through different networks via bridges embedded in the structures of these networks. When it comes to contagiousness, distinguishing simple contagion in which transmission can occur with single source exposure (e.g., infectious diseases such as measles) from complex contagion in which multiple sources of exposure (e.g., most behaviors such as being vaccinated) are required for transmission is necessary (Centola, 2018). In simple contagion, the infectiousness of what is being spread is crucial in determining whether the phenomenon is transmissible or not and how many exposures are required for it to spread. For example, a weather report on a thunderstorm is more infectious than the result of a not-much-anticipated sports match. In complex contagion, the fraction of reinforcers to all existing sources (i.e., reinforcers and those who are not reinforcers) is critical in determining the adoption threshold. For example, while a piece of complex information such as rumor can be easily dismissed if there is only one source of exposure, it can be adopted if, let's say, 60 percent (for the sake of argument) of someone's contacts reinforce it (Centola, 2018). Violence as news or a communication medium can be a simple contagion with an infection level that depends on the brutality of the violent act. In contrast, violence as power manifestation and epiphany of one's control over many is a complex behavior with complex contagion that requires the affirmation of a large number of one's contacts in order to diffuse in a system.

Regardless of contagion mechanism, the network's structure and shape have a central role in how violence spreads. With global networks being dynamic, the evolution of subsystems occasionally contributes to the spread of violence. The spread of violence takes place by an increase in connectivity and density of the global network which also increases homophily by connecting like-minded individuals to each other. With an increase in homophily, the variety of information input becomes limited. Accordingly, a positive feedback loop can potentially intensify false information and community consensus as well divergence across different communities. This process will cause the global network to end up with a polarized structure (Jackson, 2019). As a result of the polarized structure, any internal and external perturbations can push the system to the edge of chaos by feeding the violent communicating networks. An immediate outcome of such fragmented networks is high levels of uncertainty and low levels of capacity for adaption, which threatens the system's integrity. The extreme polarization of the United States' political firmament and the situation in Ukraine after Russia's invasion of Crimea are examples of how fragmented networks contribute to violence and war.

Complexity: control systems

The impact of violent systems is not limited to society only. One way or another, these systems will interact with political systems and will drag the formal and semiformal governance systems to the duet of peace and conflict. One side of the story is about power and control, and like it or not, governance and control systems are the entangled parts of the process. Apart from the initial condition, predefined mechanisms (game rules), types of government (e.g., democratic, autocratic), governing mechanisms, and governing system's structure and behavior in conflict-infested regions will adapt to the situation and the perturbation that the system is faced with. Therefore, the system will produce a unique response set that cannot be explained by any linear process (Kramer, 2017). Due to various error components, these controlling systems sometimes fail to synchronize with their respective systems that they are attempting to control and, hence, will end up in a condition known as the complexity gap. The complexity gap is the space between the controlling regime (governing system) and the population/mass system in a state that, if not closed, will create instability, unrest, and revolutions (if amplified with positive feedback loops). The inability of the governing system or the unwantedness of the governing system (due to the benefits that violence has for them) to effectively control the networks and close the gap will result in violence becoming the dominant communication method in the network. Afghanistan is an example of a complexity gap that has existed for a very long time (Kramer, 2017).

Finally, violence and conflict are born and die in the network of relationships. Recognition and rationalization of violence in various forms of conflicts without perceiving the role of underlying network structure is extremely challenging, if not impossible. For example, why do Sunnis and Shiites kill each other in civil wars such as those in Syria and Iraq, while in a developed European city, these two groups live peacefully next to each other? The answer is in the underlying networks that codify, regulate, and sanction violence in the above-mentioned environments (Kramer, 2017). Therefore, elimination of the disintegrating effects of wars, conflicts, and any other violent conduct is only possible if we can reprogram/control the network (Kramer, 2017). Networks in large numbers, nested, interrelated, and representing a broad range of systems, exist in any state/nation/player. Their program design, structure, and function, however, are different and unique. These networks are the most significant threats, yet the greatest assets of these players, to keep or disturb the global peace (Kramer, 2017). Furthermore, the importance of networks is not limited to the time of conflict; the role, adaptability, and persistence of informal ethnic/economic post-conflict networks in the process of peacebuilding have been observed on multiple occasions in sub-Saharan Africa, the Balkans, South Caucasus, as well as Central and South Asia (Bojicic-Dzelilovic et al., 2022). From an international relation perspective, the decision and mechanism of link-creation by an actor in a network, although to some extent depends on the individual actor's choice, is actually the outcome of network structure and other actors' influences. These links are critical in the network's structure and function as they have a tremendous effect on the network's future and how it contributes to the diffusion of conflict/peace (Maoz, 2012a).

Complexity: the final curtain

By now, we should have a grasp of complexity notions in the contexts of trade/tourism and peace/conflict. Even in their most classic conceptions (i.e., interactions, emergence, dynamics, self-organization, and adaptation), both tourism and conflicts/peace systems show various characteristics of complex adaptive systems (de Domenico et al., 2019). In view of that, both tourism and conflict/peace are a system of systems (SoS); the tourism system is SoS due to its umbrella nature and multilevel actors such as destinations, and the conflict/peace system is SoS due to its variety of components such as violence. The components of these two SoSs constantly interact within and between systems, leading to these two systems' high levels of interconnectedness and interdependence. In both systems, actors are changing and relationships are evolving. All forms of connections and links are continuously created and terminated which is the indication of systems' dynamicity. Both SoSs are self-organized because actors follow a set of rules and decision-making criteria to maximize their gain at any given time. Accordingly, these systems have specific network structures. It should be noted here that no single actor is capable of determining the structure of the entire network. Because of systems' self-organization characteristic, we observe a unique and complex behavior emerging with synergic outcomes concerning value creation and capacity for obliteration. The behavior of both systems also continuously changes in response to environmental forces/perturbations in order to create adaptive capacity for the systems to ensure the continuity of their survival (i.e., homeostasis) and integrity.

Thus far, the complexity of all systems involved, and the complexity of these systems' interconnections have been established. Moreover, I have discussed the presence of networks on numerous occasions and scales, from local to international. In addition to what has been presented so far, there are some natural alignments and overlaps among various subjects related to trade/ tourism and peace/conflict with network science which make it (i.e., network science) the only suitable candidate to be employed for studying tourism relations with peace. For instance, homophily and assortativity as classic subjects of social network analysis (Scott & Carrington, 2014) have also been used to study critical topics of international conflicts literature such as the role of homophily in alliances and dissimilarity of political systems in conflicts (Cranmer et al., 2012). Moreover, the role of proximity in border disputes (e.g., Iran/Iraq, India/Pakistan, the Korean peninsula, Israel/Palestine, Crimea) as another significant topic in international conflict literature (Cranmer et al., 2012) is closest to Euler's Königsberg bridges problem, which is the origin of graph theory and network science (Börner et al., 2007). Furthermore, the successful examples of utilizing network science in studying subjects relevant to peace/conflict and trade/tourism also testify to the suitability of network science and complex adaptive systems approach to be employed in tourism and peace studies. For example, many international conflicts are rooted in the interactions among various states. These interactions are mainly guided by state preferences, which are continuously evolving. It is not possible to directly observe and measure the state preferences; therefore, proxy measures such as alliances and United Nations voting behavior are commonly employed to estimate these preferences. These measures, however, are not good proxies due to the dynamism of state preferences. On this note, recently, some scholars suggested utilizing the network approach as an effective measurement tool for revealing the actual preferences (Gallop & Minhas, 2021). Another example is social network analysis, which has been extensively used in studying terrorist organizations and tracking their members ever since the 9/11 attacks (OECD/SWAC, 2021). Networks are effective in studying various forms of extremist and terrorist organizations, including overt or covert and profit- or value-driven ones (OECD/SWAC, 2021). In addition, social network analysis has been employed by states as a tool for counterinsurgency (Mac Ginty, 2010). Another example is conflicts that even in their most dyadic form are not only under the impact of third parties but are also under the influence of the entire system's structure. The inception and termination of conflicts are better understood if and only if we study them through an extradyadic (e.g., triadic) relations lens since excluding the extradyadic interdependence increases the likelihood of type-I error because of the confounding effects (Dorussen et al., 2016). Based on this discussion then, the type and likelihood of a third party's intervention and its stability (i.e., balanced vs. unbalanced) can only be investigated through the network perspective (Corbetta & Grant, 2012). For instance, the concept of shared enemy (a form of triadic relationship) (Cranmer et al., 2012) has been abundantly studied via structural balance theory and signed networks to show cooperation and opposition in various networks of rivalries and alliances (OECD/SWAC, 2021).

Finally, various models and tools are developed in network science to yield more accurate and representative analyses of real-world problems. I have already reviewed some of the most appropriate models under the concept of multilayer networks, which have the highest utility in modeling complex systems. The four classes of network science models known as random networks, lattice graphs, small-world networks, and scale-free networks and the subsets of each class plus the combination of these models result in an extensive library of network models to be used according to various conceptualizations of real-world networks (Khalilzadeh, 2022; Strogatz, 2001). Moreover, different statistical models in social network analysis can be employed in inferential analyses. An excellent example of these statistical representations is the family of exponential random graph models (ERGMs), which provides a powerful tool for modeling networks from the perspectives of structural, endogenous, and exogenous variables (Scott & Carrington, 2014). For instance, in international conflicts and alliances studies, by using ERGMs, it is possible to statistically test various dyadic and network-structure-related hypotheses that we couldn't test otherwise (Cranmer et al., 2012). Another example is Maoz (2012b), who studied the evolution of alliances and trade networks and concluded that while trade networks mainly follow the preferential attachment principle and form a scale-free network over time, alliance networks mostly evolve around the concept of homophily and can be modeled using a broad range of generative models (Pham et al., 2016). In the same vein, despite some evidence of preferential attachment in tourism (Khalilzadeh, 2022), a new study by Khalilzadeh (2022) has shown that the tourism system follows a precise small-world regime in its evolution and becomes strictly a small-world network as time elapses.

Conclusion

We should not always look for the cause of conflicts, and instead, we should look for methods to reprogram the networks and establish a communication network beyond violence, as doing so is the only way that even the most complex forms of conflict, such as civil wars, will cease to exist (Kramer, 2017). In fact, looking for causation and predicting the system's future state via linear systems' perspectives are fruitless efforts. Finding a simple solution to complex problems, more often than not, leads to the Cobra effect and makes the issue worse (Attarha et al., 2018). Network reprogramming and control-based solutions are usually absent in military, political, and economic interventions, resulting in failed attempts. We cannot study the relationship between tourism and peace by ignoring the trade, financial, infrastructure, risk, communication, control, violence, and power networks and their interactions. Therefore, network science is the only approach that can yield meaningful results, which unfortunately, is missing from the literature on tourism and peace.

Network theory can be as valuable as relational data in advancing the tourism and peace research agenda. In studying peace/conflict and tourism, networks can be used in various capacities as a theoretical tool, a measurement tool and methodological toolkit, or a modeling, statistical testing/inferential tool (Dorussen et al., 2016). There are a few research streams in this realm that scholars should pursue as they can revolutionize our understanding of tourism and peace. For example, the impacts of trade and conflict networks on one another can be studied by network science (Dorussen et al., 2016). As briefly discussed above, theoretically, violence can transmit by following both simple and complex contagions. Nevertheless, we do not have any empirical evidence of violence networks' diffusion mechanisms and interaction with the tourism network. The same goes for most of the networks mentioned above (except for financial ones). Future studies should focus on the transmission of peace, conflict, and violence when studying tourism and peace. Over the past 20 years, various diffusion models have been employed in network science that can be useful in tourism and peace cases as well especially that these models have improved tremendously because of the COVID-19 pandemic. Also, agent-based modeling can be employed on or alongside network modeling to model various contingency configurations during or after a shock and external perturbations in systems (Dorussen et al., 2016). Since war and armed conflicts are subject to uncertainty, reaction, and incomplete information (Kramer, 2017), utilization of game theory in networks could be a remarkable research stream as well. Game theory and network science have been used together before and have resulted in groundbreaking studies (Jusup et al., 2022). Future studies can also combine game theory, network science, and agent-based modeling to test and simulate scenarios that have never occurred in the real world so that we have an appropriate response set for future states of tourism and peace complex systems. Finally, control systems can be studied in the networked systems mentioned above to improve our intervention efforts. Detection of influential nodes (i.e., driver nodes) along with structural control is another well-developed area of network science that can yield valuable outcomes if applied to tourism and peace as it can tell us whether the system is controllable or not and how we can plan for sustainable interventions (Liu et al., 2011).

As a closing note, it is important to mention that the successful implementation of network science and achieving valuable and practical results depend on the selection of suitable models. In fact, the famous saying of *"garbage in, garbage out"* that is frequently used in computer science and statistics is also a useful concept to consider in network science. Selecting the correct model has the utmost importance in getting accurate results. Unlike simple linear models in which parsimony and simplicity are the main principles of modeling, in network science and complex networks, similarity of the model to the reality is the main focus for better representation of real-world complexities. Moreover, the relevancy of a network science study is also about its conceptualization and operationalization which highly depends on the skills, creativity, and knowledge of the scholars. Lastly, the irresponsible use of network science in peace/ conflicts can harm the peace process and postwar construction by destroying the social capital needed for peacebuilding and community cohesion (Mac Ginty, 2010). Therefore, scholars who study the relationship between tourism and peace should consider ethical obligations when designing their research and be aware of the potential negative impacts of their practices on the peacebuilding process.

References

Attarha, M., Bigelow, J., & Merzenich, M. M. (2018). Unintended consequences of white noise therapy for tinnitus – Otolaryngology's Cobra effect. *JAMA Otolaryngology-Head & Neck Surgery, 144*(10), 938. https://doi.org/10.1001/jamaoto.2018.1856.

Baggio, R. (2013). Oriental and occidental approaches to complex tourism systems. *Tourism Planning & Development, 10*(2), 217–27. https://doi.org/10.1080/21568316.2013.783731.

Barabási, A.-L., & Albert, R. (1999). Emergence of scaling in random networks. *Science, 286*(5439), 509–12. https://doi.org/10.1126/science.286.5439.509.

Bojicic-Dzelilovic, V., Kostovicova, D., & Suerdem, A. K. (2022). Persistence of informal networks and liberal peacebuilding: evidence from Bosnia and Herzegovina. *Journal of International Relations and Development, 25*(1), 182–209. https://doi.org/10.1057/s41268-021-00220-4.

Börner, K., Sanyal, S., & Vespignani, A. (2007). Network science. *Annual Review of Information Science and Technology, 41*(1), 537–607. https://doi.org/10.1002/aris.2007.1440410119.

Cai, M., Cui, Y., & Stanley, H. E. (2017). Analysis and evaluation of the entropy indices of a static network structure. *Scientific Reports, 7*(1), 9340. https://doi.org/10.1038/s41598-017-09475-9.

Centola, D. (2018). *How Behavior Spreads: The Science of Complex Contagions.* Princeton University Press.

Corbetta, R., & Grant, K. A. (2012). Intervention in conflicts from a network perspective. *Conflict Management and Peace Science, 29*(3), 314–40. https://doi.org/10.1177/0738894212443343.

Cranmer, S. J., Desmarais, B. A., & Menninga, E. J. (2012). Complex dependencies in the alliance network. *Conflict Management and Peace Science, 29*(3), 279–313. https://doi.org/10.1177/0738894212443446.

de Domenico, M., Brockmann, D., Camargo, C., Gershenson, C., Goldsmith, D., Jeschonnek, S., Kay, L., Nichele, S., Nicolás, J. R., Schmickl, T., Stella, M., Brandoff, J., Martínez Salinas, A. J., & Sayama, H. (2019). *Complexity explained* (Version 1.0). http://hdl.handle.net/10871/124302.

Dorussen, H., Gartzke, E. A., & Westerwinter, O. (2016). Networked international politics: complex interdependence and the diffusion of conflict and peace. *Journal of Peace Research, 53*(3), 283–91. https://doi.org/10.1177/0022343316637896.

Dorussen, H., & Ward, H. (2010). Trade networks and the Kantian peace. *Journal of Peace Research, 47*(1), 29–42. https://doi.org/10.1177/0022343309350011.

Farmaki, A., Khalilzadeh, J., & Altinay, L. (2019). Travel motivation and demotivation within politically unstable nations. *Tourism Management Perspectives, 29*, 118–30. https://doi.org/10.1016/J.TMP.2018.11.004.

Gallop, M., & Minhas, S. (2021). A network approach to measuring state preferences. *Network Science, 9*(2), 135–52. https://doi.org/10.1017/nws.2020.44.

Hafner-Burton, E. M., & Montgomery, A. H. (2012). War, trade, and distrust: why trade agreements don't always keep the peace. *Conflict Management and Peace Science, 29*(3), 257–78. https://doi.org/10.1177/0738894212443342.

Hammoud, Z., & Kramer, F. (2020). Multilayer networks: aspects, implementations, and application in biomedicine. *Big Data Analytics, 5*(1), 2. https://doi.org/10.1186/s41044-020-00046-0.

Jackson, M. O. (2019). *The Human Network: How Your Social Position Determines Your Power, Beliefs, and Behaviors.* Pantheon Books.

Jusup, M., Holme, P., Kanazawa, K., Takayasu, M., Romić, I., Wang, Z., Geček, S., Lipić, T., Podobnik, B., Wang, L., Luo, W., Klanjšček, T., Fan, J., Boccaletti, S., & Perc, M. (2022). Social physics. *Physics Reports, 948*, 1–148. https://doi.org/10.1016/j.physrep.2021.10.005.

Khalilzadeh, J. (2018). Demonstration of exponential random graph models in tourism studies: is tourism a means of global peace or the bottom line? *Annals of Tourism Research.* https://doi.org/10.1016/j.annals.2017.12.007.

Khalilzadeh, J. (2022). It is a small world, or is it? A look into two decades of tourism system. *Physica A: Statistical Mechanics and Its Applications, 606*, 128061. https://doi.org/10.1016/j.physa.2022.128061.

Kramer, C. R. (2017). *Network Theory and Violent Conflicts.* Springer International. https://doi.org/10.1007/978-3-319-41393-8.

Liu, Y.-Y., Slotine, J.-J., & Barabási, A.-L. (2011). Controllability of complex networks. *Nature, 473*, 167. http://dx.doi.org/10.1038/nature10011.

Mac Ginty, R. (2010). Social network analysis and counterinsurgency: a counterproductive strategy? *Critical Studies on Terrorism, 3*(2), 209–26. https://doi.org/10.1080/17539153.2010.491319.

Maoz, Z. (2012a). How network analysis can inform the study of international relations. *Conflict Management and Peace Science, 29*(3), 247–56. https:// doi .org/ 10 .1177/0738894212443341.

Maoz, Z. (2012b). Preferential attachment, homophily, and the structure of international networks, 1816–2003. *Conflict Management and Peace Science, 29*(3), 341–69. https://doi.org/10.1177/0738894212443344.

OECD/SWAC (2021). *Conflict Networks in North and West Africa.* https://doi.org/10.1787/896e3eca-en.

Pham, T., Sheridan, P., & Shimodaira, H. (2016). Joint estimation of preferential attachment and node fitness in growing complex networks. *Scientific Reports, 6*(1). https://doi.org/10.1038/srep32558.

Rainie, L., & Wellman, B. (2012). *Networked: The New Social Operating System.* The MIT Press.

Scott, J., & Carrington, P. J. (2014). *The SAGE Handbook of Social Network Analysis.* SAGE Publications. https://doi.org/10.4135/9781446294413.

Strogatz, S. H. (2001). Exploring complex networks. *Nature, 410*(6825), 268–76. https://doi.org/10.1038/35065725.

Su, L., Stepchenkova, S., & Dai, X. (2020). The core-periphery image of South Korea on the Chinese tourist market in the times of conflict over THAAD. *Journal of Destination Marketing & Management, 17*, 100457. https://doi.org/10.1016/j.jdmm.2020.100457.

Walther, O. J., Radil, S. M., & Russell, D. G. (2021). Mapping the changing structure of conflict networks in North and West Africa. *African Security, 14*(3), 211–38. https://doi.org/10.1080/19392206.2021.1996173.

WTTC (2016). Tourism as a driver of peace. https://www.americansforthearts.org/sites/default/files/TourismPeace.pdf.

8 Reflections on researching tourism and peace

Jack Shepherd and Mónica Guasca

Introduction

Despite several decades of investigation into tourism's relationship to peace, there has been little reflection on the ontological, epistemological and methodological challenges of conducting research on peace-through-tourism (PTT). This should be a source of shared concern given just how complex researching the concept of peace is and how challenging fieldwork in settings of conflict can be. We are troubled by the silences in the literature about experiences of researching PTT, and feel it is time to encourage a more sensitive engagement with the concept of peace, and a more reflexive approach to researching PTT.

In this chapter, we attempt to breach this issue and answer Buda and McIntosh's (2012) call to bring our attention to the act of researching PTT. To do this, we reflect on our research experiences in the Israeli-Palestinian and Colombian contexts, highlighting the challenges we faced and the lessons we learnt. Taking this opportunity for retrospection, we engage in reflexive dialogue on conceptual, practical and ethical considerations that we believe should be part of any future research agenda for PTT.

Our chapter is constructed in a conversational style, where we both (Jack and Mónica) discuss our own experiences with PTT research and bounce ideas off one another. We were impressed by the readability and dialogical nature of similar academic work (e.g. Pearce & Dietrich, 2019; Grant & Zeeman, 2012), and are convinced of the benefits of dialogue in a community of practice such as our own (Frank, 2005). Much of our discussion focuses on two key subjects. The first is the slipperiness of the concept of peace, which is only now starting to gain attention in the PTT literature (e.g. Shepherd & Laven, 2022). The second is, as Acar et al. (2020) point out, the messy nature of research in settings of conflict. This includes its emotional aspects, the political and contested nature of the field and its data, and the risks to both researcher and informants. Navigating such terrain is challenging, and we deign not to proffer *the* answer to researching tourism in conflict settings. What we do hope to provide, however, are reflections that help scholars push forward a research agenda for PTT.

The concept of peace: ontological and epistemological challenges

Jack: I will start this conversation by focusing on the contested nature of peace, which I consider one of the main points that we wish to convey within this chapter. The PTT debate has tended to take a normative approach to what peace means – assuming that what peace means to one person is what it is going to mean to someone else. I find this testified to in the numerous articles that have probed the question, "does tourism lead to peace"? (e.g. Becken & Carmignani, 2016; Khalilzadeh, 2018). I think our contribution here is to stress that peace does not mean the same thing to everyone, and that it can look different in different times and spaces. Peace studies literature reveals that peace should not be thought of in the singular, but in the plural. This means there are "many peaces" (Dietrich, 2012, p. 2), with peace meaning anything from harmony of man with nature, to a state of security ensured by nation states. Such literature has helped me put words to what I have witnessed in Israel/ Palestine.

In 2019, I was researching a tourism initiative called the Abraham Path. The path was established by an American non-governmental organisation (NGO) called the Abraham Path Initiative, and is a hiking trail that follows in the footsteps of the biblical patriarch Abraham across the Middle East. The idea was that the path would be infrastructure for peace in that it celebrates the shared cultural touchstone that is Abraham, who is central to the Jewish, Christian and Muslim faiths. In my research, I wanted to understand how such an attempt at PTT is received, and in what ways tourists, and those working and living on the trail, see the trail as infrastructure for peace. My findings revealed a variety of opinions, not only in terms of whether the trail "does" or "does not" work for peace, but also in terms of "in what ways" it might or might not do so (Shepherd, 2022). For some visitors, the trail worked for peace in celebrating a cultural commonality and in materialising a hope for inter-faith tolerance and respect. For other visitors, the trail worked for peace in educating international tourists about the heinousness of the Israeli occupation – tourists who might return home and pressure their politicians to act towards bettering the Palestinian condition. Other tourists saw walking the path as constitutive of peace work in that their presence protected Palestinian farmers, as Israeli settlers would be less likely to attack if tourists are around. However, the majority of those living and working on the trail were pessimistic as to the trail's ability to promote peace. For them, peace meant justice for their cause – an end to the Israeli occupation and respect for human rights enshrined in United Nations resolutions. For many of them, the unifying approach to PTT that the trail represented was inappropriate and irrelevant. Therefore, just in this project, we can see that peace is understood in very different ways by different people. It would be impossible for us to say "does the Abraham Path promote peace through tourism?" – it would all depend on who you ask and whose voice you are prioritising.

Mónica: Exactly. We need research that demonstrates the complexity of the peace concept and addresses the interconnections between tourism and peace in a more nuanced way. I also share your concern about the normative approach to peace taken by some researchers. I want to delve into this argument by reflecting on how the researcher's understanding of peace might, inadvertently, silence other voices and even set impossible standards for local actors. Admittedly, this was one of my biggest mistakes when I started researching tourism in conflict-affected areas in Colombia.

When I first went into the field in 2018, Colombia was considered a peacebuilding reference after the signing of the peace agreement between the government and the largest guerrilla group in the country, the Revolutionary Armed Forces of Colombia (FARC). The images of the then president Santos shaking hands with the FARC representative was in the forefront of most Colombians' minds, and the word reconciliation occupied the news headlines. Immersed in this optimism and influenced by what I had read about other post-conflict cases (e.g. Causevic & Lynch, 2013), I set foot in the field eager to find joint tourism ventures between antagonists.

My understanding of peace at the time was closely related to healing the wounds of the past. Peace for me was characterised by images of ex-combatants and victims shaking hands, leaving a violent past behind and working together for a better future. The reality on the ground exposed my naivety. Community-based tourism projects were indeed flourishing, but dealing with the history of armed conflict was not necessarily part of their objectives. Instead, these projects were more concerned with raising awareness of new manifestations of violence that had appeared in the aftermath of war (Guasca et al., 2022). My interviewees were not immediately referring to their resilience to survive wartime, but to the struggles of surviving in "peace" times. The threats to their tourism initiatives and their livelihoods ranged from the expansion of monocultures in their regions, to the stigmatisation that reduces them to victims without any agency, to having to follow rules imposed by new illegal groups, such as drug trafficking organisations. There was a clear clamour for peace *with* social justice, which you also saw reflected in Palestine, and I quickly realised that peace was not just a matter of harmonious relationships, but also of dignified livelihoods.

Seen in retrospect, my fixation with reconciliation might have impacted my research participants, to whom I perhaps gave the impression that forgiveness was their moral duty. I am not going to canvass whether forgiveness is necessary for peace, but this realisation made me aware of the risk of imposing frames of reference on the participants. So, we should acknowledge the political, intellectual and religious beliefs underpinning our own understanding of peace. As Dalby (1991, p. 265) suggests, academics "are inevitably enmeshed in a cultural grid derived from their historical and cultural circumstances", and we are far from being "detached, sovereign, ahistorical researcher[s]".

Jack: I am glad you have brought this up because it sums up how I also was thinking about PTT when I started my field work. Historically, the focus in the PTT literature has tended to be on how tourism can provide opportunities for cross-cultural contact and leads to changes in attitudes between formerly hostile groups (e.g. Pizam et al., 2002). This is also the message that the International Institute for Peace through Tourism (IIPT) has forwarded most keenly (IIPT, n.d.). I therefore entered my PTT research by taking transformations in attitudes between hostile groups as the key variable by which PTT was to be understood and measured. My early experiences in Palestine disavowed me of such simplistic notions. I arrived at my first research site in January 2018 – the Area D hostel in Ramallah – following a bus ride from Jerusalem where the view from the bus window was characterised by giant concrete walls, checkpoints and guns. After such an introduction, I felt incredibly uncomfortable then sitting down to interview Palestinian staff members about how their work might contribute to cross-cultural understanding and reconciliation. The brutality of life under Israeli occupation made the question seem not only bizarre but also inappropriate. While in the end I did find tentative signs of how this youth hostel was engaging in cooperative efforts with Israelis (Shepherd & Laven, 2020), my findings were still far from the happy-clappy vision of PTT that I had hoped to find. I remember feeling deflated by this early experience and found myself asking, "What does PTT really mean in a context such as this?". In reality, however, it was only my own conceptualisation of peace that had not been fulfilled.

Mónica: This is why we should approach the study of peace with sensitivity. As you have properly exemplified, we should think of peace in the plural, but we also have to think of the multiple violences that take place in the lives of conflict-affected communities. Communities in conflict may find themselves able to escape direct physical violence with the arrival of a peace agreement, but other forms of violence, such as structural violence (violence inherent in a system that perpetuates social injustice) and cultural violence (social norms that make direct and structural violence appear acceptable) may remain, or even emerge in "peace time". It is therefore important that we are aware that just as there are many peaces, there are also many forms of violence that struggle to be placed within the war–peace dichotomy (Galtung, 1996).

Like you, I was also faced with situations that raised profound questions. How to approach community-based ecotourism projects that are promoting an environmental and peace pedagogy while the expansion of monocultures threatens to take over these lands? How to assess the role of tourism ventures that provide opportunities for socio-economic development, but are nonetheless facilitated by far-right neo-paramilitary groups? I understood that it was not sufficient to study PTT with a purely tourism-centric focus (Higgins-Desbiolles et al., 2022). I therefore looked for other disciplines that could help me better grasp the connection between tourism spaces and broader dynamics of peace and violent, and found it enlightening to engage with critical scholarship in political science, human geography and developmental studies (e.g. Escobar, 2008; Koopman, 2020; Mac Ginty, 2021). These insights could certainly enrich the PTT debate.

Jack: Our discussions would certainly benefit from greater transdisciplinary influence. I would like to return to the example you raised of a PTT initiative that is simultaneously facilitated by far-right militias. To me, this once again underlines the sensitivity with which we must approach the concept of peace. Peace is usually seen as synonymous with stability, yet such stability is often grounded in violence. Peace is not guaranteed to be a universal good that has occurred through consent with local communities. Historically, periods of stable peace have often resulted from the annihilation of one side in a conflict or the solidification of an empire, for example, the famed *Pax Romana* (Allan, 2010). As your example demonstrates, peace can be rooted in violence (Shinko, 2008), and can bring with it new violences that may be less direct than the violence of open warfare but perhaps no less damaging. We should keep our eyes peeled for the possibility that PTT can develop in supposedly peaceful, post-conflict settings, where violence might be lurking behind the facade of peace.

Building on this problematisation of peace as a normative good, I think we often gloss over the fact that in settings of conflict, peace can be a dirty word.

This is characteristic of intractable conflicts where the cyclical nature of prom-ising peace talks giving way to yet more violence leads people to see peace as either impossible or a trap set by a disingenuous opposing side (Coleman, 2003). This creates problems for us who wish to research PTT, as the very subject of our inquiry is taboo or treated with suspicion. In my fieldwork, tourism stakeholders have routinely shown a reluctance to see their work as promoting peace. Peace for them is either an unreachable utopia, or a term too sullied by the charade of a peace process that has continued for almost two decades (Turner, 2015). When I have interviewed Israelis and Palestinians, and asked whether they see their work as promoting peace, the following state-ments are rather typical:

> I don't see why tourism should be [working towards peace] and that's what a lot of international NGOs are aspiring for … No it's not a work for peace. Peace is peace. It is a state. [There] is peace or not.[1]

> Tourism is good for the local people, [but] from a purely Palestinian perspective, I don't see it as a tool for peace-making.[2]

While I understand the political implications of being associated with peace in this region, I have nonetheless been left uneasy by these denials of peace-building agency. I very much view these tourism initiatives as building peace. I see them building peace in that they challenge the cultural violence of the Israeli-Palestinian context and play a role in an ongoing process of peace-building that has no start and will have no end (Koopman, 2011). This leaves me with a dilemma that I cannot answer in any satisfactory way: if informants do not see peace as possible or reflective of their work, should we be framing what they do within the lexicon of peace? Is it possible that labelling something PTT does more harm than good? Although there are undoubtedly different opinions as to how to answer that question, what is undeniable is that we should become better at understanding the palatability of the peace concept in the areas we work in. We should be aware of the potential weaponisation of discourses of peace, and how our own use of the term may indicate bias, naivety or insensitivity (Höglund & Öberg, 2012).

Mónica: Discourse is a key word you mention because the peace concept could also serve to conceal interventions that ultimately threaten the well-being of local communities; a sort of "peacewashing", which relates to your argument about the "dirtiness" of the concept. This was the case for the far-right militias in one of my research areas, where state institutions presented the increase in community-based tourism as evidence of the return to peace while violent land dispossession led by these illegal groups continued to take place around tourism spaces.

You also ponder the appropriateness of framing initiatives as conducive to peace when not even those behind it perceive it as such, and it makes me think of the methodological implications of the peace ontologies and epistemologies we have been discussing. How can we acknowledge these multiple interpretations of peace (or its absence) in our work? As you rightly mentioned, peace can be seen as a process, and it is a process that requires contextual knowledge. That is why I believe we should strive for more qualitative research, which is better at capturing processes and explaining the whys and hows. Qualitative research has certainly helped me deal with the multi-faceted nature of peace, by allowing me to form a nuanced understanding of local contexts, which also allowed me to avoid falling into generalising discourses of tourism as a promoter of world peace. The challenge remains in recognising whose interpretations of peace take centre stage in academic narratives.

In my view, trying to reach a conclusion on causality between the phenomenon of tourism and the presence of peace through quantitative analysis will not lead us to a productive discussion. Attempts to operationalise peace by measuring proxy indicators have left us with contradictory results (Becken & Carmignani, 2016; Pratt & Liu, 2016) while reinforcing the peace and war dichotomy that is best avoided. This was the case of studies using questionnaires to measure attitude change among tourists visiting formerly enemy territory (Milman et al., 1990), and of more recent studies using the Global Peace Index – a compound indicator of the level of national peace, together with international tourist arrival data (Pratt & Liu, 2016). Such positivist approaches to studying PTT are tempting because of our craving for certainty; for a theory with explanatory power reached through value-free science. However, these approaches falsely give the impression that there is *one* peace ready to be confirmed by the objective scientist.

Jack: While I wholeheartedly agree with you about the advantages of qualitative methods in this regard, the question still remains, as you rightly point out: whose peace is being forwarded in our academic narrative? Qualitative work can be equally, if not more, guilty when it comes to hiding whose interpretation of peace is centre stage. I therefore do not believe that we should shun quantitative approaches and thus jettison half the available methodological toolbox. For me, what is most important is for authors to be open about what frame of reference is being used in their work. In other words, how do they interpret the word "peace" in their research and make clear their "peace positionality" (Shepherd & Laven, 2022, p. 178). This should go on to dictate their choice of methods. If you view peace and violence as a dichotomy, or peace as envisaged by the Global Peace Index, then causal quantitative experiments can make sense. Yet if, like us, you view peace as a continually ongoing process, then perhaps qualitative tools are better placed to understand these processes of becoming.

Researching PTT: impacts on informants and researchers

Mónica: While discussing the conceptual challenges associated with PTT, we hinted at the various difficulties we faced in the field. I want us to reflect on those struggles, the process of conducting research in violence-stricken contexts, and the potential impacts it can have on us as researchers and on our informants. By impacts, I primarily refer to the consequences it can have on people's emotional well-being and physical safety.

I will begin by considering the dangers that local communities may face in the research process. I would like to return to your thinking on the "dirtiness" of peace and the fact that some of your participants were reluctant to associate their work with peacebuilding. This reminds me of a tourism entrepreneur and peace activist who told me, "working on any issue that is community-related is a tremendous risk because this clashes with the interests of those who do not benefit from a strengthened community that protects the territory".[3] At that moment, I understood that tourism entrepreneurs who work under the peacebuilding emblem could be considered social leaders with leftist ideals, which can be life threatening. Colombia is a dangerous country for social and environmental leaders. Between January and September 2022, 128 leaders were killed, and the grim statistics exceed a thousand murders when counting back to the signing of the peace agreement in 2016 (INDEPAZ, 2022). Therefore, talking about peace tourism is not a light subject precisely because peace is a concept that has very strong political connotations.

Jack: Thank you for pointing this out, Mónica. I think that often it is assumed that because tourism is perceived as a hedonic phenomenon, those who work with tourism live in a similarly detached and apolitical world. In reality, those using tourism to work for peace are just as politically implicated, and therefore vulnerable, as those who work for peace in ways that would be of more interest to political scientists.

Helping me think about the ethical ramifications of my research is Brinkmann and Kvale's (2005) division of research ethics into "micro" and "macro" ethics. Micro ethics refer to how informants are treated at the point of contact, for example, whether consent has been gained, whether the informants have the right to withdraw from the study, and whether they have been offered the option of anonymity. Macro ethics refer to how "the knowledge produced will circulate in the wider culture and affect humans and society" (Brinkmann & Kvale, 2005, p. 167).

These different scales of research ethics can clash in settings of conflict. For example, whereas good research practice suggests that the researcher keeps detailed field notes to ensure the accuracy of the data (Patton, 2002), such notes can pose safety risks for those who are mentioned in them. Therefore, as others have suggested, in order to ensure the macro ethics of research in settings of conflict, we may have to adjust our common understandings of the micro ethics of research by, for example, ensuring that any field notes are swiftly transcribed, sent to a secure place and then deleted (Kovats-Bernat, 2002; Leuenberger, 2015).

I have always tried to follow this approach in Israel/Palestine. While the consequences of working for peace are not usually as gruesome as you mention in Colombia, to be associated with peace work certainly risks social ostracism given the sullied nature of peace as described earlier. Peace work in such settings is often conducted in secret, behind closed-doors or within private friendships (Mac Ginty, 2021). It would thus be dangerous to informants if their identities become known and attached to peace work without their consent. This is one of the reasons why Cohen and Arieli (2011) argue that snowball sampling is the only effective and ethical sampling method in conflict settings because peace workers remain largely hidden and suspicious of outsiders, and need to know there are trusted individuals between themselves and the researcher.

While our focus is predominantly on those living in conflict, tourists can also be put at risk. In my context, tourists visiting Palestinian areas can receive a five-year ban from Israel. This is not because visiting Palestine is illegal, but it is certainly frowned upon and can be punished by more parochial border officials (Shepherd & Laven, 2020). I think that what we are both getting at here is that the ethics of researching PTT are as much about what we do after we have been in contact with our informants as it is about satisfying the micro ethics associated with ethical review boards (Kovats-Bernat, 2002).

Mónica: Precisely, and one crucial aspect of macro ethics is the ethics of representation that are at stake in the writing up and dissemination of our findings. Admittedly, we research from a privileged position and produce texts and speeches that have the power to portray a version of our research participants. It is therefore worth asking ourselves what kind of representation we are supporting. Do our writings reproduce disempowering narratives that reduce people's lives to victimhood? Or are we perhaps further silencing our participants in our quests for objectivity?

Time and time again my interviewees mentioned that they were tired of the narrative of the conflict being imposed over their lives; as if there was no past other than war and the present could only be understood through the suffering experienced during war. I remember how several of my research participants mentioned their frustration at being treated only as victims and hearing how they were referred to as "those poor communities". In the words of one tourism entrepreneur:

> It is such a tabloid thing that we need to always mention the conflict because that is what attracts attention. Selling [the territory] from that feeling of pity (…) Why can't we just say that we have some great assets that we need to preserve? That should be enough. But we need to mention the dead, the displaced, the victims.[4]

There is the danger of reproducing this type of discourse also in our academic output, but there is not enough reflection on this issue as most of our attention goes to the ethical concerns during data collection (Pickering & Kara, 2017).

Jack: The macro-ethical consequences of the ethics of representation should be in the forefront of our minds as we write about those living in areas of conflict. As you suggest, representations of people living in conflict tend to create essentialised portrayals of suffering peoples, in much the same way as has been noted in fields such as nursing and mental health (Grant & Zeeman, 2012). My experience in the field has told me that those living in conflict, although deeply affected by it, do not wish to be solely represented as victims or in need of charity or sympathy. Conflict is rarely totalising, even if it aims to become so, and people's lives have to go on (Mac Ginty, 2021). It seems respectful therefore to allow these people the narrative space to carve out different lives from tourism than just what the conflict gives them. As one stakeholder in Palestine told me, this is why it is equally important to celebrate tourism to Roman archaeological sites and donkey treks as it is to show tourists the impact of the Israeli occupation. For, as he says, "it would be sad if we focus most of our hearts on negative emotions because it eventually gets back to us" (Shepherd & Laven, 2020, p. 863). It is important to bear this in mind so that our representations do not make the conflict more totalising than those enduring it wish it to be.

If I may, I would like to add another comment here. Earlier you described the benefits of qualitative research to understand PTT and I think there is an ethical representational benefit for using such methods in conflict-affected areas. I see it as undeniable that the experience of living in a conflict-affected area, of visiting such areas, and of being involved in any kind of peace process, are deeply emotional experiences. Too often we talk of our hopes for PTT or the obstacles facing it, and in the process, we lose the messy and emotive dimensions of life in conflict-affected areas. The representation of emotions is lacking in tourism studies more generally (Pritchard & Morgan, 2007), and this is equally true when it comes to tourism in settings of conflict (Buda & McIntosh, 2012). If conflicts and peace work are deeply emotional affairs, it seems wrong to remove that emotion through sterile quantitative analysis or lifeless qualitative prose. This not only creates an inauthentic representation of what we have been researching (Gilbert, 2000), but "constitutes a form of betrayal of the people we question and the experiences and the stories they chose to share" with us (Leuenberger, 2015, p. 27).

Mónica: I am glad you point out the emotive dimension of conducting PTT research because the focus tends to be on how the researcher's positionality affects the research, but very little has been said about how the research impacts the researcher (Buda & McIntosh, 2012). Of course, the purpose of discussing our feelings is not to indulge ourselves, but to help us better prepare for the inevitable array of emotions that come with working in conflict-affected environments.

I particularly struggled with the anxiety of entering regions that in the collective imaginary were no-go areas. Coming from Bogotá and growing up seeing in the news all the violence that was unleashed in those "red zones", it was inevitable for me to feel unsafe. Even if I was in my home country, I felt like a complete outsider. I remember the continuing tension that came with not knowing if my behaviour was in accordance with local norms or customs, if I was crossing an invisible border, or if I could trust the person who was taking me to some remote place. Surely my fears also stemmed from being a woman doing fieldwork by myself, but over time I felt more at ease. I think I was never in danger and I never had to face a threatening situation. People who I imagined as distrustful were actually kind, talkative, empathetic people. Where I expected to find insecurity and rejection, I found communities full of hope, strength and resilience.

Another big challenge was dealing with the emotional baggage that comes with listening to war-related stories (Theidon, 2014). Even though my participants' experiences of the conflict were not the subject of my interviews, I was often under the impression that they used the interview as a cathartic moment. I was naive about my ability to handle their painful stories. This was emotionally draining, not just because I had to respond to accounts of violence with empathy without being confused with pity, but because it was inevitable that I developed affinity or even affection with the participants and, to a certain extent, I felt helpless that I could not do more for them at that moment than offer a listening ear. We are frequently lectured about not letting our emotions interfere with the study, but we are bound by our humanity, and I believe that recognising and sharing the emotional dimensions of our research can only make us better researchers.

Jack: I love what you said about being bound by our humanity. Researching tourism and peace can be emotionally challenging, and like Buda and McIntosh (2012), I have found my research in Israel/Palestine characterised by a whole range of emotions from anger to sadness to joy and empathy. Rather than bracket out these emotions (Fischer, 2009), I have seen them as a resource to better understand the intensity of feeling conflict arouses and how such feelings can work towards the benefit of PTT, or indeed, work against it (e.g. Shepherd et al., 2020; Shepherd, 2022).

Like you, I have never felt in real physical danger conducting research on PTT in Israel/Palestine. I have certainly felt uncomfortable and afraid, most noticeably when crossing Israeli military checkpoints, or when leaving Israel, out of fear for an Israeli entry ban that has affected other researchers (Kadari-Ovadia, 2021). The conflict has certainly had peaks of violence in recent years, and common sense tells you to avoid the study area when open warfare is afoot.

For the most part though, the risks have been emotional. It has been the difficulty of knowing how to respond to someone describing how their neighbours were incinerated in a terrorist attack. It has concerned the difficulty of recalibrating to "normal" life back home after being in a conflict-affected context. It has centred on how to navigate moving between informants in Israel and Palestine, occupied and occupier, in a research project that has engaged both sides of a conflict – something uncommon in this context (Ram et al., 2017).

Adding to these challenges is my position as an outsider in Israel/Palestine. I am unable to speak the local languages, and often fear the consequences of erroneous slights of tongue that may betray a bias or a naivety (Cohen & Arieli, 2011). I found it interesting that this outsider role is not confined to being foreign. You describe yourself as an outsider despite being a Colombian national. This alone should help us contemplate how peace is an "uneven socio-spatial process" (Koopman, 2020, p. 10), meaning that all citizens in a state are not equally affected by a conflict or by subsequent peace agreements. Peace and conflict will look different and feel different in different parts of a territory, and again, this is something that is hard to capture in quantitative approaches that seek generalisability.

Finally, there are those pangs of guilt that come with researching the lives of conflict-affected people, knowing you are not bound to the conflict and its privations. This is something aggravated by blending the roles of tourist and researcher, roles that in theory are supposed to be kept apart but that all too often awkwardly clash. This was highlighted by Buda and McIntosh (2012), where Buda explains how her expectations for service as a tourist sometimes clashed with her role as the insentient, undemanding researcher.

Concluding thought: the contribution of PTT research

Mónica: I propose that we close our discussion by reflecting on how we, as peace researchers, could also commit ourselves to being peacemakers. This book's central objective is to outline future perspectives in researching PTT, but we need to ask ourselves the questions of why do we want to advance this research agenda and what outcomes do we expect to achieve.

I believe that our contribution cannot stop at debating whether tourism is good or bad, successful or not. Our job is not to reveal truths, but to offer perspectives, reflections, in-depth analyses and, above all, to make visible realities that otherwise would remain unknown. I welcome the shift in more recent PTT contributions that highlight the achievements of local communities working for peace instead of glorifying tourism as a peacebuilding industry in and of itself. Our discussion should not be about tourism, it should be about the people behind it. It is about the people who, as Theidon (2014, p. 9) put it, "do not sit in tragic heaps waiting for the next blow life will send their way". Accordingly, it is about people using tourism to challenge the legacy of apartheid in South Africa (Muldoon & Mair, 2022) or about small farmers defending their ecotourism projects from the expansion of monocultures (Guasca et al., 2022).

Moreover, our work should not be limited to our academic production. We should be peace activists by participating in demonstrations, signing petitions, speaking to the media, promoting a pedagogy of peace, or even supporting the communities' objectives more directly. I therefore support Kobayashi (2003, p. 346) in her call for being part of "social change as it occurs on the ground" instead of hoping that by "our own wisdom alone we make significant contribution to society". I trust that PTT scholarship will continue to evolve towards more committed research that not only seeks to expand knowledge, but above all contribute to more just societies.

Jack: I wholeheartedly welcome your call for a more engaged stance from tourism scholarship in relation to tourism's role in peace. Our work should help influence policy, provide encouragement and offer solidarity to those challenging violence, raise awareness of their bravery, and dare I say market their enterprises. I would argue that we must respond to what Frank (1997, p. 132) calls the "ethic of solidarity and commitment", to report as truthfully as we can what we have seen, to speak with and not about others, and to encourage action. This entails moving away from trying to be omniscient and objective about tourism's role in peacebuilding and to instead focus on how our research helps communities enact visions of peace in their community.

While questions of peace and conflict can seem too grand for us to contribute to, we should be careful not to undersell the importance of tourism as a vehicle for promoting peace in all its forms. Peace work concerns everything from nuclear weapons treaties to the accessibility of incontinence pads in refugee camps. It can be seemingly grand or mundane, extraordinary or every day. Tourism is one tool of many that can be utilised to envision less violent futures for communities exhausted by conflict.

The bulk of this chapter has been to highlight the challenges of researching PTT. This has ranged from the challenges of working with the highly con-tested concept of peace to the interpersonal safety and emotional problems of research in a conflict zone. Our motivation, however, has never been to scare people off from researching PTT. Although we see a need for more sensitivity in dealing with this topic, and that necessitates more transdisciplinary work into PTT, we also believe that there is scope for an even broader discussion on tourism's role in peace, when peace can mean so many different things and tourism can be thought of in so many different ways.

To end this discussion, we therefore forward a research agenda characterised by this broadening of the PTT debate. For us, this should involve research that critically examines PTT ventures and discourse, both in academia and on the ground, in ways that interrogate who PTT is working for, what type of peace is being envisioned, and whether or not such tourism becomes implicated in new forms of violence. We also believe this agenda should be characterised by reflexivity over our biases as researchers, over how we choose to represent those living in conflict, and over which methods to use. In particular, we would appreciate seeing researchers engaging with both creative qualitative methods that might be able to capture the messy and emotional nature of conflict settings, and with mixed methods that seem left by the wayside in the PTT debate. We look forward with hope and confidence to the continued emergence of such a research agenda.

Notes

1. Interview with a Palestinian stakeholder conducted in December 2019.
2. Interview with a Palestinian stakeholder conducted in December 2019.
3. Interview with a Colombian entrepreneur and activist conducted in October 2019.
4. Interview with a Colombian entrepreneur conducted in October 2019.

References

Acar, Y. G., Moss, S. M, & Ulug, Ö. M. (Eds.) (2020), *Researching Peace, Conflict, and Power in the Field: Methodological Challenges and Opportunities.* Springer.

Allan, P. (2010). Measuring international ethics: a moral scale of war, peace, justice, and global care. In P. Allan, & A. Keller (Eds.), *What is a Just Peace?* (pp. 90–129). Oxford University Press.

Becken, S., & Carmignani, F. (2016). Does tourism lead to peace? *Annals of Tourism Research, 61,* 63–79.

Brinkmann, S., & Kvale, S. (2005). Confronting the ethics of qualitative research. *Journal of Constructivist Psychology, 18*(2), 157–81.

Buda, D. M., & McIntosh, A. J. (2012). Hospitality, peace and conflict: 'doing fieldwork' in Palestine. *Journal of Tourism and Peace Research, 2*(2), 50–61.

Causevic, S., & Lynch, P. (2013). Political (in)stability and its influence on tourism development. *Tourism Management, 34,* 145–57.

Cohen, N., & Arieli, T. (2011). Field research in conflict environments: methodological challenges and snowball sampling. *Journal of Peace Research, 48*(4), 423–35.

Coleman, P. T. (2003). Characteristics of protracted, intractable conflict: toward the development of a metaframework – I. *Peace and Conflict: Journal of Peace Psychology, 9*(1), 1–3.

Dalby, S. (1991). Critical geopolitics: discourse, difference, and dissent. *Environment and Planning D: Society and Space, 9*(3), 261–83.

Dietrich, W. (2012). *Interpretations of Peace in History and Culture.* Palgrave Macmillan.

Escobar, A. (2008). *Territories of Difference.* Duke University Press.

Fischer, C. (2009). Bracketing in qualitative research: conceptual and practical matters. *Psychotherapy Research, 19*(4–5), 583–90.

Frank, A. (1997). *The Wounded Storyteller: Body, Illness, and Ethics.* The University of Chicago Press.

Frank. A. (2005). What is dialogical research, and why should we do it? *Qualitative Health Research, 15*(7), 964–74.

Galtung, J. (1996). *Peace by Peaceful Means: Peace and Conflict, Development and Civilization.* Peace Research Institute Oslo.

Gilbert, K. (2000). *The Emotional Nature of Qualitative Research*. Routledge.

Grant, A., & Zeeman, L. (2012). Whose story is it? An autoethnography concerning narrative identity. *The Qualitative Report*, *17*(36), article 2.

Guasca, M., Vanneste, D., & Van Broeck, A. M. (2022). Peacebuilding and post-conflict tourism: addressing structural violence in Colombia. *Journal of Sustainable Tourism*, *30*(2–3), 427–43.

Higgins-Desbiolles, F., Blanchard, L. A., & Urbain, Y. (2022). Peace through tourism: critical reflections on the intersections between peace, justice, sustainable development and tourism. *Journal of Sustainable Tourism*, *30*(2–3), 335–51.

Höglund, K., & Öberg, M. (2011). *Understanding Peace Research Methods and Challenges*. Routledge.

INDEPAZ [Instituto de Estudios para el Desarrollo y la Paz] (2022). *Líderes sociales, defensores de dd.hh y firmantes de acuerdo asesinados en 2022*. https://indepaz.org.co/lideres-sociales-defensores-de-dd-hh-y-firmantes-de-acuerdo-asesinados-en-2022/.

IIPT [International Institute for Peace through Tourism] (n.d.). About the International Institute for Peace through Tourism (IIPT).https://peacetourism.org/about-iipt.

Kadari-Ovadia, S. (2021, November 28). Israel denies entry to German students who 'tried hiding' plans to visit Palestinian university. *Haaretz*. https://www.haaretz.com/israel-news/twogerman-students-intending-to-visit-ramallah-denied-entry-intoisrael-1.1042074.

Khalilzadeh, J. (2018). Demonstration of exponential random graph models in tourism studies: is tourism a means of global peace or the bottom line? *Annals of Tourism Research*, *69*, 31–41.

Kobayashi, A. (2003). GPC ten years on: is self-reflexivity enough? *Gender, Place and Culture*, *10*(4), 345–9.

Koopman, S. (2011). Let's take peace to pieces. *Political Geography*, *30*, 193–4.

Koopman, S. (2020). Building an inclusive peace in an uneven sociospatial process: Colombia's differential approach. *Political Geography*, *83*. https://doi.org/10.1016/j.polgeo.2020.102252.

Kovats-Bernat, J. C. (2002). Negotiating dangerous fields: pragmatic strategies for fieldwork amid violence and terror. *American Anthropologist*, *104*(1), 208–22.

Leuenberger, C. (2015). Knowledge-making and its politics in conflict regions: doing research in Israel/Palestine. *Studies in Symbolic Interaction*, *44*, 19–41.

Mac Ginty, R. (2021). *Everyday Peace: How So-Called Ordinary People Can Disrupt Violent Conflict*. Oxford University Press.

Milman, A., Reichel, A., & Pizam, A. (1990). The impact of tourism on ethnic attitudes: the Israeli-Egyptian case. *Journal of Travel Research*, *29*(2), 45–9.

Muldoon, M. L., & Mair, H. L. (2022). Disrupting structural violence in South Africa through township tourism. *Journal of Sustainable Tourism*, *30*(2–3),444–60.

Patton, M. (2002). *Qualitative Research and Evaluation Methods*. SAGE.

Pearce, J., & Dietrich, W. (2019). Many violences, many peaces: Wolfgang Dietrich and Jenny Pearce in conversation. *Peacebuilding*, *7*(3), 268–82.

Pickering, L., & Kara, H. (2017). Presenting and representing others: towards an ethics of engagement. *International Journal of Social Research Methodology*, *20*(3), 299–309.

Pizam, A., Fleischer, A., & Mansfeld, Y. (2002). Tourism and social change: the case of Israeli ecotourists visiting Jordan. *Journal of Travel Research*, *41*(2), 177–84.

Pratt, S., & Liu, A. (2016). Does tourism really lead to peace? A global view. *International Journal of Tourism Research*, *18*(1), 82–90.

Pritchard, A., & Morgan, N. (2007). De-centering tourism's intellectual universe, or traversing the dialogue between change and tradition. In I. Ateljevic, A. Pritchard, & N. Morgan (Eds.), *The Critical Turn in Tourism Studies: Creating an Academy of Hope* (pp. 11–28). Elsevier.

Ram, Y., Isaac, R., Shamir, O., & Burns, P. (2017). Geopolitics of tourism and academia in the Holy Land. *Tourism Planning and Development, 14*(3), 411–29.

Shepherd, J. (2022). Exploring a unifying approach to peacebuilding through tourism: Abraham and Israel/Palestine. *Journal of Sustainable Tourism, 30*(2–3), 482–99.

Shepherd, J., & Laven, D. (2020). Providing counter-narratives: the positive role of hostels in the Israeli-Palestinian context. *Tourism Geographies, 22*(4–5), 848–71.

Shepherd, J., & Laven, D. (2022). The impact of tourism on peace. In A. Stoffelen & D. Ioannides (Eds.), *Handbook of Tourism Impacts: Social and Environmental Perspectives* (pp. 166–82). Edward Elgar Publishing.

Shepherd, J., Laven, D., & Shamma, L. (2020). Autoethnographic journeys through contested spaces. *Annals of Tourism Research, 84.* https://doi.org/10.1016/j.annals.2020.103004.

Shinko, R. (2008). Agonistic peace: a postmodern reading. *Millennium: Journal of International Studies, 36*(3), 473–91.

Theidon, K. (2014). How was your trip? Self-care for researchers working and writing on violence. *Drugs, Security and Democracy Program Working Papers on Research Security, 2,* 1–20.

Turner, M. (2015). Peacebuilding as counterinsurgency in the occupied Palestinian territory. *Review of International Studies, 41*(1), 73–98.

9 The metaphorical perceptions of tourism students on the relationship between tourism and peace

Dilara Bahtiyar Sari and Metin Sürme

Introduction

Tourism is a massive industry as more than 1 billion people travel every year, generating over US$1 trillion in revenue (UNWTO, 2022a). Therefore, tourism represents an important economic industry that, despite fluctuations in demand due to crises and external factors (e.g., health crises, inflation), continues to grow steadily worldwide. In fact, tourism has managed to recover following the COVID-19 pandemic, with approximately 250 million international arrivals recorded in the first months of 2022 (UNWTO, 2022a). In addition, tourism is perceived as a social activity with national and international aspects, which affects the society and social structure. One of the socio-cultural outputs of tourism is its contribution to social peace (Dilek, Dilek & Gümüş, 2016).

The concept of peace through tourism is not new as it has been discussed since the 1920s. The British Travel and Holiday Association's theme back in 1929 was titled "Travel for Peace" (Becken & Carmignani, 2016), implying that the relationship between peace and tourism is initiated by travelling. This travel-induced contact between tourists and the host community may, subsequently, positively affect international politics and support world peace, as the interaction between tourists and the host community has the ability to reduce cultural and psychological gaps among people. Thus, tourism may ultimately contribute to the development and maintenance of a peace environment around the world. While various studies agree that the interaction brought about by travel can eliminate obstacles between people and encourage international cooperation (Askjellerud, 2003; Causevic, 2010), there are scholars that contest this view (Farmaki, 2017; Pratt & Liu, 2016).

The critics of the peace through tourism tenet suggest that tourism benefits from peace rather than contributing to it. Relevant studies posit that the effects of conflicts and wars on tourism are deeply rooted to a society (Farmaki, 2017) and, hence, inhibit peacebuilding attempts as they cause animosity perceptions among people that often extend beyond the country affected by the conflict. The Russia–Ukraine war, for example, which was still ongoing at the time of writing seems to affect the global tourism industry, mostly through the loss of the Russian-Ukrainian outbound tourist market that represented 3 per cent of global expenditure for international tourism in 2020 (UNWTO, 2022b), as well as the rapid increase in fuel prices following the sanctions imposed on Russia. Although the possibility of a long-term conflict could turn into a global tourism crisis, estimated to cost US$14 billion, effects may go beyond economic problems as animosity perceptions are developing in various countries around the world (Campo & Alvarez, 2019). Such negative perceptions not only influence intention to visit a country but also impede peacebuilding opportunities that may be brought about by the tourism activity.

While relevant studies have looked at the perceptions of tourists travelling to post-conflict destinations (e.g., Campo & Alvarez, 2019; Sánchez et al., 2018), the peace-related perceptions of other important groups in tourism including employees and students have been ignored. To this end, the aim of this study is to examine the perceptions of tourism students, who represent the future employees in tourism, towards peace. It is the future generations that will be most affected by the current wars and conflict the world is experiencing. It is, thus, necessary to take steps today so that future generations can live in an environment of peace. In light of this need, the United Nations issued an Agenda which outlines peace as one of the sustainable development goals that need to be achieved by 2030. In this context, the importance of how tourism students interpret the concepts of tourism and peace is evident. Education was recognized as a great influencer on economic, social and cultural development as well as the formation of individuals (Monteiro, Lopes & Carbone, 2021). There is not only pedagogical value in understanding how tourism education can contribute to an environment of intercultural exchange and peace but also social value as education carries the potential for change at a social level. According to Kelly (2006), tourism education provides opportunities for conscientization, implying that tourism students' perceptions may be integral in how peace through tourism eventually unfolds. Drawing from student groups studying tourism at a university in Turkey, this chapter uses the metaphor analysis method to propose metaphors that underline the peace and tourism relationship. The chapter, thus, offers significant implications that may help to redesign tourism education and improve the peace through tourism goal.

Tourism, peace and education

Tourism brings many socio-economic benefits to destinations, especially in developing regions. For instance, tourism provides the transformation from the agricultural sector to the service sector, increases the quality of employment, eliminates the imbalance between regions and preserves the architectural style unique to the region (Mason, 2003; Özekici, 2019). Tourism activities have also been argued to reduce political tensions and disagreements between societies and create a peaceful environment (Çakıcı, Benli, Üzülmez & Kaynak, 2015). The tenet that tourism contributes to peace is not new. Scholars have asserted years ago that as tourism involves the movement of people from country to country, it can lead to economic, social and cultural exchanges that reinforce world peace. The rationale for this proposition lies on the contact hypothesis which implies that contact brought about by tourism eventually improves understanding between different cultural groups and strengthens the relations between countries (Farmaki, 2017).

In October 1988, academics and practitioners from various fields evaluated this proposal for the first time in Vancouver, Canada at a conference dedicated to peace and tourism (Burnett & Uysal, 1990). Since then, a burgeoning number of studies on the role of tourism in consolidating peace have been published, the findings of which suggest that the peace through tourism narrative remains inconclusive (Moufakkir, 2010; Pernecky, 2010; Seabra, Kastenholz, Abrantes, & Reis, 2018). First, conditions such as peace and security are considered important for a successful tourism industry (Becken & Carmignani, 2016), with several scholars arguing that peace benefits from peace rather than leading to peace (Pratt & Liu, 2016; Seabra et al., 2018). Indeed, tourism can rarely be successful when there is no peace (Yeşiltaş, Öztürk & Türkmen, 2008). Therefore, in order for people to travel and engage in touristic activities, first of all, a safe environment of peace must be provided, as tourism movements will increase in a destination where an environment of peace is provided (Gelbman, 2010). Ending the conflict in a tourism destination and reducing tensions will enable people to create a perception of a safe environment. This perception of security plays an important role in the selection of the destination by tourists (Anson, 1999; Çakıcı, Benli, Üzülmez & Kaynak, 2015).

Second, it is not enough for tourism to have a peaceful environment only in the tourist-receiving region but the welfare level of the tourist-sending region should also be considered (Smith, 1998; Yenişehirlioğlu et al., 2016; Güney, Göktepe & Kokonalıoğlu, 2022). The tourism industry is immediately affected by events such as war, political instability, turmoil and terrorism. In addition, wars are destructive not only in the countries where the wars take place but also in neighbouring countries and their effects are often evidenced on a global scale in terms of tourism. Unpredictable, ubiquitous warfare has a very negative impact on tourism. For example, the effects of the Russia–Ukraine war that erupted in 2022 are reflected on a global scale (Güney, Göktepe & Kokonalioğlu, 2022) as sanctions imposed on Russia led to fuel price increases, disruptions in trade and the loss of the Russian–Ukrainian outbound tourist market. In this context, the perceptions of people of countries accused of initiating war are affected as animosity grows among certain groups, be they in the tourist receiving or tourist generating region.

While animosity perceptions have been studied previously in terms of intentions to visit a destination (Sanchez et al., 2018; Yu et al., 2020), less academic attention has been paid to people working in the tourism industry or to tourism students who represent the tourism workers of the future. This omission is surprising considering the interaction that tourism employees have with tourists. The importance of peace education to tourism studies has been previously highlighted. Embedding peace in tourism education is vital as education exerts great influence on economic, social and cultural development and is, to a great extent, responsible for the formation of individuals' perceptions and attitudes (Monteiro, Lopes & Carbone, 2021). By understanding how tourism education can contribute to an environment of intercultural exchange and peace, not only pedagogical but also social value can be gained as education carries the potential for change at a social level. As Kelly (2006) postulated, tourism education provides opportunities for conscientization; thereby, tourism students' perceptions of peace are significant predictors of the dynamics of peace through tourism.

To this end, this chapter aims to examine the metaphorical perceptions of tourism students about the relationship between tourism and peace. Knowing how the concepts of tourism and peace are perceived by tourism students is expected to guide public institutions, local governments and private sector representatives towards the peacebuilding goal by embedding peace in tourism education.

Methodology

To achieve the aim of the research, we drew from the perceptions of students at the Gaziantep University Vocational School of Tourism and Hotel Management in Turkey in terms of the relationship between tourism and peace. Using the phenomenology research design, the metaphors the students produced for the following expressions were analysed:

1. "Tourism is like ...; because ..."
2. "Peace is like ...; because ..."
3. "Tourism and peace are like ...; because ...".

In the study, we tried to find answers to the following questions with the metaphors produced for these expressions:

a. What are the perceptions of "tourism", "peace" and "tourism-peace" of the associate degree students studying tourism?
b. Under which conceptual categories can the metaphors produced by the students regarding the tourism-peace relationship be gathered?

For the preparation of the questions used in the research, the metaphorical study of Kulakoğlu Dilek and her colleagues (2016) on the relationship between tourism and peace on hotel workers was used. This study was structured on the basis of the phenomenology model, a popular method of qualitative research. Phenomenology is a qualitative research design that enables the revealing of phenomena that we are aware of but which requires in-depth research in order to gain detail on them (Patton, 2002; Sanders, 1982). Facts are events, experiences, perceptions and concepts about which we do not have full knowledge of, even though we have encountered them in various forms in the world we live in and have, somehow, experienced. Phenomenology is an appropriate research design that can be used to investigate these concepts that are not foreign but cannot be fully defined (Sönmez & Alacapınar, 2011; Yıldırım & Şimşek, 2008).

Data collection and analysis

Research data were collected from 31 students between August and September 2022. The sentences "Tourism is like ...; because ...", "Peace is like ...; because ..." and "Tourism and peace are like ...; because ..." were directed to tourism students who were asked to fill in the blanks with a metaphor. The relationship between the subject and the source of the metaphor was determined with the word "like". With the word "because", the meaning and the reason attributed to this metaphor were revealed (Schmitt, 2005; Pitcher, 2013).

While categorizing the data, attention was paid not only to the metaphors that were produced but also to their justification as, sometimes, the same metaphor produced by two different people can be used with different meanings. For this reason, content analysis was carried out considering the justification of the metaphor produced. The data obtained from the study group was analysed in five stages: (i) coding and extraction, (ii) sample metaphor compilation, (iii) category development, (iv) validity and reliability, and (v) data transfer to a computer environment (Çoğaltay & Aras, 2018). Specifically, at the *Coding and Debugging Phase*, the metaphors produced by the tourism students in the forms were transferred to the Microsoft Excel program and listed in alphabetical order. Thus, the temporary list created was carefully examined and it was determined whether tourism students could produce any metaphor clearly. At the *Sample Metaphor Collection Stage*, the new list that passed the first stage was written again in alphabetical order and was re-examined. During the examination, the statement that is assumed to best represent the metaphor was taken from the forms filled by the participants representing a metaphor, and a "sample metaphor list" was created. Thus, the list, which was thought of as a suitable reference source for use in the next stage of the research was reached. At the *Category Development Stage*, the metaphors produced were examined in terms of source-subject-justification, significance and the relationship they contain. At the *Validity and Reliability Stage*, the reliability and validity of measurement results was tested to verify the credibility of the findings obtained. In qualitative research, reporting in detail how the data were collected and how the obtained data were analysed positively affects the validity. However, how objective one is when reaching the results is related to the reliability at the first level (Yıldırım & Şimşek, 2008). In our research, an expert on the qualitative approach was used to test the reliability in the context of consistency. Finally, at the stage of *Transferring the Data to a Computer Environment*, all the metaphors and categories whose reliability was tested were transferred to the computer environment, and by doing so the frequency and percentage calculations representing the relevant categories were considered.

Findings

Overall, 31 metaphors were developed. The distribution of the participants included in the study according to their demographic characteristics is shown in Table 9.1.

Table 9.1   Demographic characteristics of the participants

Gender	f	%
Female	18	58.1
Male	13	41.9
Age Group		
18–21	20	64.5
22–25	8	25.8
26–29	1	3.2
30–33	1	3.2
34 and above	1	3.2
Marital status		
Single	25	80.6
Married	6	19.4
Total	31	100

As seen in Table 9.1, the majority of the tourism students participating in the research are in the 18–21 age group (64.5 per cent) and mostly female (58.1 per cent).

Table 9.2   Metaphors produced for the concept of tourism

Metaphor Name	f	%
Life	5	16.10
Carnival	2	6.44
The heart of countries	1	3.22
Oil	4	12.88
Factory	1	3.22
Dream	1	3.22
Peace	2	6.44
Sun	2	6.44
Culture	1	3.22
Breath	1	3.22

Metaphor Name	f	%
Adana	1	3.22
Mill	1	3.22
Love	1	3.22
Education	1	3.22
Fun	1	3.22
Flower	2	6.44
Power station	1	3.22
Trade	1	3.22
The World	1	3.22
Socialization	1	3.22
Total	31	100

The findings obtained regarding the metaphors that tourism students produced for the concept of "tourism" are presented in Table 9.2. The most frequently repeated metaphors for the concept of "tourism" by the participants included: life (f=5), oil (f=4), peace (f=2), sun (f=2), flower (f=2) and carnival (f=2). The examples of the metaphors created for the concept of tourism by students are given in Table 9.3.

Table 9.3   Examples of tourism metaphors

"Tourism is like life, life gets better as you travel."

"Tourism is like life because one season ends, another season begins."

"Tourism is like oil because it has an important place."

"Tourism is like life because everything you seek is in tourism."

"Tourism is like the sun because as you participate in tourism activities, you become enlightened."

"Tourism is like love because it grows and develops with love."

"It's like oil because it contributes about 30 billion dollars to the country every year."

"Tourism is like a flower because if it is not taken care of, it withers and loses its beauty."

"Tourism is like Turkey's oil; because it is a source of income."

Table 9.4   Metaphors produced for the concept of peace

Metaphor Name	f	%
Plane tree	1	3.22
Bird	1	3.22
War	1	3.22
Summer	1	3.22
Happiness	3	9.66
Victory	1	3.22
Peace	2	6.44
Flower	1	3.22
Winning	1	3.22
Brotherhood	2	6.44
Child	1	3.22
Life	2	6.44
Strength	1	3.22
Tourism	1	3.22
Justice	1	3.22
Smile	1	3.22
Weather	1	3.22
Partnership	1	3.22
Sea	1	3.22
An infectious disease	1	3.22
Quality time	1	3.22
Rules	1	3.22
Freedom	1	3.22
Friendship	3	9.66
Total	31	100

Similarly, metaphors produced by students for the concept of "peace" are shown in Table 9.4. According to Table 9.4, tourism students produced a total of 31 metaphors for the concept of "peace". The most frequently repeated metaphors for the concept of "peace" by the participants included: happiness (f=3), friendship (f=3), peace (f=2), brotherhood (f=2) and life (f=2). In this respect, it is revealed that the students have a positive perception of peace as can be understood from the positive metaphors they bring to the concept of peace. Table 9.5 shows examples of the metaphors created for the concept of peace through tourism students.

Table 9.5   Examples of peace metaphors

"Peace is like a plane tree because it holds many people in its shade."

"Peace is like a bird because being able to fly in the endless sky is the greatest freedom."

"Peace is like the happiness hormone because it feels good."

"Peace is like peace because where there is peace there is peace and happiness."

"Peace is like brotherhood. Because it is to love without making religion, language or race."

"Peace is like happiness because it makes everyone happy."

"Peace is like a child; because it knows no barriers."

"Peace is like life because without it there is no peace."

"Peace is like power because he who holds power makes peace."

"Peace is actually like a smile. Because peace is a state that brings great peace and happiness when its name is announced to humanity."

"Peace; happiness, love, peace, etc. Because: if there is peace, there will be happiness, if there is peace, there will be peace, if there is peace, there will be love.

"Peace is like people spending quality time with each other; because with good communication, peace is possible."

"Peace is like rules because it brings order and peace wherever it goes."

"Peace is like freedom because where war ends there is freedom."

"Peace is like happiness; because it digests everything."

Table 9.6 shows information about the metaphors produced for the "Tourism–Peace" relationship; Table 9.7 depicts relevant examples.

Table 9.6   Metaphors produced for the relationship between tourism and peace

Metaphor Name	f	%
Sibling/brother-sister	6	19.32
Quetzal bird	1	3.22
Paradise	1	3.22
Excitement	1	3.22
Family	2	6.44
Hour-minute hand	1	3.22
Friend	3	9.66
Love	1	3.22
Stadium	1	3.22
Culture	1	3.22
Adrenaline-fun	1	3.22
Fairness	1	3.22
Reflection of the heart	1	3.22
Human	1	3.22
Key-lock	1	3.22
Peace	1	3.22
Baklava-pistachio	1	3.22
Goodness	1	3.22
Unifying force	1	3.22
Inseparable duo	1	3.22
A free world	1	3.22
Cultural exchange	1	3.22
Development	1	3.22
Total	31	100

Table 9.7   Examples of tourism–peace metaphors

"Tourism and peace are like brothers because they combine many different ideas."

"Tourism and peace are like the Quetzal bird, the Quetzal bird is the most beautiful bird in the world in carnival colour."

"Tourism and peace are like brotherhood because they are inseparable."

"Tourism and peace are like family because they both provide beauty and unity."

"One. Space: it's like a clock. 2nd space: one is the hour and the other is the minute hand, and without one, the clock won't be right."

"Tourism and Peace are like friends. Because they support each other and produce better results."

"Tourism and Peace is like a stadium; because it unites everyone."

"Tourism and peace are like brothers because they complement each other."

"Tourism and Peace is like a reflection of the heart. Because people can be happy when they have fun, travel, rest, travel to countries and meet new people, and most importantly, when they can 'smile', in fact, it is the peace of people that brings peace to the world."

"Tourism and peace are like keys and locks because for tourism to exist, tourism is necessary for peace to exist."

"Tourism and Peace are like inseparable pairs; because they complement each other, they are relational."

"Tourism and peace is like a free world because it provides a chance for all people to visit each other's country in beauty."

"Tourism and Peace is like cultural exchange; because it brings out different meanings."

When we look at the metaphors produced for the relationship between tourism and peace, it shows parallelism with the metaphors produced for both the concept of tourism and the concept of peace. Considering the most produced metaphors, emotional perceptions such as sibling (f=6), friend (f=3) and family (f=2) came to the fore. In this respect, three conceptual categories have been created, namely emotional, relational and holistic for the relationship between tourism and peace (Table 9.8).

Table 9.8 Conceptual categories and metaphors for the relationship between tourism and peace

Emotional	Relational	Holistic
• Siblings/brother–sister	• Hour and minute hand	• Human
• Brother	• Adrenaline–fun	• A free world
• Friend	• Key–lock	• Development
• Love	• Baklava–pistachio	• Quetzal bird
• Goodness	• Inseparable duo	• Paradise
• Peace	• Unifying force	• Stadium
• Excitement		• Culture
• Reflection of the heart		• Cultural exchange
		• Fairness

In this context, the perceptions of the participants regarding the relationship between tourism and peace also show parallelism with previous studies in the literature (Kulakoğlu Dilek et al., 2016; Kelly, 2006; ATA Fellows, 2011).

Discussion and conclusion

Tourism, as a social phenomenon, enables two or more people who do not know each other to interact; hence, bringing about greater socio-cultural understanding between groups of people as well as improved perceptions of one another. As such, tourism has been argued to contribute to peace as improved perceptions of people can lead to stronger relations among nations (D'Amore, 1988). Despite a burgeoning number of studies on people's perceptions in post-conflict travel situations, little is known of the perceptions of the peace–tourism relationship of people related to the tourism industry including employees and students. In particular, the importance of examining student perceptions of the relationship between tourism and peace should not be ignored considering the power that education has in shaping individuals' attitudes (Monteiro, Lopes & Carbone, 2021). Tourism students are the future employees of the industry and, hence, bound to interact closely with tourists. In this study, the metaphorical perceptions of tourism students about the relationship between tourism and peace were uncovered.

What findings reveal is that students' perception of the "tourism–peace" relationship can be evaluated along three basic dimensions. Firstly, the tourism–peace relationship is considered as emotional. Perspective-taking consists of three dimensions: perceptual, cognitive, and emotional. Emotional perspective taking is defined as evaluating or understanding another's emotion (Kurdek & Rodgon, 1975). According to participants, the relationship between tourism and peace is complementary. This duality, which they perceive emotionally from their perspective may be a solution to conflicts in today's world. Various scholars have presented tourism as the most appropriate tool for promoting world harmony and peace (e.g., D'Amore, 1988; Cho, 2007). Çakıcı and his colleagues (2015) also, aiming to determine the relationship between tourism and peace from the perspective of postgraduate tourism students, found that tourism generally affects peace along four dimensions (social, political, economic and cultural). In this regard, the authors emphasized the view that tourism will increase interpersonal communication and empathy, develop mutual understanding, reduce prejudices, be an important industry in establishing economic and political cooperation, and positively affect peace.

Secondly, the tourism and peace interface is found to be relational. Tourism students have expressed tourism and peace in relation to many metaphors (e.g., Scorpio–sail–hand, adrenaline–entertainment, key–lock, baklava–pistachio, inseparable duo, unifying power). The resulting metaphors show parallelism with a similar study of Kulakoğlu Dilek et al. (2016) which highlights the importance of the relational dimension to tourism and peace interaction as one influences the other. Indeed, peace affects tourism as tourism movements will increase in a destination where an environment of peace is provided (Gelbman, 2010). Likewise, it has been argued that tourism affects peace by reducing political tensions between nations and improving people's perceptions through travel-induced contact (Çakıcı et al., 2015; Yeşiltaş, Öztürk & Türkmen, 2008). Third, the tourism–peace relationship is holistic. In this respect, peace and tourism act like a puzzle, combining the various pieces together and becoming a whole. Evidently, the potential of tourism to create peace is emphasized in students' metaphorical perceptions.

In this context, the role of tourism education is emphasized as it can play an important part in influencing students' awareness of the potential contribution of tourism to peace and, thereby, help shape student perceptions of the peace and tourism relationship. As students represent the industry's future employees, it is vital that tourism educators are included in peacebuilding efforts. Tourism education will determine the quality of the service provided and that includes the attitudes of employees towards visitors. Tourism students may also represent the industry's future employers; hence, it is important that positive perceptions exist that will eliminate inequalities persistent in societies, especially against ethnic minorities. For example, if tourism students understand and appreciate the role of the industry in shaping peaceful environments and providing a framework of justice (Farmaki & Stergiou, 2021), then they may become fairer managers and employers recruiting members of ethnic minorities.

Notwithstanding, tourism has the potential to provide direct and indirect employment to a wide range of people in various social strata, especially in developing countries such as Turkey. Tourism can also generate additional income for people who already have other jobs. Taken as a whole, this broad network of employment opportunities can generate income for many layers of society (Honey & Gilpin, 2009). Income generation leads to an increase in per capita income and is one of the preventive factors that reduces the escalation of internal conflicts. In case of low incomes, increased inequality is noted in society and if these inequalities are based on ethnicity, it can trigger more social unrest. Therefore, income inequalities can lead societies to more structural inequalities and prolong reigning civil wars. For this reason, it can be argued that tourism is a forward-looking alternative for developing countries to reduce the dangers of impending internal conflict (Collier, Hoeffler & Söderbom, 2004). In the study on peace tourism and tourism education, duties and responsibilities fall on tourism trainers. Instructors who help students determine their perspectives should approach different communities and elements such as language, religion, and belief without prejudice but with tolerance. The awareness that tourism is one of the ways to ensure peace should thus be given to students by instructors is in several ways including curriculum redesign, case studies, real-life scenarios and group projects.

Overall, by explaining that tourism and peace are meaningful emotionally, relationally and holistically, tourism students emphasized the necessity of a peaceful environment in order to generate economic and social benefits from tourism. In addition to contributing to the tourism and peace literature, this study highlights the significance of the future to tourism stakeholders. Although young people use different metaphors for tourism and peace, each of them stated that the two are inseparable. The main purpose of education is, therefore, to increase the knowledge and skills of people and to bring them into society as good citizens. Since tourism is a service sector, its content and features should be learned within the scope of an appropriate curriculum and tourism education should be evaluated within general education. Tourists want to know and understand the country or region they visit. People residing in the region or a country the tourist visits should have an attitude suitable for this purpose, and they should be understanding and respectful towards the tourist.

The literature recognized the purpose of tourism education as being to raise tourism awareness in the public, to increase productivity in the labour-based tourism sector, to provide professional knowledge and behaviour to the personnel who directly serve tourists, and to establish a balance between the personnel's authority, skills and responsibilities (Olcay, 2008). However, this study acknowledges that tourism education should include discussions about tourism and peace. In this context, tourism educators should consider these while preparing students for the tourism sector through education. Specifically, the addition of courses on tourism and peace to the tourism education curricula will further develop the sensitivity of the students on this issue. It is also important that the private sector – in which many students do internships – aligns with government policies concerning tourism development and which may contribute to establishing a peaceful environment at a destination.

Despite its insightful conclusions, this study is not without limitations. First of all, the study draws from a specific cultural context where the metaphors used are linguistically bound. Second, the results in question cannot be generalized as qualitative research was employed. Therefore, future research is required to investigate the role of tourism education in peacebuilding further and, especially, examine the perceptions and attitudes of students in terms of the peace through tourism tenet. As a suggestion, future studies can employ quantitative research on the subject to allow for greater generalization. In addition, comparative studies may be undertaken to examine if there are any differences in student perceptions from various cultural contexts or socio-economic backgrounds, using a variety of analysis methods beyond the one adopted in this study. Furthermore, other stakeholders' perceptions on the peace and tourism relationship may be analysed and compared to student perceptions for a holistic view of how tourism education can contribute to the goal of peace.

References

Anson, C. (1999). Planning for peace: the role of tourism in the aftermath of violence. *Journal of Travel Research*, 38(1), 57–61.
Askjellerud, S. (2003). The tourist: a messenger of peace? *Annals of Tourism Research*, 30(3), 741–4.
ATA [American, Turkey and Armenian] Fellows (2011). Tourism for peace: theory put in practice for Turkey and Armenia. *The Journal of Tourism and Peace Research*, 2(2), i–viii.

Becken, S., & Carmignani, F. (2016). Does tourism lead to peace? *Annals of Tourism Research, 61*, 63–79.

Burnett, G. W., & Uysal, M. (1990). On the nature of peace in relationship to tourism: three cases. *The Tourist Review, 45*(1), 2–7.

Çakıcı, A. C., Benli, S., Üzülmez, M., & Kaynak, M. (2015). Turizm ve barış ilişkisi üzerine lisansüstü turizm öğrencilerinin algısı. 16. Ulusal Turizm Kongresi 12–15 Kasım 2015, Çanakkale/Türkiye.

Campo, S., & Alvarez, M. D. (2019). Animosity toward a country in the context of destinations as tourism products. *Journal of Hospitality & Tourism Research, 43*(7), 1002–24.

Causevic, S. (2010). Tourism which erases borders: an introspection into Bosnia and Herzegovina. *Tourism, Progress and Peace*, 48–64. https:// doi .org/ 10 .1079/ 9781845936778.0048.

Cho, M. (2007). A re-examination of tourism and peace: the case of the Mt. Gumgang tourism development on the Korean Peninsula, *Tourism Management, 28*(2), 556–69.

Çoğaltay, N., & Aras, Z. N. (2018). Öğretmen adaylarının öğretmen atamalarında kullanılan sözlü sınava ilişkin algıları: metafor analizi örneği. *BEÜ SBE Derg, 7*(1), 211–30.

Collier, P., Hoeffler, A., & Söderbom, M. (2004). On the duration of civil war. *Journal of Peace Research, 41*(3), 253–73. https://doi.org/10.1177/0022343304043769.

D'Amore, J. L (1988). Tourism—a vital force for peace. *Tourism Management, 9*(2), 151–4.

Dilek, N. K., Dilek, S. E., & Gümüş, M. (2016). Otel çalışanlarının turizm ve barış ilişkisine yönelik metaforik algıları. *Batman Üniversitesi Yaşam Bilimleri Dergisi, 6*(2/1), 1–15.

Farmaki, A. (2017). The tourism and peace nexus. *Tourism Management, 59*, 528–40.

Farmaki, A., & Stergiou, D. (2021). Peace and tourism: bridging the gap through justice. *Peace & Change, 46*(3), 286–309.

Gelbman, A. (2010). Border tourism attractions as a space for presenting and symbolizing peace. *Tourism, Progress and Peace*, 83–98. https:// doi .org/ 10 .1079/ 9781845936778.0083.

Güney, T., Göktepe, S., & Kokonalıoğlu, H. T. (2022). Rusya-Ukrayna Savaşı'nın Türkiye turizmine olası etkileri. *Batman Üniversitesi Yaşam Bilimleri Dergisi, 12*(1), 92–104.

Honey, M., & Gilpin, R. (2009). Special report on tourism in the developing world: promoting peace and reducing poverty (Washington, DC: United State Institute of Peace). http:// www .responsibletravel .org/ resources/ documents/ reports/ USIP %20Tourism%20in%20the%20Developing%20World.pdf.

Kelly, I. (2006). Tourism education, the peace proposition and the conscientization of the tourism industry. *Journal of Teaching in Travel & Tourism, 6*(1), 1–16.

Kulakoğlu Dilek, N., Dilek, S. E., & Gümüş, M. (2016). Otel çalışanlarının turizm ve barış ilişkisine yönelik metaforik algıları. *Batman Üniversitesi Yaşam Bilimleri Dergisi, 6*(2/1), 1–15.

Kurdek, L. A., & Rodgon, M. M. (1975). Perceptual, cognitive, and affective perspective taking in kindergarten through sixth-grade children. *Developmental Psychology, 11*(5), 643–50.

Mason, P. (2003). *Tourism İmpacts, Planning and Management (Birinci Baskı)*. Oxford: Butterworth Heinemann.

Monteiro, A., Lopes, S., & Carbone, F. (2021). Academic mobility: bridging tourism and peace education. In J. T. da Silva, Z. Breda, & F. Carbone (Eds.), *Role and Impact of Tourism in Peacebuilding and Conflict Transformation* (pp. 275–301). Hershey, PA: IGI Global.

Moufakkir, O. (2010). Peace through domestic tourism and tourism rights: ınclusion of Muslim ethnic minorities in the context of social tourism. *The Journal of Tourism and Peace Research, 1*(1), 42–59.

Olcay, A. (2008). Türk turizminde eğitimin önemi. *Gaziantep Üniversitesi Sosyal Bilimler Dergisi, 7*(2), 383–90.

Özekici, Y. K. (2019). Yerli halk-turist etkileşimi ve bir model önerisi. Gazi Üniversitesi Sosyal Bilimler Enstitüsü, Turizm İşletmeciliği Anabilim Dalı, Doktora Tezi.

Patton, M. Q. (2002). *Qualitative Evaluation and Research Methods* (3rd edn). Thousand Oaks, CA: Sage.

Pernecky, T. (2010). The being of tourism. *The Journal of Tourism and Peace Research, 1*(1), 1–15.

Pitcher, R. (2013). Using metaphor analysis: MIP and beyond. *The Qualitative Report,* 18, article 68, 1–8.

Pratt, S., & Liu, A. (2016). Does tourism really lead to peace? A global view. *International Journal of Tourism Research, 18*(1), 82–90.

Sánchez, M., Campo, S., & Alvarez, M. D. (2018). The effect of animosity on the intention to visit tourist destinations. *Journal of Destination Marketing & Management, 7,* 182–9.

Sanders, P. (1982). Phenemology: a new way of wieving organizational research. *The Academy of Management Review, 7*(3), 353–60.

Schmitt, R. (2005). Systematic metaphor analysis as a method of qualitative research. *The Qualitative Report, 10*(2), 358–94.

Seabra, C., Kastenholz, E., Abrantes, J. L., & Reis, M. (2018). Peacefulness at home: impacts on international travel. *International Journal of Tourism Cities, 4*(3). https:// doi.org/10.1108/IJTC-10-2017-0050.

Smith, V. L. (1998). War and tourism: an American ethnography. *Annals of Tourism Research, 25*(1), 202–27.

Sönmez, V., & Alacapınar, V. G. (2011). *Bilimsel Araştırma Yöntemleri.* Ankara: Anı Yayıncılık.

UNWTO (2022a). International tourism and Covid-19. https:// www .unwto .org/ tourism-data/international-tourism-and-covid-19.

UNWTO (2022b). Impact of the Russian offensive in Ukraine on international tourism. https://www.unwto.org/impact-russian-offensive-in-ukraine-on-tourism.

Yenişehirlioğlu, E., Salha, H., & Şahin, S. (2016). Politik krizlerin turizm talebi üzerindeki etkisine yönelik bir araştırma: Rusya'nın değişen yüzü ve bu değişimin Türkiye turizmine etkileri. *Balkan ve Yakın Doğu Sosyal Bilimler Dergisi, 2*(3), 74–83.

Yeşiltaş, M., Öztürk, İ., & Türkmen, F. (2008). Terör faaliyetlerinin turizm sektörüne etkilerinin çözüm önerileri perspektifinde değerlendirilmesi. *Sosyal Bilimler Dergisi, 10*(1), 180.

Yıldırım, A., & Şimşek, H. (2008). *Sosyal Bilimlerde Nitel Araştırma Yöntemleri.* Ankara: Seçkin Yayıncılık.

Yu, Q., McManus, R., Yen, D. A., & Li, X. R. (2020). Tourism boycotts and animosity: a study of seven events. *Annals of Tourism Research,* 80, 102792.

10 Women and peace: a gender approach to peace through tourism

Fiona Bakas and Anna Farmaki

Introduction

The death of Mahsa Amini on 16 September 2022, while she was in the custody of Iranian 'morality' police on the pretext that she had not adequately covered her hair (Reuters, 2022), led to a series of protests against the Iranian government in both Iran and the rest of the world. These events remind us that the role of women is irrevocably linked to peacebuilding and security as female empowerment and gender equality are prerequisites of a peaceful and stable society (World Bank, 2022). According to Crespo-Sancho (2017), the larger the gender gap in a society the more likely people will enter into violent conflict whereas greater gender equality has been associated with decreased possibility of military force being used to resolve disputes as it minimises the severity of violence in a society. Correspondingly, the goal of the United Nations' INSTRAW Gender, Peace and Security programme has been to enable nations to increase women's participation in peace processes and incorporate gender equality in post-conflict reconstruction mechanisms (UN, 2022).

Although several studies have been undertaken over the years to examine the role of women in peacebuilding (e.g., Charlesworth, 2008; Goyol, 2019), scarce attention has been paid to gender issues in the context of peace through tourism. Tourism has long been considered a tool for bridging social, economic and political inequalities that divide societies, as travel brings people together encouraging interaction and mutual understanding while fostering cooperation opportunities (Seyfi et al., 2022). Consequently, tourism has the potential of improving the relations among nations and rebuild societies affected by conflict (Causevic & Lynch, 2011). Although numerous studies exist investigating a range of issues pertinent to peace through tourism, a focus on gender remains largely absent in the peace and tourism literature. This omission is surprising for numerous reasons. First, approximately 55 per cent of workers employed in the tourism industry are women (UN, 2019a). Second, tourism has been argued to provide empowerment opportunities to women (WTO, 2019) which are regarded as contributing to the peacebuilding goal as female empowerment minimises inequalities that divide societies. Likewise, women are considered to be more compassionate and understanding than men (Benenson et al., 2021); thus, they are more likely to achieve positive and meaningful host–guest exchanges that are fruitful for reconciliation and peacebuilding. It is, hence, imperative that gender is considered in peace and tourism research and, specifically, that women's role and contribution to peace through tourism is examined.

The aim of this chapter is to address this gap in the research and conceptually examine the role of gender in peace through tourism. First, we explain the importance of women in peacebuilding by acknowledging the influence of gender on peacebuilding mechanisms and post-conflict reconstruction. Then, we analyse the role that women may play in peace through tourism using a feminist economics approach. The chapter concludes by discussing how the relevant research agenda can be advanced and what practical insights arise that need to be taken into consideration if the peace through tourism goal will be more appropriately addressed in terms of gender.

Gender and peacebuilding

Gender refers to the characteristics that distinguish men and women, boys and girls (WHO, 2022) and carries great importance socially as it influences how people behave. Contrary to sex which has biological connotations, gender is socially constructed as expectations, behaviours and roles are assigned to men and women in a society and these, in turn, influence the relationships among genders. Therefore, gender is not a constant variable as it changes according to times and varies from one society to another depending on the assumed roles and perceptions each society has of men and women. In this sense, gender produces inequalities as some societies are patriarchal, valuing men as more important, stronger or superior to women. Inequalities may also stem from economic discrepancies between men and women as in many societies men are considered the breadwinners and women the housekeepers; such perceptions prevent or discourage women from working and becoming financially independent. To this day, it is reported worldwide that men receive higher salaries than women for the same job performed (World Bank, 2021).

Gender is also deeply rooted to situations of war and conflict. Traditionally, it is men that are considered the warriors, the fighters or the community leaders responsible for decisions of entering into a war or not. Wars are considered a male practice with masculinity being culturally antecedent to war and men are thought of as more prone to enter into violence than women (Ferguson, 2021). Women, to the contrary, have played different roles in conflict situations including that of a nurse or more often that of the victim, although in many cases gender dichotomies in war are not that binary, especially nowadays that women have been encouraged to take part in combat. Even so, to a great extent, women have been excluded from conflict and simultaneously they have also been excluded from peacebuilding processes and conflict prevention attempts (Human Rights Watch, 2022).

In light of this, the United Nations has called for the need to include women in post-conflict restructuring and peacebuilding processes and to maximise gender equality to ensure more peaceful and stable societies, free of social and economic inequalities (UN, 2022). The relationship, thus, between gender and peace is two-fold. First, if gender inequalities are reduced societies may emerge as more peaceful and secure. To this end, the empowerment of women is necessary for gender inequality reduction and by extent peace. Second, if women are encouraged to participate more in post-conflict reconstruction and peacebuilding efforts there are higher chances of peace being durable and positively active, with meaningful exchanges between the parties involved taking place. According to the UN (2019b) the inclusion of women in peacebuilding will create sustainable peace, which is more inclusive, hopeful and just than other forms of peace identified (e.g., positive and negative peace as conceptualised by Galtung, 1995) as it addresses structural inequalities that often lead to conflict re-emergence (Farmaki and Stergiou, 2021). Peace and justice, therefore, go hand in hand and the discussion on women's role in peacebuilding needs to address gender inequalities at its core.

Although women are known as being active in informal grassroots peacebuilding activities, they are less likely to participate in formal peace processes (Porter, 2008) as they remain in many societies politically marginalised from decision-making processes. This is an oxymoron considering that women are more likely to focus on reconciliation, economic development, justice and education rather than the spoils of war (Lindborg, 2017). The inclusion of women in peacebuilding efforts is equally important for women themselves as they are greatly affected by war and conflict; thus, their needs and interests should be taken into account in negotiation and conflict resolution processes. In this context, the term 'gender responsive peacebuilding' was coined by the UN as a goal aiming to highlight gender balancing approaches to peacebuilding that include participation, protection, prevention and recovery.

Despite the increasing literature on women's role in peace and security and the efforts of inter-governmental organisations in promoting a gender responsive agenda in peacebuilding, gender issues have received scant attention in the peace through tourism research context. This is surprising considering that tourism – an industry in which 55 per cent of the workforce comprises women – is seen as being inextricably related to peace. The tourism activity implies contact between hosts and guests, which in turn may elicit improved understanding and relations between the parties involved (Becken & Carmignani, 2016). In this context, tourism has been characterised as a force for peace (D'Amore, 1988) capable of bridging social, economic and political inequalities among societies by encouraging cooperation and mutual socio-economic exchanges. In this regard, tourism is perceived as a track II diplomacy activity aiming at fostering a positive form of peace, which is peace that is sustainable and eradicates the structural inequalities that often fuel and sustain a conflict (Galtung, 1995). Thus, a consideration of gender in relevant examinations may help to illuminate understanding of the contributory role of tourism to peace. In the section below, we discuss the role of gender in peace through tourism, adopting a feminist economics approach, an approach which focuses on what is required to produce a gender equal society.

Gender in tourism and peace: a feminist economics approach

Peacebuilding can be achieved through intercultural exchanges benefiting both the travelled and travelling cultures. Tourism that is ethical, equitable and responsible is capable of promoting peace and justice in destinations, a concept known as 'socialising tourism' (Higgins-Desbiolles et al., 2021). Tourism can especially help to promote positive peace: a form of peace that evolves through addressing structural violence, which in this chapter is perceived as the economic structures contributing to gender inequality. Similar to Everingham et al.'s (2022) approach to peace through volunteer tourism and Cave and Dredge's (2020) approach to regenerative tourism, we take a diverse economies approach (Gibson-Graham, 2006) to imagine how postcapitalist economies, with a greater focus on equality that highlights invisibilised gendered economic operations, can exist and work towards more ethical forms of the tourism economy.

Feminist political economics critiques the neo-liberal, patriarchal, capitalist structures which are deemed to be at the root of the various global crises that society is facing, such as war. Kalisch and Cole (2022) argue that it is through feminist alternative economic critiques, addressing the root causes for gender inequality, that major global crises can be mitigated by reducing crisis vulnerability while increasing resilience and sustainability. Past research on gender in tourism has largely focused on economic and management approaches to tourism labour discourse, instead of attempting to understand the underlying causes of inequality and how they relate to wider social, cultural, economic and political considerations, with some exceptions (Ladkin, 2011). The present chapter responds to the call for more critical research that challenges hegemonies and affects social change, by focusing on how gender influences peace through tourism in terms of the stereotypes affecting women's empowerment though tourism (Ren et al., 2010). Thus, this chapter contributes to the discussion by focusing on how gender analyses of peace through tourism can increase the social and economic benefits for tourism stakeholders (including women).

Gender equality and tourism

Over the past 50 years, there has been an increase in women's employment and education rates globally. This increase has been fuelled by legal changes that make gender-based discrimination illegal and by a shift in social attitudes towards women working (England, 2010). Despite this change, women continue to perform 66 per cent of the world's work and produce 50 per cent of the food while earning 10 per cent of the income and owning only 1 per cent of property worldwide (UN WOMEN, 2015). Addressing gender issues in the economic arena benefits both women and the economy as a whole as it may result in lower discrimination at work, less household violence and decreased poverty rates. According to OECD (2012, p. 3), "higher female earnings and bargaining power translate into greater investment in children's education, health and nutrition, which leads to economic growth in the long term". Tourism can and should contribute to realising the 17 sustainable development goals (SDGs) identified in the United Nation's Agenda 2030 (Boluk et al., 2019), wherein SDG 5 refers to achieving greater gender equality. Gender equality means that women and men have equal conditions for realising their full human rights and for contributing to, and benefiting from, economic, social, cultural and political development (Baum, 2013). Achieving greater gender equality is not only a basic human right that aids social cohesion, but it also makes 'smart economic' sense by increasing productivity and efficiency (Ferguson & Alarcón, 2014).

Tourism can have a significant positive impact on gender equality as can be seen in research that investigates changes in women's income, employment and education in the development of tourism, based on regional (Alarcón & Cole, 2019; Alrwajfah et al., 2020) but also national case studies (Zhang & Zhang, 2020). The role gender plays within tourism is of special interest as women are often encouraged to enter tourism employment due to its flexibility and its 'suitability' for women to engage in this activity, without challenging gender norms regarding women's roles as home-based carers. However, one of the criticisms that Swain (1995, p. 251) made is that by failing to define gender one fails to show how "interlocking dimensions of gender" operate within tourism. Bibliometric research finds that a focus on gender in tourism studies remains marginal and disarticulated from wider feminist and gender-aware research, lacking the critical mass of publications and multi-institutional networks which characterise other tourism sub-fields (Santero-Sanchez et al., 2015). Whilst tourism is often seen as a vehicle for women's empowerment, there are still many obstacles to the realisation of gender equality in tourism. In some cases, tourism has been found to lead to a decline in women's power. For example, ecotourism may exert a potential disempowerment effect on Botswana's rural women (Lenao & Basupi, 2016). In relation to this point, Scheyvens (2000) concluded that ecotourism has the potential to disadvantage and marginalise local women. Duffy et al. (2015) point out that as women gain economic and social independence, new gender roles and status changes lead to conflicts between women's actual needs and family relationships, which in turn limit women's further involvement in tourism. The argument that economic empowerment through tourism is not sufficient, brings forward the issue of how gender roles influence peace through tourism.

Gender roles in tourism

Gender roles represent beliefs about behaviours that are appropriate for members of each sex (Eagly & Wood 2011), influencing behaviours ranging from sexual behaviour to leadership style and entrepreneurial behaviour. Gender is not exactly something that someone is or something that a person has, it is the mechanism by which notions of what constitutes masculine and feminine are produced and normalised (Butler, 2004). Gender roles involve behaviours that are repeated over time, thus becoming internalised as a natural way of being (Beauvoir et al., 2000). Gender can be considered society's "most pervasive organising principle" (Ahl & Nelson, 2010, p. 7) as it is a form of social power, and thus crucial to investigate in social studies of tourism such as this one. In relation to this point, gender essentialism becomes relevant. Gender essentialism is the notion that men and women are innately and fundamentally different in interests and skills (Ridgeway, 2009). According to gender essentialism, gender typically acts as a background identity that biases, in gendered directions, the performance of behaviours undertaken in the name of organisational roles and identities. Looking at personality traits that are supposedly 'masculine' or 'feminine' is in itself a technique of debatable effectiveness and vigour since such essentialisations only serve to perpetuate gendered stereotypes regarding what a 'man' or a 'woman' is like.

Gender relations in economic organisations are a well-established area of research and feminist studies show that tourism organisations are not gender-neutral spaces (Carvalho et al., 2019; Figueroa-Domecq et al., 2020). To the contrary, they actively reinforce gender differences, gendered power relations and the male-dominated gender order, both in paid and non-paid work (Acker, 2012; Bakas, 2014). Gender operates, often invisibly, in numerous ways (Figueroa-Domecq & Segovia-Perez, 2020). For example, definitions of who constitutes the 'ideal tourism worker' are influenced by tourism managers' gendered perceptions of female workers' "availability-related flexibility" as seen in a study based in Portugal (Costa et al., 2017, p. 73). Indeed, tourism processes exhibit high levels of gendering, ranging from the sexualised images used to promote tourism destinations (Pritchard, 2014) to tourism labour, where women occupy positions such as maids and cleaners which they are 'naturally' good at (Swain, 1995), to tourism recruitment processes often being gendered (Costa et al., 2017) and the continuing existence of a gender wage gap in tourism (Bakas et al., 2018a).

Therefore, whilst tourism is often depicted as having the potential to empower women due to its diverse, dynamic and flexible nature, it remains a highly gendered activity that reinforces traditional gendered performances by offering temporary and part-time employment in traditionally gendered skills (Figueroa-Domecq, de Jong & Williams, 2020). Tourism labour is a particularly pertinent place to look at gender roles and relations, as work is a key discursive site for the enactment of gender (Bakas et al., 2018b; Bruni et al., 2005). Today, gender in tourism labour has moved past the empowerment discourse to more nuanced understandings of how gender roles and economic roles interact in the tourism arena (Cole, 2018), building upon investigations into the role of gender in tourism (Kinnaird & Hall, 1996) and questioning "who controls what" and "how hierarchies are built and maintained" (Swain, 2004, p. 102). This highlights the need for an understanding of current gender roles in terms of policy and development in tourism which in turn impact peace through tourism research.

Progressing the research agenda

Alternative economy and gender

The feminist movement brought about a focus on conceptualisations of 'the economy' in terms of social actors dynamically influencing interdependent economic processes, which is known as a turn towards a focus on 'social provisioning' (Power, 2013). The social reproduction economy is built of all the acts that people complete in order to maintain life on a daily basis and intergenerationally (Gibson-Graham, 2006). Social reproductive roles, that is, responsibility for completion of these largely unpaid labour acts, are highly gendered, with women completing most social reproductive tasks globally. Consequently, social reproductive gender roles (e.g., carer for an elderly relative) can influence productive roles in tourism. Despite a drive for conceptual change, mainstream economic theorising is still characterised by hidden assumptions relating to gender, such as overlooking the significance of social reproductive activities within the economy and viewing all economic activities as the "self-interested exchange between rational economic agents" (Barker & Kuiper, 2003, p. 3).

Viewing individual choice as a myth, the politico-economic conditions that inform people's actions according to gender roles they are expected to perform, may be explored. The myth of individual choice has been analysed by various feminist economists (Badgett & Folbre, 2003; Elias, 2013; England, 1993; Folbre, 2012) who highlight the importance of politico-economic conditions that mould people's actions according to the gender roles they are expected to perform. For example, a study on the gender wage gap in Spain points out how a higher incidence of the traditional male-breadwinner model combined with low public provision for childcare for preschool children, increases the gender wage gap as women have more career interruptions in order to provide childcare because of the politico-economic structures like welfare (Cebrián & Moreno, 2015). In another example, it is revealed that horizontal segregation, gendered geographical mobility, and the prevalence of men in hierarchical positions contribute to the maintenance of the gender wage gap in tourism in Portugal (Bakas et al., 2018a). In India (Rinaldi & Salerno, 2020), when rural women were encouraged to enter the tourism job market they saw improvements in their income generation and, consequently, self-esteem and bargaining power within the family. However, politico-economic structures make it difficult for these rural women in India to have bank accounts in their name and socio-cultural norms that give men free rein over how finances are used water-down the perceived empowerment these women have.

Gender roles and norms are influenced by cultural structures but there are more complex forces at work involving politico-economic structures that favour expressions of masculinity within tourism labour at the detriment of feminine expressions. As women tend to have different interpretations of economic activity due to their social reproductive roles (Bakas, 2014), they often keep their businesses small, without this entailing that they are less 'valid' as economic agents or 'underperforming' (Marlow & McAdam, 2013). Since economic theory is based on conventionally masculine beliefs about the economically efficient person being a rational and independent adult, the influence of values socially attributed to work need to be reconsidered. The emergence of the 'rational economic woman' (Rankin, 2001) illustrates how the masculine persists, since the concept of 'rational economic woman' is created simply by adding some essentialising feminine sensibilities, such as concern for the family, to the utility maximising rational economic man model. Mooney (2020) notes that in tourism, female leadership is different from the male norm and that traditional theoretical framings relating to women's prioritisation of domestic commitments acts to their detriment, suggesting a new research agenda. Hence, there is a need for alternative conceptualisations of discourses surrounding women consuming and producing tourism, which are less based on the male model and more on women's lived experiences.

Invisibility of gender inequality in tourism

Creating gender analyses of tourism processes is essential for a more holistic representation of today's reality (Ferguson & Alarcón, 2014). This is because gender roles and relations silently order social dynamics, hence invisibly influencing economic structures. Women working in tourism are confronted with invisible barriers that prevent them from climbing the organisational ladder, namely the 'glass ceiling' and 'glass cliff' phenomena, occupational segregation and limitations of access to informal organisational networks (Bakas et al., 2018b). The invisible and informal nature of the barriers presented to women in the organisational environment makes their identification and eradication difficult. Increased attention to how stereotyped gender roles, as an 'invisible hand', can influence tourism discourse (Alarcón & Cole, 2019; Costa et al., 2017) encourages a deeper investigation into how gender roles influence tourism production and consumption. For example, in research conducted in Saudi Arabia (Elshaer et al., 2021) it is found that only if robust women's empowerment is consolidated into tourism planning and implementation processes can tourism then act as a vehicle for encouraging gender parity. In a study conducted in three countries, United Arab Emirates, Egypt and Oman, the importance of how women's work is perceived in terms of value are significant predictors of women's psychological and economic empowerment in the tourism sector (Abou-Shouk et al., 2021). Such findings illustrate the importance of having better understandings of the productive work that women in tourism conduct, in terms of the challenges they face at work because of gender stereotypes.

Drawing on post-structuralist theorising which addresses issues of visibility/invisibility, it is useful to address the concept of gender essentialism as a mechanism by which gender becomes, and continues to be, invisible. As individuals themselves are embedded in this discourse, it is difficult to distinguish discrimination based on gender roles, which also means that the organisation itself faces difficulty in being 'gender-aware'. An example of this invisibility is shown in a study where participants who are tourism leaders in Portugal express the idea that the goal of achieving gender equality at work was in fact a non-goal, as they see little influence of gender on business processes (Costa et al., 2015). Many development programmes, such as the ones implemented by the World Bank, specifically target women encouraging them to engage with tourism entrepreneurship, in fulfilling their objectives to increase economic growth (Ferguson, 2011; Griffin, 2010). However, as women are often encouraged to partake in economic growth initiatives but continue to be held responsible for all household labour (Momsen, 2004), conflict arises. It is especially pertinent to investigate *how* gender equality influences the tourism industry and, by extent, peace through tourism.

Increasing gender equality through tourism

A more practical way of increasing gender equality in the hospitality industry is through implementing mentoring of female hospitality workers (Dashper, 2020) to challenge gendered discourses of success in hospitality careers and play a role in confronting gender inequality in the hospitality industry. Recent research on 21 Asia-Pacific Economic Cooperation (APEC) member states (Hutchings et al., 2020) reveals continued segregation of women across the economies, suggesting that better integration of gender into human resource management strategies, policy interventions and provision of equal employment opportunities are needed to achieve greater gender equality. Lomazzi et al. (2019) also showed that in Europe, institutional and workplace arrangements supporting the dual-earner/dual-caregiver family model, which promotes better work–family balance, is an indicator for gender equality associated with more egalitarian gender-role attitudes. Hence, it is suggested that in order to promote the aim of achieving peace through tourism, policies should be created at the constitutional level to combat gender-based discrimination, that will help as the tourism industry benefits from increased gender equality which will in turn increase the goals of social cohesion.

Recently, the nexus between seemingly unrelated topics such as that between tourism, water and gender have been explored (Cole et al., 2020), revealing important new insights into how gender operates within tourism and one of the most important resources on Earth, water. Similarly, investigating how gender roles affect and are affected by peace through tourism represents a fruitful new topic for further investigation. For example, the role of women as producers, service providers, entrepreneurs and consumers of tourism needs to be examined in relation to peace, for their respective roles may play an essential part in bringing about peace in post-conflict destinations. Although all genders are affected by wars and conflict, women in particular have been acknowledged as victims of violent acts (e.g., rape); hence, research needs to investigate peace constituencies within women's capacity as important tourism stakeholders. Understanding of women's role in peacebuilding via tourism production and consumption activities can ultimately advance knowledge of sustainable development processes and practices.

Conclusions and implications

Women are often depicted as being a vulnerable societal group, a portrayal that is still persistent today despite feminist movements worldwide highlighting the existence of gendered stereotypes. In relation to wars and conflict, women have been traditionally portrayed as the victims of violent acts including rape. In tourism, the root of such violent acts is often gender-based violence, wherein people are attacked because of gendered beliefs and stereotypes (Eger et al., 2020). Indeed, conflicts are generally seen as a masculine practice (Ferguson, 2021). On the contrary, women have been acknowledged as being more caring in nature and, hence, recently identified as being potentially ideal for contributing to reconciliation and peacebuilding once a conflict ceases (Goyol, 2019). Correspondingly, women can play a significant role in peace talks and reconciliation processes, especially if they are empowered through their involvement in tourism. The role of women in peacebuilding is also important for another reason. Given that peace requires the eradication of structural inequalities at the social, economic and political levels, it is evident that for peace to be maintained gender equality needs to be promoted. In this context, tourism becomes relevant to peace. Tourism has been argued to contribute to peace because travel elicits contact between people which, in turn, improves perceptions and attitudes towards a hostile outgroup (D'Amore, 1988). Likewise, tourism may help to eliminate inequalities between groups in a society and, thus, improve peace prospects (Farmaki & Stergiou, 2021).

As tourism is "built on human relations" (Aitchison, 2001, p. 134), the relationship of gender to peace through tourism is an important but under-researched topic. Hence, it is necessary to look more deeply at the reasons underpinning the role of gender in tourism and peace in order to improve understanding on the ways gender influences peacebuilding via tourism activities. In this chapter, we have attempted to examine the role of gender in peace through tourism using a feminist economics approach. We have identified the areas of inequalities between men and women as applied in the tourism industry and which relate to employment conditions and benefits and stereotypes of gender roles which determine both the production and consumption of tourism. We, then, propose that research attention shifts towards the examination of the political and economic structures that impact women producers and consumers within tourism settings as well as the definition of gender roles and how they manifest in peace through tourism. In addition, we propose that researchers investigate gender equality in all the facets of women's lives within tourism in terms of employment, travelling and entrepreneurial pursuits.

Undoubtedly, examinations of gender issues in peace through tourism research will uncover an array of important topics that may not only advance our knowledge of how tourism can more effectively address the peace goal, but also enlighten stakeholders as to how women in the tourism industry can assist the peace through tourism process and how gender equality in tourism can be achieved to improve peace prospects. We hope that, with this chapter, we open up the discussion on gender roles and gender quality as an important factor to be acknowledged and considered in peace through tourism analyses.

References

Abou-Shouk, M. A., Mannaa, M. T., & Elbaz, A. M. (2021). Women's empowerment and tourism development: a cross-country study. *Tourism Management Perspectives*, *37*, 100782. https://doi.org/10.1016/j.tmp.2020.100782.

Acker, J. (2012). Gendered organizations and intersectionality: problems and possibilities. *Equality, Diversity and Inclusion: An International Journal, 31*(3), 214–24.

Ahl, H., & Nelson, T. (2010). Moving forward: institutional perspectives on gender and entrepreneurship. *International Journal of Gender and Entrepreneurship, 2*, 5–9.

Aitchison, C. (2001). Theorizing other discourses of tourism, gender and culture. *Tourist Studies, 1*, 133–47.

Alarcón, D. M., & Cole, S. (2019). No sustainability for tourism without gender equality. *Journal of Sustainable Tourism, 27*(7), 903–19. https://doi.org/10.1080/09669582.2019.1588283.

Alrwajfah, M. M., Almeida-García, F., & Cortés-Macías, R. (2020). Females' perspectives on tourism's impact and their employment in the sector: the case of Petra,

Jordan. *Tourism Management, 78*, 104069. https://doi.org/10.1016/j.tourman.2019
.104069.

Badgett, L. M. V., & Folbre, N. (2003). Job gendering: occupational choice and the
marriage market. *Industrial Relations, 42*(2), 270–98. https://doi.org/10.1111/1468
-232X.00290.

Bakas, F. E. (2014). Tourism, female entrepreneurs and gender: crafting economic
realities in rural Greece (PhD thesis, University of Otago). http://hdl.handle.net/
10523/5381.

Bakas, F. E., Costa, C., Breda, Z., & Durão, M. (2018a). A critical approach to the gender
wage gap in tourism labor. *Tourism, Culture and Communication, 18*(1). https://doi
.org/10.3727/109830418X15180180585167.

Bakas, F. E., Costa, C., Durão, M., Carvalho, I., & Breda, Z. (2018b). "An uneasy truth?":
female tourism managers and organizational gender equality measures in Portugal.
In S. Cole (Ed.), *Gender Equality and Tourism: Beyond Empowerment* (pp. 34–44).
Wallingford: CABI.

Barker, D. K., & Kuiper, E. (2003). Introduction. In D. Barker & E. Kuiper (Eds.),
Toward a feminist philosophy of economics. Abingdon: Routledge.

Baum, T. (2013). International perspectives on women and work in hotels, cater-
ing and tourism (Working Paper 1/2013). https://www.ilo.org/gender/Information
resources/WCMS_209867/lang--en/index.htm.

Beauvoir, S. D., Parshley, H. M., & Crosland, M. (2000). *The second sex*. New York:
David Campbell Publishers.

Becken, S., & Carmignani, F. (2016). Does tourism lead to peace? *Annals of Tourism
Research, 61*, 63–79.

Benenson, J. F., Gauthier, E., & Markovits, H. (2021). Girls exhibit greater empathy
than boys following a minor accident. *Scientific Reports, 11*(1), 1–8.

Boluk, K. A., Cavaliere, C. T., & Higgins-Desbiolles, F. (2019). A critical framework
for interrogating the United Nations Sustainable Development Goals 2030 Agenda
in tourism. *Journal of Sustainable Tourism, 27*(7), 847–64. https://doi.org/10.1080/
09669582.2019.1619748.

Bruni, A., Gherardi, S., & Poggio, B. (2004). Entrepreneur-mentality, gender and the
study of women entrepreneurs. *Journal of Organizational Change Management,
17*(3), 256–68.

Butler, J. (2004). *Undoing gender*. Abingdon: Routledge.

Carvalho, I., Costa, C., Lykke, N., & Torres, A. (2019). Beyond the glass ceiling: gendering tourism management. *Annals of Tourism Research, 75*, 79–91. https://doi.org/10
.1016/j.annals.2018.12.022.

Causevic, S., & Lynch, P. (2011). Phoenix tourism: post-conflict tourism role. *Annals of
Tourism Research, 38*(3), 780–800.

Cave, J., & Dredge, D. (2020). Regenerative tourism needs diverse economic practices.
Tourism Geographies, 22(3), 503–13.

Cebrián, I., & Moreno, G. (2015). The effects of gender differences in career interruptions on the gender wage gap in Spain. *Feminist Economics*, 1–27. https://doi.org/10
.1080/13545701.2015.1008534.

Charlesworth, H. (2008). Are women peaceful? Reflections on the role of women in
peace-building. *Feminist Legal Studies, 16*(3), 347–61.

Cole, S. (Ed.) (2018). *Gender equality and tourism: beyond empowerment*. Wallingford:
CABI.

Cole, S. K. G., Mullor, E. C., Ma, Y., & Sandang, Y. (2020). "Tourism, water, and gender"—an international review of an unexplored nexus. *WIREs Water, 7*(4), e1442. https://doi.org/10.1002/wat2.1442.

Costa, C., Bakas, F. E., Breda, Z., Durão, M., Carvalho, I., & Caçador, S. (2017). Gender, flexibility and the 'ideal tourism worker'. *Annals of Tourism Research, 64*, 64–75. http://dx.doi.org/10.1016/j.annals.2017.03.002.

Costa, C., Bakas, F., Durão, M., & Breda, Z. (2015). Gender equality measures in tourism: organisational awareness and strategies. *Journal of Tourism & Development, 23*, 91–103.

Crespo-Sancho, C. (2017). The role of gender in the prevention of violent conflict. Background paper for the United Nations/World Bank Flagship Study, Pathways for Peace: Inclusive Approaches to Preventing Violent Conflict. Washington, DC: World Bank.

D'Amore, L. J. (1988). Tourism: a vital force for peace. *Tourism Management, 9*(2), 151–4.

Dashper, K. (2020). Mentoring for gender equality: supporting female leaders in the hospitality industry. *International Journal of Hospitality Management, 88*, 102397. https://doi.org/10.1016/j.ijhm.2019.102397.

Duffy, L. N., Kline, C. S., Mowatt, R. A., & Chancellor, H. C. (2015). Women in tourism: shifting gender ideology in the DR. *Annals of Tourism Research, 52*, 72–86. https://doi.org/10.1016/j.annals.2015.02.017.

Eagly, A., & Wood, W. (2011). Feminism and the evolution of sex differences and similarities. *Sex Roles, 64*(9–10), 758–67. https://doi.org/10.1007/s11199-011-9949-9.

Eger, C., Vizcaino Suarez, L. P., & Jeffrey, H. (2020). Introducing critical debates on gender-based violence in tourism. In P. Vizcaino, H. Jeffrey, & C. Eger (Eds.), *Tourism and gender-based violence : challenging inequalities* (pp. 1–13). Wallingford: CABI. https://doi.org/10.1079/9781789243215.0001.

Elias, J. (2013). Davos woman to the rescue of global capitalism: postfeminist politics and competitiveness promotion at the World Economic Forum. *International Political Sociology, 7*(2), 152–69. https://doi.org/10.1111/ips.12015.

Elshaer, I., Moustafa, M., Sobaih, A. E., Aliedan, M., & Azazz, A. M. S. (2021). The impact of women's empowerment on sustainable tourism development: mediating role of tourism involvement. *Tourism Management Perspectives, 38*, 100815. https://doi.org/10.1016/j.tmp.2021.100815.

England, P. (1993). The separative self: androcentric bias in neoclassical assumptions. In M. A. Ferber & J. A. Nelson (Eds.), *Beyond economic man: feminist theory and economics* (pp. 37–54). Chicago, IL: The University of Chicago Press.

England, P. (2010). The gender revolution: uneven and stalled. *Gender & Society, 24*(2), 149–66. https://doi.org/10.1177/0891243210361475.

Everingham, P., Young, T. N., Wearing, S. L., & Lyons, K. (2022). A diverse economies approach for promoting peace and justice in volunteer tourism. *Journal of Sustainable Tourism, 30*(2–3), 618–36. https://doi.org/10.1080/09669582.2021.1924179.

Farmaki, A., & Stergiou, D. (2021). Peace and tourism: bridging the gap through justice. *Peace & Change, 46*(3), 286–309.

Ferguson, L. (2011). Tourism, consumption and inequality in Central America. *New Political Economy, 16*, 347–71.

Ferguson, L., & Alarcón, D. M. (2014). Gender and sustainable tourism: reflections on theory and practice. *Journal of Sustainable Tourism*, 1–16. https://doi.org/10.1080/09669582.2014.957208.

Ferguson, R. B. (2021). Masculinity and war. *Current Anthropology*, *62*(S23), S108–S120.

Figueroa-Domecq, C., de Jong, A., & Williams, A. M. (2020). Gender, tourism & entrepreneurship: a critical review. *Annals of Tourism Research*, *84*, 102980. https://doi.org/10.1016/j.annals.2020.102980.

Figueroa-Domecq, C., & Segovia-Perez, M. (2020). Application of a gender perspective in tourism research: a theoretical and practical approach. *Journal of Tourism Analysis: Revista de Análisis Turístico*. https://www.emerald.com/insight/content/doi/10.1108/JTA-02-2019-0009/full/html.

Folbre, N. (2012). Should women care less? Intrinsic motivation and gender inequality. *British Journal of Industrial Relations*, *50*(4), 597–619.

Galtung, J. (1995). Nonviolence and deep culture: some hidden obstacles. *Peace Research*, *6*(3), 21–37.

Gibson-Graham, J. K. (2006). *The end of capitalism (as we knew it): a feminist critique of political economy*. Minneapolis: University of Minnesota Press.

Goyol, Y. I. (2019). The role of women in peace-building: Liberia in perspective. *International Journal of Development and Management Review*, *14*(1), 123–35.

Griffin, P. (2010). Gender, governance and the global political economy. *Australian Journal of International Affairs*, *64*, 86–104.

Higgins-Desbiolles, F., Doering, A., & Bigby, B. C. (2021). Socialising tourism: reimagining tourism's purpose. In F. Higgins-Desbiolles, A. Doering, & B. C. Bigby (Eds.), *Socialising tourism*. New York: Taylor & Francis.

Human Rights Watch (2022). Women and armed conflict. Available at https://www.hrw.org/topic/womens-rights/women-and-armed-conflict (accessed 21 September 2022).

Hutchings, K., Moyle, C., Chai, A., Garofano, N., & Moore, S. (2020). Segregation of women in tourism employment in the APEC region. *Tourism Management Perspectives*, *34*, 100655. https://doi.org/10.1016/j.tmp.2020.100655.

Kalisch, A. B., & Cole, S. (2022). Gender justice in global tourism: exploring tourism transformation through the lens of feminist alternative economics. *Journal of Sustainable Tourism*, 1–18. https://doi.org/10.1080/09669582.2022.2108819.

Kinnaird, V., & Hall, D. (1996). Understanding tourism processes: a gender-aware framework. *Tourism Management*, *17*(2), 95–102.

Ladkin, A. (2011). Exploring tourism labor. *Annals of Tourism Research*, *38*(3), 1135–55.

Lenao, M., & Basupi, B. (2016). Ecotourism development and female empowerment in Botswana: a review. *Tourism Management Perspectives*, *18*, 51–8.

Lindborg, N. (2017). The essential role of women in peacebuilding. United States Institute of Peace. https://www.usip.org/publications/2017/11/essential-role-women-peacebuilding (accessed 21 September 2022).

Lomazzi, V., Israel, S., & Crespi, I. (2019). Gender equality in Europe and the effect of work-family balance policies on gender-role attitudes. *Social Sciences*, *8*(1). https://doi.org/10.3390/socsci8010005.

Marlow, S., & McAdam, M. (2013). Gender and entrepreneurship: advancing debate and challenging myths; exploring the mystery of the under-performing female entrepreneur. *International Journal of Entrepreneurial Behaviour & Research*, *19*, 114–24.

Momsen, J. H. (2004). *Gender and development*. London: Routledge.

Mooney, S. K. (2020). Gender research in hospitality and tourism management: time to change the guard. *International Journal of Contemporary Hospitality Management*, *32*(5), 1861–79. https://doi.org/10.1108/IJCHM-09-2019-0780.

OECD (2012). *Closing the gender gap: act now!* OECD Publishing. https://www.oecd.org/gender/closingthegap.htm.

Porter, E. (2008). Why women's contribution to peacebuilding matters. *International Studies Review*, *10*(3), 632–4.

Power, M. (2013). A social provisioning approach to gender and economic life. In D. M. Figart & T. L. Warnecke (Eds.), *Handbook of research on gender and economic life* (pp. 7–17). Edward Elgar Publishing.

Pritchard, A. (2014). Gender and feminist perspectives in tourism research. In A. Lew, M. Hall, & A. Williams (Eds.), *The Wiley Blackwell companion to tourism* (pp. 314–24). Chichester: Wiley Blackwell.

Rankin, K. N. (2001). Governing development: neoliberalism, microcredit, and rational economic woman. *Economy and Society*, *30*(1), 18–37.

Ren, C., Pritchard, A., & Morgan, N. (2010). Constructing tourism research: a critical inquiry. *Annals of Tourism Research*, 37, 885–904.

Reuters (2022). The death of Iranian woman Mahsa Amini sparks protests worldwide. Reuters. Available at https://www.reuters.com/news/picture/death-of-iranian-woman-mahsa-amini-spark-idUSRTSBJUNK (accessed 3 September 2022).

Ridgeway, C. L. (2009). Framed before we know it: how gender shapes social relations. *Gender & Society*, *23*(2), 145–60.

Rinaldi, A., & Salerno, I. (2020). The tourism gender gap and its potential impact on the development of the emerging countries. *Quality & Quantity*, *54*(5), 1465–77.

Santero-Sanchez, R., Segovia-Pérez, M., Castro-Nuñez, B., Figueroa-Domecq, C., & Talón-Ballestero, P. (2015). Gender differences in the hospitality industry: a job quality index. *Tourism Management*, *51*, 234–46. http://dx.doi.org/10.1016/j.tourman.2015.05.025.

Scheyvens, R. (2000). Promoting women's empowerment through involvement in ecotourism: experiences from the Third World. *Journal of Sustainable Tourism*, *8*(3), 232–49.

Seyfi, S., Hall, C. M., & Vo-Thanh, T. (2022). Tourism, peace and sustainability in sanctions-ridden destinations. *Journal of Sustainable Tourism*, *30*(2–3), 372–91.

Swain, M. B. (1995). Gender in tourism. *Annals of Tourism Research*, *22*, 247–66.

Swain, M. B. (2004). (Dis)embodied experience and power dynamics in tourism research. In J. Phillimore & L. Goodson (Eds.), *Qualitative research in tourism: ontologies, epistemologies and methodologies* (pp. 102–18). London: Routledge.

UN [United Nations] (2019a). *Women in tourism*. Madrid: UNWTO.

UN [United Nations] (2019b). *The power of women as peacebuilders*. Available at https://www.unwomen.org/en/news/stories/2019/10/compilation-the-power-of-women-peacebuilders (accessed 15 September 2022).

UN [United Nations] (2022). *Gender, peace and security*. Available at https://trainingcentre.unwomen.org/instraw-library/2009-I-PEA-GLO-UNI.pdf (accessed 3 September 2022).

UN WOMEN (2015). *Handbook on costing gender equality*. http://www.unwomen.org/%7B~%7D/media/headquarters/attachments/sections/library/publications/2015/handbook.

WHO [World Health Organization] (2022). Gender and health. Available at https://www.who.int/health-topics/gender#tab=tab_1 (accessed 15 September 2022).

World Bank (2021). Wage and salaried workers. Available at https://data.worldbank.org/indicator/SL.EMP.WORK.MA.ZS (accessed 15 September 2022).

World Bank (2022). Gender equality and development. Available at https:// www .worldbank.org/en/topic/gender/brief/gender-equality-at-a-crossroads (accessed 3 September 2022).

WTO [World Tourism Organization] (2019). Global report on women in tourism. Available at https://www.e-unwto.org/doi/pdf/10.18111/9789284420384 (accessed 5 September 2022).

Zhang, J., & Zhang, Y. (2020). Tourism and gender equality: an Asian perspective. *Annals of Tourism Research*, *85*, 103067. https://doi.org/10.1016/j.annals.2020 .103067.

11   Peace prospects through border and cross-border tourism

Rohit Chauhan

Introduction

Borders and boundaries can be seen from two different perspectives. One perspective tells us that two nations are divided by the border and each nation is safeguarding its territory through its border or creating a space (Okyay, 2017; Rumford, 2006; Smith, Swanson, & Gokariksel, 2015). Another perspective is that cross-border cooperation may occur, leading to mutual benefits for both nations (Castanho et al., 2018; Hardi et al., 2021; Kurowska-Pysz, Castanho, & Loures, 2018; Noferini et al., 2020; Stoffelen, 2018). Tourism presents itself as an activity that takes place beyond borders as tourists travel from one place to another. Thus, tourism has been presented in the literature as a force eliciting cross-border cooperation between two countries (Kozak & Buhalis, 2019; Kropinova, 2021; Tambovceva et al., 2020; Timothy, 1999) which in turn yields numerous benefits to bordering countries (Kropinova, 2019; Prokkola, 2010; Sergeyeva et al., 2022). The value of tourism has been particularly highlighted in cases where conflict exists across the border between two countries. In this context, if the perspective of peace is taken into consideration, then the border represents a line that is restricting the opportunities for various associations to arise between two countries. In this regard, cross-border tourism can act as an agent for building cooperation and eventually normalizing the relations between countries; hence, contributing to a peaceful environment (Gelbman, 2019; Jamgade, 2021; Mansfeld & Korman, 2015).

In border areas, tourism activities can take shape in two forms: (a) border and (b) cross-border tourism which are two types of tourism that deal with a country's geopolitical situation. In the case of border tourism, destinations on the border are prioritized for tourism development as the border provides both fears and hope to tourists, especially when the border is in conflict (Gelbman, 2008). Cross-border tourism, on the other hand, refers to the passage of borders by tourists which helps in the integration of two or more politically divided countries through institutional embedding (Timothy, 1999; Stoffelen, 2018; Hardi et al., 2021). A matter of fact remains that the regions across the border share common historical and cultural traditions and the natural landscape (Livandovschi, 2017) despite political differences and tensions being present. Thus, border tourism and cross-border tourism offer great opportunities for cultural affinity to strengthen and for social stability and peace to develop across borders through cooperation initiatives and the mutual exchange of socio-economic benefits (Kozak & Buhalis, 2019).

Despite a burgeoning number of studies on border and/or cross-border tourism (Gao, Ryan, & Cave, 2019; Gelbman & Timothy, 2017; Mansfeld & Korman, 2015; Nunkoo & Ramkisson, 2013), less attention has been paid to the ability of these types of tourism to contribute to peace. This chapter draws from the India–Pakistan border, which represents one of the conflict zones of the twenty-first century, to examine the peace prospects of the border and cross-border tourism. In so doing, two factors have been identified in terms of the people living on the borders and the tourists. On the side of potential hosts (or the people living on the borderlands), the cultural affinity between the people on both sides of the border was acknowledged as a factor that would help the development of border and cross-border tourism. From the perspective of tourists, opening up borders in the remote areas of two countries may result in a unified destination with more capital attractions.

Borders, tourism and peace

Borders are generally used to define the geographic boundaries of countries. Typically, borders restrict tourism as they produce barriers to human interaction (Weidenfeld, 2013) either because of travel restrictions as seen in the case of global health crises including COVID-19 (Sofield, 2006) or because borders are characterized by vulnerabilities that often make them become places of risk such as terrorist attacks. Borders between nations who share uncomfortable relationships are though the most vulnerable and are, thus, often locations with increased security measures including substantial deployment of armed forces. Likewise, borders can take any shape ranging from political to psychological. In this context, tourism activities are restricted to the border areas of countries whereas the imbalance of tourism development between two neighbouring areas might lead to border formation. This border formation is initially economic in nature but might transform into a psychological one (Xu,

Huang, & Zhang, 2018). As a result, the hope of peace or cohesion between neighbouring countries is minimized.

Tourism in the border region of a country is affected by two different circumstances. In the border region, nations are always desirous of a trade-off between debordering for economic benefits and rebordering for security. In such cases, debordering means the removal of restrictions and rebordering means the imposition of restrictions (Su & Li, 2021). Bordering, on the other hand, means the initial phase of demarcating boundaries. Rebordering in normal circumstances means the deployment of security and checks at the border, but in the case of the Germany–Poland border, for example, after the success of debordering rebordering was introduced as a tourist attraction (Wieckowski & Timothy, 2021). Elsewhere, on the US–Canada border, debordering for tourism and rebordering for security occurred simultaneously at two different locations (Gelbman & Timothy, 2017). Therefore, while it could be said that debordering gives hope for border tourism development, rebordering can also be used as a tourist attraction facility.

The motivation for tourism activities in border areas can vary as per tourist interest. The border of Israel and Palestine, for instance, was a heritage tourist attraction for tourists when visiting the region (Mansfeld & Korman, 2015). In Switzerland, border tourists are visiting borders looking for cheaper fuel, an activity termed "fuel tourism" (Banfi, Filippini, & Hunt, 2005). Another form of tourism possibility lying at the border is enclave tourism. In enclave tourism research, studies found that the motivations for tourists to visit these enclaves are numerous: (a) the demarcation of international borders, (b) cultural, social, and economic similarities and differences, (c) differences and similarities in law and regulations, (d) cooperation, (e) differences between the administration and the landscape and (f) nature (e.g., Gelbman & Timothy, 2011). Enclave tourism benefits communities through empowering women, offering opportunities for entrepreneurs, and providing macroeconomic conditions whilst fostering the adoption of sustainable practices (Nunkoo & Ramkissoon, 2013).

Tourism attractions in the border area also work as a catalyst for peace between two nations. Peace can be positive or negative, with the first representing the things we have when creative conflict transformation takes place in a non-violent way (Galtung, 1996) and the second meaning simply the absence of violence. Therefore, while negative peace is frequently established with the help of violence, in the case of positive peace violence is not used for settling border-related disputes. The most effective type is positive peace where tourism has been argued to act as a catalyst as it helps in conflict resolution or transformation processes (Farmaki, 2017). However, peace at the border lays the foundation for using the border attractions as a tourism resource. There is the case of the Israel–Palestine border, where heritage sites in the border areas with conflicts acted initially as a tourism attraction and paved the path for cross-border tourism (Mansfeld & Korman, 2015). The China–Vietnam border too was closed for 10 years after the border war between the two countries in 1979, only to reopen once diplomatic relations normalized and excursion tours across the border started (Chan, 2006).

Notwithstanding, there are some negative consequences associated with the development of border tourism. These consequences are in the form of showcasing of power distance between the two countries with the help of tourism development efforts on the border. Yet, the examples of Israel and China communicate that border tourism not only helps in the development of border areas, but also helps in a strong geopolitical positioning against neighbouring countries (Gao, Ryan, & Cave, 2019). Overall, what can be concluded from these cases is that, firstly, if the borders of two nations are silent for a long time and attractions on the border exist, there are favourable conditions for tourism to arise. Secondly, it may be concluded that cross-border tourism is possible even after a war between the two nations.

Cross-border tourism

Cross-border tourism can help countries on both sides of the border to develop as destinations and increase their attraction capital for tourists. When two countries share a harmonious border, then there is fertile scope for cross-border tourism. In this situation, tourists from one side of the border would be visiting the other side and vice versa. Cross-border tourism is particularly useful in cases of previous armed conflict at the border, as it can restore normalcy on the border even after the conflict. Generally, the more time that has passed since a conflict, the more opportunities for peace on the border are available (Mansfeld & Korman, 2015).

Cross-border tourism could be developed by using various strategies and by some commonalities shared by the neighbouring countries. For successful cross-border destination management, five factors were identified by Blasco, Guia and Prats (2014), namely institutional similarity, bridging actors, leadership and entrepreneurial capacities, close relationships and serendipity. The practical implementation of cross-border tourism requires the help of developing common tourism infrastructure on both sides of the border. For the development of cross-border tourism, for instance, in Eastern Europe greenways were created with the help of materials used during the world wars (Tambovceva et al., 2020). Another development of cross-border tourism was possible with the help of cycling routes in two neighbouring countries in the European borderland (Stoffelen, 2018). This also helps in the development of a framework for cross-border institutional integration. Another way of cross-border integration is through cultural tourism offering cultural values and monuments and heritage (Hardi et al., 2021).

The cooperative management of tourism resources on the border is seen as a potential way of cross-border tourism development for two major reasons. One is the attainment of peace between nations, which were at war in the past. Another is that cross-border attraction management addresses the joint development of border areas. The possibility of such integration is evident in the common management of international parks called 'peace parks' available on the US–Canada border (Timothy, 1999). When the border areas on both sides of any border share less development, as compared to its towns, then managing a cooperative attraction at the border helps the development of the border areas also. On the Finland–Sweden border, for example, the development of cooperative tourist attractions resulted in the development of the border areas (Prokkola, 2010).

Cross-border tourism seems relevant for the countries where the political and cultural divide was not significant, mostly in the case of European countries. However, there are situations where a cross-border conflict between two countries or between two communities on either side of the border exists. In case of conflict between communities within a country, cross-border tourism remains comparatively easy through the political–legal system, as was done in the case of Bosnia and Herzegovina (Causevic & Lynch, 2012). Contrary to the conflicts within a country, those between two countries seem impossible to resolve. For example, the conflict between Columbia and Ecuador endured for almost 40 years; yet, the desire to develop tourist destinations in border areas is bringing hope for future peace and tourism opportunities (Mestanza-Ramón & Jiménez-Caballero, 2021).

Nevertheless, for the development of cross-border tourism various challenges exist ranging from the history of the war to institutional support. The borders where conflict has occurred in past decades remain the dominant security discourse, which challenges cross-border tourism development and even the border areas' tourism development (Arieli, 2012). In the case of India and Pakistan, for instance, common attributes connect both countries but they are still in conflict. The solution that was provided in previous studies is cross-border tourism (Timothy, 2019). Another identified challenge to the development of cross-border tourism is the lack of institutional support (Causevic & Lynch, 2012). Economic support from the other side of the border might raise various concerns among the citizens of that country where development is taking place. Incentivization for cross-border tourism raises doubt in the minds of people at the destination where the destination region was always suspicious of territorialization efforts by the tourist's origin country (Rowen, 2014).

Evidently, cross-border tourism is not solely dependent on the efforts made by the countries sharing the border through the cooperative management of an attraction or by the development of a destination on the border for the tourists. Such integration is possible with the help of the culture shared by the same ethnic community living on both sides of the border (Livandovschi, 2017). It could be said that a common culture across the border acts as a force for cross-border integration. Culture is related to the host community but in terms of tourists, a major role may be played by the attraction capital. Attraction capital refers to the number of attractions available at a destination: the greater the number of attractions at a destination, the greater the possibility of tourist satisfaction. Thus, cross-border tourism integration holds hope for tourists to have a broader base of attractions. This becomes critical when the attraction is at a considerable distance from the place of origin of the tourists. In the following section, these forces of integration are discussed.

Cultural affinity

Borders are formed to enclave political or cultural territory. Boundaries of political territories are protected by the political system that exists in the form of military presence on the border. Political borders are sometimes shaped by cultural boundaries while these borders also divide peoples following the same culture. The border of countries established out of the political situation and the culture shared by the border communities on both sides force the communities to sustain the hope of a harmonious border. Thus, cultural affinity for the community on the other side of the border is an agent which can help in the formation of a harmonious border. If the national border is opened for the development of cooperative attraction development, village communities play a proactive role in associating with communities on the other side of the border (Prokkola, 2010).

Heritage sites were earlier considered the reason for conflict between the nations, but now these are seen as sites with the capability of increasing cross-border tourism activity (Gelbman & Laven, 2016). If the same ethnic community inhabits both sides of the border, then the heritage sites on both sides can act as catalysts for cross-border tourism development. In cross-border tourism, where the combination of attractions from both sides of the border is presented as one, destinations can have a broader attraction base. This attraction base or attraction capital might include products related to cultural heritage history, gastronomy and other cultural characteristics (Kozak & Buhalis, 2019; Radoi, 2020).

In addition to all of the cultural benefits of tourism on the borders, cultural similarity was also identified as one of the major reasons for the development of cross-border tourism (Blasco, Guia, & Prats, 2014). It was previously mentioned in the literature that cultural similarity among the border destinations could play a major role in cross-border cohesion (Timothy & Tosun, 2003). Culture is of utmost importance when it comes to debordering or cross-border tourism development. Even differences based on political culture or religious sects could be overcome with the help of other cultural components like language, common religion or ethnic events shared by those on both sides of the border (McCall, 2011). Cultural similarity also plays an important role in a tourist's selection of a destination. This also includes the religious similarity between tourists and the community living at a destination (Fourie, Rossello, & Santana-Gallego, 2015). The religion of the community staying at a destination could attract tourists of the same religion, for instance.

A few challenges to integration efforts through cultural affinity could therefore emerge. This might be in the form of the ideology of a political party in power or of the major opposition. The political ideology of the ruling government in a country also plays a major role in attracting tourists from neighbouring countries (Moufakkir, 2014). Apart from these challenges, cultural affinity on both sides of the border brings hope of a harmonious border. Tourism works as a peace force even in territories that have witnessed previous conflicts. Among the things that matter in such a case is the time which has elapsed since the conflict. The over-dominant political and public view of security in post-conflict regions could be penetrated with the tourism-centric approach from both sides of the border (Arieli, 2012). Thus, the tourism-centric approach and cultural similarity can work as a force for integration even at borders that have witnessed conflicts in the past.

Border geographical isolation as an opportunity

In normal circumstances, borders are not the most developed areas in the majority of countries. Generally, border areas are considered peripheral and rural (Prokkola, 2010; Tambovceva et al., 2020). Geographically, the lesser development of a border area in some countries limits the avenues for tourists, especially when the tourist has travelled a long distance to reach a country's border. Tourism development in the border areas holds the possibility to act as a catalyst for development. Tourism is also seen as a tool for the development of rural areas (Briedenhann & Wickens, 2004). This is not only limited to the development of simple cross-border tourism attraction development, but it also holds a benefit for tourists in the form of bigger attraction capital in the border region (Kozak & Buhalis, 2019).

Distance plays a major role in the selection of a destination by the tourist (Cao et al., 2019). Tourists tend to choose destinations that are closer to their origin. The loss of interest in choosing a destination according to its proximity from the origin is called "distance decay" (McKercher & Lew, 2003; McKercher, Chan, & Lam, 2008). In terms of international tourism, tourists are more inclined towards choosing a destination which is in spatial proximity to their current location. It has been proven in the case of international travel that countries at a distance of more than 5000 km only attracted 3 per cent of tourists (McKercher & Mak, 2019).

In border areas, residents living in the proximity of an attraction might find it interesting to visit that attraction. This has already been established in earlier studies and the campaigns by the national government of Australia and Belgium which are motivating their citizens to tour their neighbouring destinations (Jeuring & Haartsen, 2016). The interest of potential tourists rises when this visit is related to a neighbouring destination that has previously been inaccessible. The impact of distance decay decreases with an increase in the duration of a tour or the distance or an attraction from the origin point of the tourist. Once reaching the destination, even from a longer distance, it seems comfortable for a tourist to visit a few other neighbouring destinations. This is applicable even in situations in which tourists seem reluctant to visit far distances for the first time (Jin, Cheng, & Xu, 2017). So, an increase in attraction capital at the destination can help in attracting more tourists.

Contrary to the concept of distance decay is the concept of "distance desire". Distance desire means the desire for a psychologically and spatially distant attraction (Cao et al., 2019). Even in situations where distance decay is restricting the will to travel, on the contrary distance desire can help in attracting tourists. But for distance desire to arise, there is a requirement for more attraction capital at the destination. This attraction capital is possible with the integration of attractions across the border in the geographically remote destination of two countries.

Portraying tourism as an agent of peace between India and Pakistan

The beauty of Kashmir is represented by phrases like paradise or heaven on earth (Bhat, Majumdar, & Mishra, 2020; Malik & Bhat, 2015). The territory of Kashmir in South Asia is a reason for conflict between the two countries of India and Pakistan (Figure 11.1). The line of control represents the present border between India and Pakistan. This conflict started in 1947 because of territorial disputes in the Kashmir valley immediately after the separation of India and Pakistan. Since then, India and Pakistan have fought four wars because of this issue. The situation in border areas has mainly remained tense and fractious, improving only since the Kargil War of 1999 (BBC, 2019). Even after the continuous tension on the border, tourists visited Kashmir, although there was a decline in the number of tourists with every conflict (Islam, 2014). On both sides of the border, there are attractions for leisure tourists and adventure tourists.

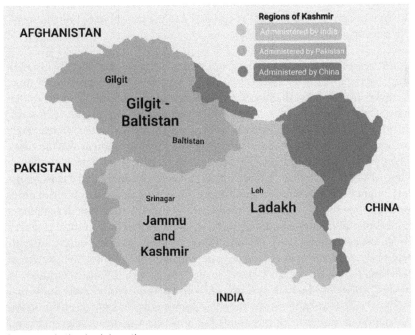

Source: Author's elaboration

Figure 11.1   Current geo-political situation of Kashmir

Where the Kashmir region in India is already a developed tourist destination; there are tourism footprints growing fast in the Gilgit Baltistan region (Hussain, Fisher, & Espiner, 2017). Here, ecotourism is one potential form of tourism with suitability in a large number of attractions (Amin et al., 2021; Niger, 2018); others are adventure tourism and cultural tourism (Arshad, Iqbal & Shahbaz, 2018).

For border tourism, there are various religious sites close to the border that might act as an agent of peace. On the Pakistan side, in Punjab, such a site is Kartarpur Sahib, which is a sacred place to Sikhs. A corridor has been constructed for pilgrims coming from India (Akhter, Jathol, & Hussain, 2019). On both sides of the border in the Punjab part of India and in the Punjab part of Pakistan live a majority of Sikhs. Hence, here culture has acted as a medium for peace. If such a breakthrough had happened in the Punjab region, then it also holds the possibility in the Kashmir region, although more time might be needed for such a thing to happen. Cross-border management of tourism attractions or cross-border tourism must thus start between India and Pakistan. This is because during the peak season time in summer, Kashmir's Srinagar receives more tourists as compared to the threshold of tourism carrying capacity (Malik & Bhat, 2015).

In the case of the disputed territory of Ladakh, Srinagar and Gilgit-Baltistan, it was observed that more factors join these two countries, irrespective of those factors which separate them, as they share a common culture. Previous studies have advised cross-border tourism as a solution to the dispute (Timothy, 2019). With an increasing gap between two conflicts on a border, which barely has remained silent, the hope of successful tourism development also increases. The development of tourism resources in such areas also catalyses the future hope of peace (Mansfeld & Korman, 2015). Between India and Pakistan, the last fought battle was in 1999 and thus the increasing time holds hope of peace through tourism. Using culture as a driver for tourism attraction development holds hope of inclusive and, therefore, sustainable tourism. Culture is shared by almost every household. This was already proved in a study on the Kashmir region that the more government brings in the initiative for the growth of tourism, the more local residents favour its growth (Bhat, Majumdar, & Mishra, 2020). In the case of Kashmir, both areas currently under India and Pakistan rule were inhibited by the same community and a tourism attraction development based on culture holds the hope for tourism development and peace between the two nations.

Hunza and Skardu districts in Gilgit-Baltistan state are Pakistan's most sought-after destinations. In terms of India, the Srinagar district of Jammu and Kashmir plays a similar role. These two states form the geographically remotest and most isolated places in both countries. But these states in their own respective countries share political boundaries and if these states are to be imagined without the political boundary, then they could be collectively seen as a geographically bigger region with more attraction capital for tourists. In the region where the same cultural values are shared by residents on both sides of the border and where top tourism destinations lie in geographically close but politically distant regions, there exists an immense hope of peace through tourism.

The cultural affinity among communities on both sides of the border and the integration of valuable tourism resources across political borders provide hope of developing an appealing destination. Cultural affinity provides hope for tourism support and peace along the political border among residents. In the case of tourists, the geographical isolation of these places in their respective countries constrains tourists to explore only a few destinations. It is a time when tourists can use their time optimally by exploring nearby destinations, separated by political borders but close in geographical distance. Tourism here could be seen as a tool for making peace among communities and providing a broader tourism resource for tourists. Thus, tourism can act as a driver for peace in geographically close but politically far regions.

Conclusion

On international borders, a trade-off exists between debordering for mutual cooperation and rebordering for concerns related to security. Tourism is an agent for peace through border and cross-border tourism. This process always gets initiated with tourism activities close to the international border as the first step. It is possible only at the borders where peace has prevailed in the past but in the case of borders with previous conflict, a different path to peace needs to be traversed. On borders where conflict has existed in history, elapsed time since the last major conflict acts as the base for this initiation. The more time that has passed since the last conflict, the more the possibility of sustaining the peace. After the successful development of tourist attractions on the border, the way forward comes in the form of cross-border tourism to the attractions beyond the international border and cooperative management of attractions by the neighbouring countries. Factors that catalyse the cohesion among the attractions across the border are the broader attraction capital for tourists and cultural affinity for the community living on both sides of the border. In addition to the benefits of tourism to peace formation, there are a few cautionary aspects related to the development of inequalities across the border and the emergence of power distance between the nations.

Tourism holds the possibility of bringing peace between destinations that are or have been in conflict. One way of achieving this goal is through border and cross-border tourism as these types of tourism stimulate cooperation and intergroup interaction. This chapter sets an agenda for the growth of tourism between India and Pakistan, which have experienced conflict in the Kashmir region for approximately 75 years. The hope for peace on the border is increasing because of the passage of time since the last major conflict and, hence, there is momentum in peace-building activities. Overall, the chapter supports the argument that the efforts for restoring peace in the region should be targeted by building attractions in the border areas. The chapter proposes that such development of attractions in border areas needs to be followed by cross-border tourism and cooperative management of tourism attractions on the border for a more efficient resolution of the conflict. In so doing, the chapter acknowledges two drivers of peace for developing border and cross-border tourism: cultural affinity and the scope for a broader attraction capital. Cultural affinity among hosts across the border is a potential for the emergence of positive attitudes among hosts. In terms of tourists, the possibility of a broader attraction capital demands the presentation of the Kashmir region as a single geographical territory.

Notwithstanding, tourism was identified as a medium for peace by earlier studies on Kashmir (Chauhan & Khanna, 2009). In the Gilgit-Baltistan region, specifically, a road project called China Pakistan Economic Corridor (Baig & Zehra, 2020) is connecting Pakistan and China. The current chapter does not put emphasis on the China Pakistan Economic Corridor but the impact of it on peace between the neighbouring countries needs to be studied in the future. Beyond the Kashmir case, future studies should look deeper into the impact of cultural affinity among hosts and the willingness to have a broader attraction capital among tourists, which were identified in this chapter as essential for border and cross-border tourism. Future research should also be carried out on destinations at border areas that have tourism potential and on the development of common attractions for which resources are shared by two or more countries, as was done in the case of the USA and Canada (Timothy, 1999). Such initiatives would lead not only to peace but also to economic profit; thus, a sustainable peace solution could be guaranteed. This was evident in the case of Thailand and Laos where cross-border tourism not only contributed to tourism but also had ripple effects in other economic sectors (Boonchai & Freathy, 2020). The initiation of such economic effects further leads to peace economics, meaning that with an increase in economic activities between two nations, the scope for sustained peace also increases (Anderton & Carter, 2007). Peace emerging out of economic interdependence is not easily affected by any other cause (Gartzke et al., 2003).

Border tourism is a topic that needs more research regarding both political and consumer perceptions about border tourism attractions. Future research is also required into the topic of cross-border cooperative management of attractions by the political systems in the neighbouring countries. Future research could be carried on the topics that would act as the catalyst for cross-border tourism (i.e., geographic isolation of border regions and the cultural affinity among communities living on both sides of the border). In order to study cross-border cultural affinity and its role in peace, research collaboration from both sides of the borders is required. For studying the problem of less attraction capital in geographically isolated regions within a country and the collaboration of attractions from across the borders, a study of tourism to the border region could be carried out in the future. This chapter also has implications for national tourism organizations which play a vital and leading role in maintaining peace between nations. Initially the process starts with the development of tourist attractions on the border and after a prolonged span of peace on the border, cross-border tourism activities could be started. In this way, tourism might act as the driver of peace between nations.

References

Akhter, D. S., Jathol, I., & Hussain, Q. A. (2019). Peace building through religious tourism in Pakistan: a case study of Kartarpur corridor. *Pakistan Social Sciences Review*, 3(2), 204–12.

Amin, G., Haroon, E., Imtiaz, I., Saqib, N. U., & Shahzad, M. I. (2021). Ecotourism potential assessment for Gilgit-Baltistan, Pakistan using integration of GIS, remote sensing, AHP and crowd-sourced data. *Geocarto International*. https://doi.org/10.1080/10106049.2021.2005157.

Anderton, C. H., & Carter, J. R. (2007). A survey of peace economics. In T. Sandler & K. Hartley, *Handbook of Defence Economics* (Vol. 2, pp. 1211–58). Elsevier. https://doi.org/10.1016/S1574-0013(06)02035-7.

Arieli, T. (2012). Borders of peace in policy and practice: national and local perspectives of Israel-Jordan border management. *Geopolitics*, 17, 658–80. https://doi.org/10.1080/14650045.2011.638015.

Arshad, M. I., Iqbal, M. A., & Shahbaz, M. (2018). Pakistan tourism industry and challenges: a review. *Asia Pacific Journal of Tourism Research*, 23(2), 121–32. https://doi.org/10.1080/10941665.2017.1410192.

Baig, S., & Zehra, S. (2020). China-Pakistan economic corridor, governance, and tourism nexus: evidence from Gilgit-Baltistan, Pakistan. *Current Issues in Tourism*, 23(23), 2884–9. https://doi.org/10.1080/13683500.2020.1763266.

Banfi, S., Filippini, M., & Hunt, L. C. (2005). Fuel tourism in border regions: the case of Switzerland. *Energy Economics*, 689–707. https://doi.org/10.1016/j.eneco.2005.04 .006.

BBC (2019, August 6). Kashmir profile. Retrieved 5 November 2022 from https://www .bbc.com/news/world-south-asia-11693674.

Bhat, A. A., Majumdar, K., & Mishra, R. K. (2020). Local sujpport for tourism development and its determinants: an empirical study of Kashmir region. *Asia Pacific Journal of Tourism Research*, 25(11), 1232–49. https:// doi .org/ 10 .1080/ 10941665 .2020.1837890.

Blasco, D., Guia, J., & Prats, L. (2014). Emergence of governance in cross-border destinations. *Annals of Tourim Research*, 49, 159–73. https:// doi.org/ 10.1016/ j.annals .2014.09.002.

Boonchai, P., & Freathy, P. (2020). Cross-border tourism and the regional economy: a typology of the ignored shopper. *Current Issues in Tourism*, 23(5), 626–40. https:// doi.org/10.1080/13683500.2018.1548579.

Briedenhann, J., & Wickens, E. (2004). Tourism routes as a tool for the economic development of rural areas: vibrant hope or impossible dream? *Tourism Management*, 25(1), 71–9. https://doi.org/10.1016/s0261-5177(03)00063-3.

Cao, J., Zhang, J., Wang, C., Hu, H., & Yu, P. (2019). How far is the ideal destination? Distance desire, ways to explore the antinomy of distance effects in tourist destination choice. *Journal of Travel Research*, 1–17. https://doi.org/10.1177/0047287519844832.

Castanho, R., Loures, L., Fernandez, J., & Pozo, L. (2018). Identify critical factors for success in cross-border cooperation (CBC) development projects. *Habitat International*, 72, 92–9. https://doi.org/10.1016/j.habitatint.2016.10.004.

Causevic, S., & Lynch, P. (2012). Political (in)stability and its influence on tourism development. *Tourism Management*, 34, 145–57. https://doi.org/10.1016/j.tourman .2012.04.006.

Chan, Y. W. (2006). Coming of age of the Chinese tourists: the emergence of non-Western tourism and host-guest interactions in Vietnam's border tourism. *Tourist Studies*, 6(3), 187–213. https://doi.org/10.1177/1468797607076671.

Chauhan, V., & Khanna, S. (2009). Tourism: a tool for crafting peace process in Kashmir, J&K, India. *TOURISMOS: An International Multidisciplinary Journal of Tourism*, 4(2), 69–89.

Farmaki, A. (2017). The tourism and peace nexus. *Tourism Management*, 59, 528–40. https://doi.org/10.1016/j.tourman.2016.09.012.

Fourie, J., Rossello, J., & Santana-Gallego, M. (2015). Religion, religious diversity and tourism. *Kyklos*, 68(1), 51–64. https://doi.org/1.1111/kykl.12066.

Galtung, J. (1996). Peace and conflict research in the age of the cholera: ten pointers to the future of peace studies. *International Journal of Peace Studies*, 1(1), 25–36.

Gao, J., Ryan, C., & Cave, J. (2019). Tourism border making: a political economy of China's border tourism. *Annals of Tourism Research*, 76, 1–13. https:// doi .org/ 10 .1016/j.annals.2019.02.010.

Gartzke, E., Li, Q., & Boehmer, C. (2003). Investing in peace: economic interdependence and international conflict. *International Organization*, 55(2), 391–438. https:// doi.org/10.1162/00208180151140612.

Gelbman, A. (2008). Border tourism in Israel: conflict, peace, fear, and hope. *Tourism Geographies*, 10(2), 193–213. https://doi.org/10.1080/14616680802000022.

Gelbman, A. (2019). Tourism, peace and global stability. In D. J. Timothy (Ed.), *Handbook of globalisation and tourism* (pp. 149–60). Edward Elgar Publishing. https://doi.org/10.4337/9781786431295.00022.

Gelbman, A., & Laven, D. (2016). Re-envisioning community-based heritage tourism in the old city of Nazareth. *Journal of Heritage Tourism*, *11*(2), 105–25. https://doi.org/ 10.1080/1743873X.2015.1044993.

Gelbman, A., & Timothy, D. J. (2011). Border complexity, tourism and international enclaves: a case study. *Annals of Tourism Research*, *38*(1), 110–31. https://doi.org/10 .1016/j.annals.2010.06.002.

Gelbman, A., & Timothy, D. J. (2017). Differential tourism zones on the western Canada-US border. *Current Issues in Tourism*, *22*(6), 682–704. https://doi.org/10 .1080/13683500.2017.1304364.

Hardi, T., Kupi, M., Ocskay, G., & Szemeredi, E. (2021). Indicator of territorial integration across the Slovak-Hungarian border. *Sustainability*, *13*(13). https://doi.org/10 .3390/su13137225.

Hussain, A., Fisher, D., & Espiner, S. (2017). Transport infrastructure and social inclusion: a case study of tourism in the region of Gilgit-Baltistan. *Social Inclusion*, *5*(4), 196–208. https://doi.org/10.17645/si.v5i4.1084.

Islam, A. U. (2014). Impact of armed conflict on economy and tourism: a study of state of Jammu and Kashmir. *IOSR Journal of Economics and Finance*, *4*(6), 55–60.

Jamgade, S. (2021). Catalytic effects of tourism in peacebuilding: sustainability and peace through tourism. In J. T. Silva & F. Carbone (Eds.), *Role and impact of tourism in peacebuilding and conflict transformation* (pp. 29–45). IGI Global. https://doi.org/ 10.4018/978-1-7998-5053-3.ch003.

Jeuring, J. H., & Haartsen, T. (2016). The challenge of proximity: the (un)attractiveness of near-home tourism destinations. *Tourism Geographies*, *19*(1), 118–41. https://doi .org/10.1080/14616688.2016.1175024.

Jin, C., Cheng, J., & Xu, J. (2017). Using user-generated content to explore the temporal heterogeneity in tourist mobility. *Journal of Travel Research*, *57*(6), 1–13. https://doi .org/10.1177/0047287517714906.

Kozak, M., & Buhalis, D. (2019). Cross-border tourism destination marketing: prerequisites and critical success factors. *Journal of Destination Marketing & Management*, *14*, 100392. https://doi.org/10.1016/j.jdmm.2019.100392.

Kropinova, E. (2021). Transnational and cross-border cooperation for sustainable tourism development in Baltic sea regions. *Sustainability*, *13*(4), 2111. https://doi .org/10.3390/su13042111.

Kropinova, E. G. (2019). The role of tourism in cross-border region formation in the Baltic region. In G. Fedorov, A. Druzhinin, E. Golubeva, D. Subetto & T. Palmowski (Eds.), *Baltic Region: The Region of Cooperation* (pp. 83–97). Springer. https://doi .org/10.1007/978-3-030-14519-4_10.

Kurowska-Pysz, J., Castanho, R. A., & Loures, L. (2018). Sustainable planning of cross-border cooperation: a strategy for alliances in border cities. *Sustainability*, *10*(5), 1416. https://doi.org/10.3390/su10051416.

Livandovschi, R. (2017). Cross-border tourism and its significance for tourism destinations. *Eastern European Journal of Regional Studies*, *3*(2), 31–40.

Malik, M. I., & Bhat, M. S. (2015). Sustainability of tourism development in Kashmir: is paradise lost? *Tourism Management Perspectives*, *16*, 11–21. https://doi.org/10.1016/ j.tmp.2015.05.006.

Mansfeld, Y., & Korman, T. (2015). Between war and peace: conflict heritage tourism along three Israeli border areas. *Tourism Grographies*, *17*(3), 437–60. https://doi.org/ 10.1080/14616688.2015.1036916.

McCall, C. (2011). Culture and the Irish border: spaces for conflict transformation. *Cooperation and Conflict*, *46*(2), 201–21. https://doi.org/10.1177/0010836711406406.

McKercher, B., Chan, A., & Lam, C. (2008). The impacts of distance on international tourist movements. *Journal of Travel Research, 47*(2), 208–24. https://doi.org/10.1177/0047287508321191.

McKercher, B., & Lew, A. A. (2003). Distance decay and the impact of effective tourism exclusion zones on international travel flows. *Journal of Travel Research, 42*, 159–65. https://doi.org/10.1177/0047287503254812.

McKercher, B., & Mak, B. (2019). The impact of distance on international tourism demand. *Tourism Management Perspectives, 31*, 340–47. https://doi.org/10.1016/j.tmp.2019.07.004.

Mestanza-Ramón, C., & Jiménez-Caballero, J. L. (2021). Nature tourism on the Colombian–Ecuadorian Amazonian border: history, current situation and challenges. *Sustainability, 13*(8). https://doi.org/10.3390/su13084432.

Moufakkir, O. (2014). What's immigration got to do with it? Immigrant animosity and its effects on tourism. *Annals of Tourism Research, 49*, 108–21. https://doi.org/10.1016/j.annals.2014.08.008.

Niger, N. (2018). Ecotourism for sustainable development in Gilgit-Baltistan. *Strategic Studies, 38*(3), 72–85.

Noferini, A., Berzi, M., Camonita, F., & Dura, A. (2020). Cross-border cooperation in the EU: Euroregions amid multilevel governance and re-territorialization. *European Planning Studies, 28*(1), 35–56. https://doi.org/10.1080/09654313.2019.1623973.

Nunkoo, R., & Ramkisson, H. (2013). Stakeholders' views of enclave tourism: a grounded theory approach. *Journal of Hospitality and Tourism Research, 40*(5), 557–8. https://doi.org/10.1177/1096348013503997.

Okyay, A. S. (2017). Turkey's post-2011 approach to its Syrian border and its implications for domestic politics. *International Affairs, 93*(4), 829–46. https://doi.org/10.1093/ia/iix068.

Prokkola, E.-K. (2010). Borders in tourism: the transformation of the Swedish-Finnish border landscape. *Current Issues in Tourism, 13*(3), 223–38. https://doi.org/10.1080/13683500902990528.

Radoi, I. (2020). European capital of culture, urban tourism and cross-border cooperation between Romania and Serbia. *Journal of Balkan and Near Eastern Studies, 22*(4), 547–59. https://doi.org/10.1080/19448953.2020.1778881.

Rowen, I. (2014). Tourism as a territorial strategy: the case of China and Taiwan. *Annals of Tourism Research, 46*, 62–74. https://doi.org/10.1016/j.annals.2014.02.006.

Rumford, C. (2006). Theorizing borders. *European Journal of Social Theory, 9*(2), 155–69. https://doi.org/10.1177/1368431006063330.

Sergeyeva, A., Abdullina, A., Nazarov, M., Turdimambetov, I., Maxmudov, M., & Yanchuk, S. (2022). Development of cross-border tourism in accordance with the principles of sustainable development on the Kazakhstan-Uzbekistan border. *Sustainability, 14*(19), 12734. https://doi.org/10.3390/su141912734.

Smith, S., Swanson, N. W., & Gokariksel, B. (2015). Territory, bodies and borders. *Area, 48*(3), 258–61. https://doi.org/10.1111/area.12247.

Sofield, T. H. (2006). Border tourism and border communities: an overview. *Tourism Geographies, 8*(2), 102–21. https://doi.org/10.1080/14616680600585489.

Stoffelen, A. (2018). Tourism trails as tools for cross-border integration: a best practice case study of the Vennbahn cycling route. *Annals of Tourism Research, 73*, 91–102. https://doi.org/10.1016/j.annals.2018.09.008.

Su, X., & Li, C. (2021). Bordering dynamics and the geopolitics of cross-border tourism between China and Mayanmar. *Political Geography, 86*. https://doi.org/10.1016/j.polgeo.2021.102372.

Tambovceva, T., Atstaja, D., Tereshina, M., Uvarova, I., & Livina, A. (2020). Sustainability challenges and drivers of cross-border greenway tourism in rural areas. *Sustainability, 12*(15). https://doi.org/10.3390/su12155927.

Timothy, D. J. (1999). Cross-border partnership in tourism resource management: international parks along the US–Canada border. *Journal of Sustainable Tourism, 7*(3–4), 182–205. https://doi.org/10.1080/09669589908667336.

Timothy, D. J. (2019). Tourism, border disputes and claims to territorial sovereignty. In R. K. Issac, E. C. Cakmak, & R. Butler (Eds.), *Tourism and hospitality in conflict ridden destinations* (chapter 3). Routledge.

Timothy, D. J., & Tosun, C. (2003). Tourists' perceptions of the Canada–USA border as a barrier to tourism at the International Peace Garden. *Tourism Management, 24*(4), 411–21. https://doi.org/10.1016/s0261-5177(02)00113-9.

Weidenfeld, A. (2013). Tourism and cross border regional innovation systems. *Annals of Tourism Research, 41*(1), 191–213. https://doi.org/10.1016/j.annals.2013.01.003.

Wieckowski, M., & Timothy, D. J. (2021). Tourism and an evolving international boundary: bordering, debordering and rebordering on Usedom Island, Poland–Germany. *Journal of Destination Marketing & Management, 22*, 100647. https://doi.org/10.1016/j.jdm.2021.100647.

Xu, H., Huang, X., & Zhang, Q. (2018). Tourism development and local borders in ancient villages in China. *Journal of Destination Marketing & Management, 9*, 330–39. https://doi.org/10.1016/j.jdmm.2018.03.007.

12 Corporate social responsibility: a contributor to peace in conflict-ridden destinations?

Anna Farmaki and Dimitrios Stergiou

Introduction

In recent years, the role of corporate social responsibility (CSR) – understood as the set of responsibilities of companies for their impacts on society – in fortifying peacebuilding efforts has been highlighted in the literature. Although, traditionally, the government was thought of as the primary stakeholder responsible in maintaining peaceful relations with other states and ensuring intra-state stability, there is growing acknowledgement that the private sector plays a vital role in sustainable development in which peace represents a key goal. In fact, the United Nations' Agenda includes peace as one of the sustainable development goals (SDG 16) that must be achieved by 2030, signifying the relevance of peace to sustainability and, by extent, CSR. Peace is important for sustainable development as its presence in a society requires the eradication of inequalities, a balanced form of power, cooperation and a just environment. In this context, CSR was recognised as a potential tool for strengthening peacebuilding efforts as CSR activities may promote distributive justice, offer the necessary capacities to disadvantaged social groups to improve their socio-economic well-being and encourage collaboration between opposing groups (Farmaki & Stergiou, 2021).

Since the early 2010s, businesses' CSR activities towards peacebuilding have become more prominent as greater socio-political instability is witnessed across the world (Rettberg, 2016). By taking a more active role in peacebuilding, businesses express a commitment to sustainable development and contribute to the elimination of the effects that conflicts may have on the economic environment (Killick et al., 2005). Likewise, by using CSR as a tool for peacebuilding, businesses take accountability and assume the role of a social agent that creates value, fosters stability and security, and provides socio-economic advancement opportunities (Joseph & van Buren, 2021); serving, thus, as a link between various actors that are key to peace including political leaders, grassroots-level stakeholders and non-governmental organisations (Farmaki, 2017). Such an inclusive participatory process is vital for building and maintaining peace.

In light of the growing importance of the private sector to peacebuilding, increasing academic attention has started to be paid on the topic of CSR as a contributor to peace. Relevant studies have looked at the business case for peace by examining the ways in which businesses can enhance peace, their motives in engaging in peacebuilding as well as the practical consideration underlying the effectiveness of their contribution (Hönke, 2014; Miklian et al., 2019; Rettberg, 2016). Despite the growing interest on the topic, little is known of the role of CSR in peacebuilding in the context of tourism. This is surprising considering the significance attributed to tourism as a peace broker (D'Amore, 1988; Causevic, 2010). The peace through tourism tenet lies on the proposition that contact brought about by travel improves perceptions and attitudes between hosts and guests and, eventually, contributes to a more peaceful society as the relations among nations are strengthened. This hypothesis remains questionable, given the fact that tourism is a global industry entrenched in capitalism (Bianchi, 2010) that often deepens inequalities rather than eliminating them (Farmaki & Stergiou, 2021).

While there is an abundance of studies looking at host and guest perceptual and attitudinal change following visitation, the role of tourism companies in promoting peace is yet to be examined. This is an important aspect of peace through tourism which to date remains unexplored. To this end, the aim of this study is to examine the potential of tourism companies to contribute to peace through their CSR activities. In doing so, we draw from the case of the Stelios Philanthropic Foundation which represents the philanthropic foundation established by Stelios Hadjioannou, the founder of Easy Group (EasyJet, EasyHotel, EasyCar), which is one of the most successful tourism corporations in Europe. Specifically, we focus on the peace awards the Foundation offers for bi-communal entrepreneurial activities in Cyprus, an island that has long been tormented by conflict. Through semi-structured interviews performed with awardees as well as tourism stakeholders in Cyprus, this study aims to illuminate the peace through tourism literature by highlighting the role of businesses and the effectiveness of their CSR activities in peacebuilding.

Theoretical background

The role of the business sector as an actor in armed conflicts and peace has been a subject of growing interest and controversy in recent decades. As a matter of fact, much scholarship regards companies as a key factor in creating new conflicts or perpetuating existing ones, especially in resource-rich developing countries or those providing labour to multinational companies (e.g., Ross, 2012; Watts, 2005). Yet, other currents of thinking explore the assertion that businesses have a role to play in promoting peace and building a larger social role in conflict-affected and fragile areas (Miklian & Schouten, 2014). This vision is not free of criticism, and some claim that corporate interests and rapid economic liberalisation are incompatible with the structural economic changes that peace often needs (Ganson, 2019; Midtgard et al., 2017; Millar, 2019).

Going beyond the debate and criticisms on the potential for businesses' roles in peace and conflict, practitioners and multilateral bodies are calling for the business world to engage more directly with issues around conflict and peace (Ford, 2015; Iff & Alluri, 2016; UNGC, 2015), through initiatives such as the Responsibility to Protect, the UN Sustainable Development Goals (SDGs), Business for Peace (B4P), and Business and Human Rights Framework. Such initiatives go beyond the old doctrine that businesses should 'do no harm' and urge the business world to deepen its involvement in peacebuilding and conflict reduction, through the implementation of responsible business conduct in conflict-sensitive regions (Miklian & Bickel, 2020; Mueller-Hirth, 2017).

Aligning to this institutional focus, there has been a proliferation of writings in the academic literature investigating business-peace interactions. This highly interdisciplinary area of study – drawn from economics, anthropology, political science, and moral theory, among other fields – has emerged to explore the linkages between business and peace. A common thread in this otherwise disparate scholarship is the recognition that businesses can be an agent for peace by promoting certain kinds of responsible, ethical and conflict-sensitive business practices (Trivedi, 2016). Providing theoretical order for this line of work, Oetzel et al. (2010) identify five main avenues through which businesses can positively promote peace: fostering economic development; undertaking diplomatic efforts; adopting principles of external valuation; contributing to social cohesion/community building; and engaging in conflict-sensitive practices. This set of recommendations remains the starting point for research around how businesses can achieve peace promotion in much of the most recent literature in the business and peace field (Joseph et al., 2021; Katsos & AlKafaji, 2019).

Such activities are most often operationalised through CSR (Miklian, 2017), which has become an important tool in guiding business involvement in peace-related activity (Rettberg, 2016). In fact, as Jamali and Mirshak (2010) argue, the contemporary CSR discourse calls for businesses to embrace voluntary initiatives that reflect specific social roles and expectations beyond legal compliance. This links well with the definition of CSR suggested by Farmaki and Stergiou (2022) who stated that CSR is conceptualised "as the business actions that provide social good beyond company interests and the requirements of law". In conflict-sensitive areas particularly, societal demands may dictate a more active involvement of business in conflict prevention and furthering peace, which may constitute a logical contextual extension or adaptation of the CSR agenda (Oetzel et al., 2010).

Accordingly, CSR-peacebuilding linkages have in the past few years received more scholarly attention. One clear and useful example in this context is a framework by Jamali and Mirshak (2010), exploring different forms of CSR engagement strategies when firms are subjected to conflict, including a coping strategy (low CSR and peacebuilding orientation), compromise strategy (moderate CSR and peacebuilding orientation), and conflict resolution strategy (high CSR and peacebuilding orientation). In their scheme, a coping strategy involves a passive reaction to conflict situations, where firms may exit the conflict zone or merely comply with new social constructs, national regulations and international laws/standards. A compromise strategy involves moving beyond basic compliance and engaging in behaviours aimed at minimising risks from business operations; although this approach does not include active participation in peace-related activity, it represents a more progressive form of CSR and peacebuilding orientation in that it involves acting on an understanding of a firm's ability to create or exacerbate violent conflict through its impacts. Conflict resolution strategy, on the other hand, comprises all intentional CSR contributions to help prevent conflict and build peace, often envisioning win-win profit and peace relationships (Dresse et al., 2021).

Numerous illustrations of this type of self-regulating practices through which businesses can engage with peacebuilding may be found throughout the literature. At the most fundamental level, CSR is generally seen to make a contribution to peace by supporting and developing communities, which in turn facilitates local capacities for building peace (Miklian & Bickel, 2020). This might involve the creation of jobs but also partnering with local stakeholders, tackling local social issues or promoting social inclusion (Miklian, 2017;

Subedi, 2013). In terms of positive social contributions to communities, CSR could also constitute a mechanism of direct philanthropic giving (monetary or in-kind) that can include (re)building infrastructures or direct support of those affected by conflict (Joseph et al., 2023). Further, through the adoption of international standards, norms and ethics – typically key features of CSR frameworks – businesses are able to promote healthier societal relations and accountability (Oetzel et al., 2010). On this view, ethical business conduct and adherence to best practice norms may have positive ripple effects by setting higher standards for and reshaping the conduct of involved actors, thus fostering a better groundwork for peace (Miklian et al., 2016). Engagement in diplomatic efforts with conflict actors is also more likely when companies have formed institutional networks that support CSR practice (Kolk & Lenfant, 2013). This represents the highest level of explicit corporate contribution to promoting peace (Miklian, 2017) and can take different forms such as participating in peace negotiations, working as mediators, or leveraging local economic power to initiate peace talks (Miklian et al., 2016; Ralph & Hancock, 2018).

While the tourism literature has dealt quite extensively with the conjunction of tourism and peace (see Farmaki, 2017 for a review of issues and debates surrounding the peace–tourism nexus), the issue of how tourism companies could contribute to peace via different types of business initiatives such as CSR, has not attracted scholarly attention. Interestingly, although to the best of our knowledge there has been virtually no analysis to date on the capacity of CSR to link tourism and peace, a few authors have explicitly acknowledged this connection – albeit abstractly and with no empirical support. For example, Alluri et al. (2014, p. 118) proposed that strengthening the engagement of the tourism private sector with peacebuilding should involve "integrating conflict sensitivity in existing CSR approaches". Along similar lines, Carbone (2022, p. 571) has recently argued that "the promotion of peace-through-tourism should be considered part of the CSR agenda in the tourism sector". One notable exception to this paucity of research is that by Levy and Hawkins (2010) who examined commerce-based tourism activities that can strengthen peaceful societies. Based on a content analysis of award-winning commercial tourism practices they concluded that CSR activities can strengthen peace in conflict-prone destinations with illustrations provided including health programmes, education initiatives, infrastructure development, direct corporate donations, community-based tourism initiatives, and institutionalising detailed CSR codes of conduct. Within this CSR and business for peace agenda, we tried to examine whether and how tourism companies' CSR activities can contribute to peace. Next, the adopted research methodology is presented followed by study findings and their implications.

Methodology

Study background

In achieving its aim, this study focused on the case of the Stelios Philanthropic Foundation which represents a non-profit organisation founded by Sir Stelios Hadjioannou, who is known for creating the Easy Group (EasyJet, EasyHotel, EasyCar). According to its mission statement, the Foundation aims to support a range of charitable activities in the countries where Stelios has lived and worked including the UK, Greece, Cyprus and Monaco. Amongst the charitable activities undertaken by the Foundation are: the "Food from the heart" programme which feeds approximately 200,000 people in Greece and Cyprus, donations to good causes including environmental protection charities, financial support to disabled entrepreneurs, scholarships to young people attending university and the peace awards which bestow €500,000 annually to Greek Cypriots and Turkish Cypriots who collaborate on bi-communal activities on the island of Cyprus (Stelios Philanthropic Foundation, 2022). The last activity is of the interest of this study as it is centred on promoting long-lasting peace on the island of Cyprus, which is known for its protracted conflict (Farmaki et al., 2019a) that has been ongoing since the 1960s between the Greek Cypriot and Turkish Cypriot communities.

The conflict climaxed in 1974 when Turkish troops landed in Cyprus and occupied one third of the island. Cyprus has been divided as a result with the two communities living in complete isolation until 2003, when the Turkish Cypriot authorities unexpectedly allowed crossings between the northern and southern parts of the island for the first time. Despite the great numbers of crossings recorded from both communities in the first years (Webster & Timothy, 2006), to date little progress has been noted in terms of reconciliation and peacebuilding primarily due to minimal political support and animosity (Farmaki et al., 2019b). Therefore, the peace awards that the Stelios Philanthropic Foundation offers to members of the two communities that collaborate on bi-communal projects and entrepreneurial activities represent an important grassroots initiative that may encourage reconciliation and enable peacebuilding. According to Kelleher & Johnson (2008), vibrant grassroot peace processes serve as a prelude to formal peace agreements. Even so, little is known of the role of businesses in peacebuilding especially within the context of tourism. Despite the increasing focus paid on CSR as a contributor to peace (e.g., Hönke, 2014; Rettberg, 2016), there is scant academic attention on CSR within the peace through tourism realm. By drawing from the Stelios Philanthropic Foundation – the charitable organisation of a colossal tourism and hospitality corporation based in Europe – this study aims to illuminate the peace through tourism literature and discuss the role of businesses and their CSR practices in peacebuilding.

Data collection and analysis

Interviews were performed with tourism stakeholders to examine their perceptions of the potential contribution of CSR to peacebuilding as well as awardees of the Stelios Philanthropic Foundation bi-communal programme, aiming to understand the opportunities and threats surrounding such awards in terms of building and maintaining peace. For the purpose of this exploratory research, eight interviews were performed between November 2022 and February 2023 with participants being selected using purposive sampling. Purposive sampling allows researchers to use their a priori theoretical understanding of the topic (Robinson, 2014) and select participants deemed knowledgeable about the study (Schutt, 2018). Table 12.1 illustrates the profile of the participants.

Table 12.1   Profile of interviewees

ID number	Gender	Role	Position in organisation
P1	F	Awardee	N/A
P2	F	Awardee	N/A
P3	M	Awardee	N/A
P4	F	Officer	Deputy Ministry of Tourism
P5	M	Chair	Tourism Association
P6	M	Director	Sustainable Tourism Association
P7	F	Marketing manager	Hotel
P8	M	Tourism academic	University

The interviews were conducted on a one-to-one basis with a member of the research team at a day and time of convenience to the interviewees. Interviewees were informed in advance that the data would remain confidential and that the interviews were conducted solely for academic purposes. Questions were framed according to the goals of the study. Specifically, in the beginning the researcher asked the participants ice-breaking questions to establish the profile of the interviewees before proceeding to questions related to the awards programme itself and its effects on peace. Questions included, among others, the following (depending on the background of the participant asked):

- Do you think that businesses have a role to play in peacebuilding? If so, how?
- What do you think that CSR can contribute to peace?
- What was your motive for applying to the peace awards?
- Which benefits did you receive from the award scheme?
- What obstacles did you face?
- Do you believe the award programme is contributing to peace in Cyprus?
- How would you evaluate the effectiveness of these kind of actions on peacebuilding?

The data collected from the interviews were analysed using thematic analysis. In particular, the transcripts produced were read many times by the researchers to identify patterns of themes. Blocks of text were copied verbatim, re-organised and cross-referenced to allow for the identification of thematic categories. Sub-categories were also produced which were combined with pre-identified themes to allow for greater elaboration on key issues (Hennink et al., 2010). The findings are presented according to the categories of the participants, namely tourism stakeholder and awardees, where their perspectives are presented.

Findings

Tourism stakeholder perspectives

Almost all tourism stakeholders agreed that tourism can have an important contribution to peacebuilding on the island of Cyprus. The participants highlighted the interaction facilitated by tourism between the visitors and the host community (referring to members of the two communities of Cyprus) as well as the potential of cooperation between tourism business. However, the participants noted that while people can travel between the two sides of the island at an individual level, official cooperation at the industry level is frowned upon with some even wondering if it is even allowed. "There are some businesses that have cooperated unofficially especially with foreign tourist groups arriving on the island on one side and holiday on the other but there can be no official cooperation unless the problem [conflict] is settled by the politicians" explained participant 5. In relation to this point, participant 8 commented that "tourism is like a double-edged sword" bearing also the risk of becoming a factor of antagonism as both communities are developing separate tourism industries. Evidently, the role of tourism in peacebuilding can have both positive and negative aspects.

In terms of the peace awards offered yearly by the Stelios Philanthropic Foundation, the participants agreed that this is a positive development that not only helps both communities but also shows the important role of the private sector in peacebuilding. As participant 6 put it, "the private sector of the tourism industry is often blamed for the negative effects it exerts on the environment and society so any initiative that can help the community achieve sustainability is positive". Indeed, the stakeholders acknowledged peace as a sustainable development goal included in the United Nation's Agenda 2030 and emphasised the pressing need to solve the 'Cyprus problem'. "... To do this [resolve the conflict] all stakeholders from both the public and private sectors need to contribute" said participant 8. In this context, participant 4 commented that the public sector supports such initiatives with bi-communal committees being established to navigate a fruitful economic and social relationship between the two communities. The participant went further to suggest that the effectiveness of such programmes depends on many factors and not solely the support from a ministry or government as "it takes two to tango".

Awardees' perspectives

Despite the cautious yet positive views of tourism stakeholders, awardees' experiences of the peace awards reveal another story. In the case of awardees, the motive for applying for the peace awards is two-fold. On the one hand, economic motives were expressed as a requirement for developing and sustaining their proposed businesses. On the other hand, the acquirement of the peace award is also seen as "symbolic ... to seal our friendship. We don't expect to make money to survive out of this" (participant 2). In this context, the awardees highlighted the monetary reward and recognition of their project as key benefits derived from the peace awards; however, they also noted several obstacles that hinder the award's effectiveness. Participant 1 mentioned inexperience of running a business as the main problem she and her co-awardee faced. The participant also identified the difficulty of developing the project further and make it sustainable financially long-term as another obstacle. Other awardees agreed and also added lack of skills in making this project successful as another hindering factor.

In relation to this issue raised, awardees pointed towards the wider structure in which reconciliation efforts and bi-communal projects evolve stating that there is very little information available for such initiatives. As participant 3 argued, "people don't know about this initiative of the Stelios Foundation and other similar ones that may exist. They are always surprised when I mention this programme so lack of awareness is a big obstacle to the effectiveness of these initiatives". Indeed, an overview of the list of awardees of the Peace Awards of the Stelios Philanthropic Foundation reveals that many win the peace award two or more times. When questioned about this, participant 2 said that this is not surprising as people don't know about this programme but also may be afraid of applying out of fear for being judged negatively so it is the same people applying for it. Participant 3 added that people not only are unaware of the peace awards, which don't receive adequate recognition in the media or government support, but may also not be eligible to apply as they didn't have the opportunity to form the necessary ties with members of the opposing community. "There are other initiatives that need to precede to bring the two communities together before these types of funded efforts for bi-communal projects take place" said the participant.

Regardless, awardees agreed that the importance of such CSR initiatives should not be underestimated especially for environmental or social related issues. In the words of participant 1, the initiative carries "symbolic significance in awarding something that is otherwise considered illegal or is frowned upon". The participant highlighted that as cooperation between the two communities in Cyprus is seen as a taboo by many, it may not facilitate a business for marketing purposes. Evidently, the support of the government was noted as was greater training and information provision to interested parties. Interestingly, participant 2 commented that such initiatives run the risk of substituting official reconciliation efforts at the political level. In her own words, "we need to be careful because the private sector often adopts strategies that may seem positive initially but replace the required foundations for peace which can't exist without political support".

Conclusion and implications

The aim of this chapter was to examine the potential of tourism companies to contribute to peace through their CSR activities. Drawing from the Stelios Philanthropic Foundation in Cyprus, the study examined the perceptions of tourism stakeholders and awardees regarding the potentiality of the peace awards offered on a yearly basis by the Foundation for bi-communal projects. Findings reveal that while support exists for such CSR initiatives, their effectiveness is limited due to lack of support from the government, lack of awareness and appropriate skills for the longevity of such projects. Participants reported the risk of CSR peace initiatives overshadowing and potentially replacing official peace efforts between divided communities, although the role of the private sector in peacebuilding was highlighted. In conclusion, CSR can help in reconciliation and peace in a conflict-ridden destination but only if it is accompanied by official support at the government level and media exposure to raise awareness and the credibility of such programmes.

In relation to these findings, a number of implications arise. First, the CSR function cannot and should not be expected to replace government reconciliation work. Instead, CSR and business peace contributions can be enhanced through collaborative mechanisms, an issue hinted at by stakeholder respondents. Abramov (2009) argues that when entrepreneurs are linked to and supported by public-private partnerships, these contributions can multiply. As Joseph et al. (2023) explain, when local officials and businesses work together, post-conflict zones can be developed in an ethical fashion, creating opportunities that have downstream pro-peace effects which positively impact surrounding communities. In this context, specific interventions such as CSR programmes and their promotion can play a role in linking responsible economic activity to peace within an ethical framework. Second, given that entrepreneurs located in fragile states often lack the skills needed to grow their businesses (Aldairany et al., 2018), as suggested by awardees' perspectives in this study, government efforts should also be directed towards supporting entrepreneurial activity through the development of educational programmes for entrepreneurs combined with socially responsible business skills training. Third, the findings reported here point to the need to involve local populations in peace education practices that explicitly promote intercommunity dialogue, considered by many as taboo, enabling a realistic adjustment to post-conflict realities, with the ultimate purpose of reconciliation and peace promotion. Such efforts are likely to lay the foundations for and cultivate bi-communal cooperation, including entrepreneurial activities and participation in CSR initiatives.

Notwithstanding, this study is not without limitations. First of all, it was exploratory in nature and hence included a very small number of interviewees in its sample. Research using larger samples is required as well as quantitative studies to enhance understanding of the motives, benefits, problems and effectiveness of the implementation of similar CSR initiatives in a peace context. Second, comparative studies are required as each context carries specific factors that influence the success of CSR initiatives. Although context specific factors may lead to a variety of studies the findings of which may be difficult to generalize, it is axiomatic that further research on the role of CSR in reconciliation and peace is mandatory. Future studies can also look at the perspectives of different stakeholders including residents, tourism employees as well as tourists. Ultimately, more research is required to understand the dimensions, aspects and potentialities of CSR in contributing to peace.

References

Abramov, I. (2009). Building peace in fragile states: building trust is essential for effective public–private partnerships. *Journal of Business Ethics, 89*, 481–94.

Aldairany, S., Omar, R., & Quoquab, F. (2018). Systematic review: entrepreneurship in conflict and post conflict. *Journal of Entrepreneurship in Emerging Economies, 10*(2), 361–83.

Alluri, R. M., Leicher, M., Palme, K., & Joras, U. (2014). Understanding economic effects of violent conflicts on tourism: empirical reflections from Croatia, Rwanda and Sri Lanka. In C. Wohlmuther & W. Wintersteiner (Eds.), *International Handbook on Tourism and Peace* (pp. 101–19). Klagenfurt: Drava Verlag.

Bianchi, R. V. (2010). Tourism, capitalism and Marxist political economy. In J. Mosedale (Ed.), *Political Economy of Tourism: A Critical Perspective* (pp. 17–37). London: Routledge.

Carbone, F. (2022). "Don't look back in anger". War museums' role in the post conflict tourism–peace nexus. *Journal of Sustainable Tourism, 30*(2–3), 565–83.

Causevic, S. (2010). Tourism which erases borders: an introspection into Bosnia and Herzegovina. In O. Moufakkir & I. Kelly (Eds.), *Tourism, Peace and Progress* (pp. 48–64). Wallingford: CABI.

D'Amore, L. J. (1988). Tourism: a vital force for peace. *Tourism Management, 9*(2), 151–4.

Dresse, A., Nielsen, J. Ø., & Fischhendler, I. (2021). From corporate social responsibility to environmental peacebuilding: the case of bauxite mining in Guinea. *Resources Policy, 74*, 102290, 1–10.

Farmaki, A. (2017). The tourism and peace nexus. *Tourism Management, 59*, 528–40.

Farmaki, A., Antoniou, K., & Christou, P. (2019a). Visiting the "enemy": visitation in politically unstable destinations. *Tourism Review, 74*(3), 293–309.

Farmaki, A., Khalilzadeh, J., & Altinay, L. (2019b). Travel motivation and demotivation within politically unstable nations. *Tourism Management Perspectives, 29*, 118–30.

Farmaki, A., & Stergiou, D. (2021). Peace and tourism: bridging the gap through justice. *Peace & Change, 46*(3), 286–309.

Farmaki, A., & Stergiou, D. (2022). CSR responses to the Covid-19 pandemic: insights from the hotel sector. *Anatolia: An International Journal of Tourism and Hospitality Research.* https://doi.org/10.1080/13032917.2022.2140442.

Ford, J. (2015). Perspectives on the evolving "business and peace" debate. *The Academy of Management Perspectives, 29*, 451–60.

Ganson, B. (2019). Business and peace: a need for new questions and systems perspectives. In J. Miklian, R. M. Alluri & J. E. Katsos (Eds.), *Business, Peacebuilding and Sustainable Development* (pp. 3–26). London: Routledge.

Hennink, M., Hutter, I. and Bailey, A. (2010), *Qualitative Research Methods.* London: Sage.

Hönke, J. (2014). Business for peace? The ambiguous role of 'ethical' mining companies. *Peacebuilding, 2*(2), 172–87.

Iff, A., & Alluri, R. (2016). Business actors in peace mediation processes. *Business and Society Review, 121*(2), 187–215.

Jamali, D., & Mirshak, R. (2010). Business–conflict linkages: revisiting MNCs, CSR and conflict. *Journal of Business Ethics, 93*, 443–64.

Joseph, J., Katsos, J., & Daher, M. (2021). Local business, local peace? Intergroup and economic dynamics. *Journal of Business Ethics, 173*, 835–54.

Joseph, J., Katsos, J., & Van Buren, III, H. J. (2023). Entrepreneurship and peacebuilding: a review and synthesis. *Business and Society, 62*(2), 322–62.

Joseph, J., & Van Buren III, H. J. (2021). Entrepreneurship, conflict, and peace: the role of inclusion and value creation. *Business & Society.* https:// doi .org/ 00076503211040238.

Katsos, J., & AlKafaji, Y. (2019). Business in war zones: how companies promote peace in Iraq. *Journal of Business Ethics, 155*, 41–56.

Kelleher, A., & Johnson, M. (2008). Religious communities as peacemakers: a comparison of grassroots peace processes in Sudan and Northern Ireland. *Civil Wars, 10*(2), 148–72.

Killick, N., Srikantha, V. S., & Gündüz, C. (2005). The role of local business in peacebuilding. In N. Killick, V. S. Srikantha & C. Gündüz (Eds.), *The Role of Local Business in Peacebuilding.* Berlin: Berghof Research Center for Constructive Conflict Management.

Kolk, A., & Lenfant, F. (2013). Multinationals, CSR, and partnerships in Central African conflict countries. *Corporate Social Responsibility and Environmental Management, 20*(1), 43–54.

Levy, S. E., & Hawkins, D. E. (2010). Peace through tourism: commerce-based principles and practices. *Journal of Business Ethics, 89*, 569–85.

Midtgard, T., Vadlamannati, K. C., & de Soysa, I. (2017). Economic liberalization via IMF structural adjustment: sowing war or reaping peace? *Review of International Organization, 9*(1), 1–28.

Miklian, J. (2017). Mapping business–peace interactions: five assertions for how businesses create peace. *Business, Peace and Sustainable Development, 5*(2), 1–17.

Miklian, J., Alluri, R. M., & Katsos, J. E. (Eds.) (2019). *Business, Peacebuilding and Sustainable Development.* London: Routledge.

Miklian, J., & Bickel, J. P. M. (2020). Theorizing business and local peacebuilding through the "Footprints of Peace" coffee project in rural Colombia. *Business & Society, 59*(4), 676–715.

Miklian, J., & Schouten, P. (2014). Broadening 'business', widening 'peace': a new research agenda on business and peace-building. *Conflict, Security & Development, 19*(1), 1–13.

Miklian, J., Schouten, P., & Ganson, B. (2016). From boardrooms to battlefields: 5 new ways that businesses claim to build peace. *Harvard International Review, 37*(2), 1–4.

Millar, G. (2019). The messy business of peace amid the tyranny of the profit motive: complexity and culture in post-conflict contexts. In J. Miklian, R. M. Alluri & J. E. Katsos (Eds.), *Business, Peacebuilding and Sustainable Development* (pp. 44–60). London: Routledge.

Mueller-Hirth, N. (2017). Business and social peace processes: how can insights from post-conflict studies help CSR to address peace and reconciliation? In S. Vertigans & S. O. Idowu (Eds.), *Corporate Social Responsibility: Academic Insights and Impacts* (pp. 137–53). Cham: Springer.

Oetzel, J., Westermann-Behaylo, M., Koerber, C., Fort, T. L., & Rivera, J. (2010). Business and peace: sketching the terrain. *Journal of Business Ethics*, *89*, 351–73.

Ralph, N., & Hancock, L. (2018). Exploring the role of alternative energy corporations in ethical supply chains and corporate peacebuilding. *Global Governance*, *24*, 81–102.

Rettberg, A. (2016). Need, creed, and greed: understanding why business leaders focus on issues of peace. *Business Horizons*, *59*(5), 481–92.

Robinson, R. S. (2014). Purposive sampling. In A. C. Michalos (Ed.), *Encyclopedia of Quality of Life and Well-Being Research* (pp. 5243–5). New York: Springer.

Ross, M. (2012). *The Oil Curse: How Petroleum Wealth Shapes the Development of Nations*. Princeton, NJ: Princeton University Press.

Schutt, R. (2018). *Investigating the Social World: The Process and Practice of Research*. Boston, MA: Sage.

Stelios Philanthropic Foundation (2022). About us. Accessed 7 October 2022 at https:// stelios.org/.

Subedi, D. P. (2013). "Pro-peace entrepreneur" or "conflict-profiteer"? Critical perspective on the private sector and peacebuilding in Nepal. *Peace & Change: A Journal of Peace Research*, *38*(2), 181–206.

Trivedi, S. (2016). Operationalizing peace through commerce: toward an empirical approach. *Business Horizons*, *59*(5), 525–32.

UNGC [United Nations Global Compact] (2015). Business for peace. Available at https:// d306pr3pise04h .cloudfront .net/ docs/ issues _doc %2FPeace _and _Business %2FB4P_Flyer.pdf.

Watts, M. J. (2005). Righteous oil? Human rights, the oil complex and corporate social responsibility. *Annual Review of Environment and Resources*, *30*, 373–407.

Webster, C., & Timothy, D. J. (2006). Travelling to the 'other side': the occupied zone and Greek Cypriot views of crossing the Green Line. *Tourism Geographies*, *8*(2), 162–81.

Index

Abraham Path 122–3
Abramov, I. 203
Acar, Y.G. 121
acceptance 70–72
accountability 6, 193, 197
actors, in system of systems (SoS) 113
adaptation 24
adaptive resilience 19
adventure, sense of 25
adventure tourism 184
affiliation, media effects on 41, 42, 43, 44
Afghanistan 56, 59, 111, 112
agency, denial of 126
agency theories, of conflict 3, 4
agent-based modelling 116
agro-tourism 24–5
alliance networks 115
Allport, G. 20
Alluri, R.M. 10, 197
alternative economy, and gender 161, 164–5
alternative stories, post-war 73
alternative tourism 10, 11
Althusser, L. 63
anarchist movements 28–9
Anastasopulos, P.G. 7
animosity 10, 34–45
Antoniou, K. 10, 77
archaeology 77, 81, 130
Arieli, T. 129
Assmann, J. 72
assortativity 114
attitudinal change 7, 9, 11, 124
attraction capital 178, 180, 181, 182, 184, 185, 186, 187
attraction management, cross-border 179, 180, 184, 185, 186, 187

Auschwitz-Berkenau 57, 58, 59, 60, 61–2, 69
Australia 182
awardees' perspectives, CSR contribution to peacebuilding 201–2, 203

Beauty and Hope for All (CEI) 93
Becken, S. 21
Beerda, E. 71
Belgium 182
best practice 45, 197
The Better Angels of Our Nature: The Decline of Violence in History and Its Causes 20
Black Heritage Tours 71
Black Lives Matter (BLM) 50
'Black Spots' concept 69
Blasco, D. 178
border disputes, proximity in 114
border geographical isolation 181–2
border tourism 23, 175, 176–8, 187
borders/boundaries 175, 176, 180, 185
Bounia, A. 77
Boyd, S.W. 23, 92
Brinkman, S. 128
broadening the mind 91
Buda, D.M. 121, 132, 133
Buddhas, destruction of 58, 59, 62
built environment, impact of monument destruction on 63
business-peace interactions 195
Butler, R. 22, 23

Çakici, A.C. 152
Canada 51, 52, 55, 56, 177, 179
cancellation of memory 72
capitalism 20, 194
Carbone, F. 197

Carmignani, F. 21
catharsis 23, 131–2
causality 127
Causevic, S. 7, 23
Cave, J. 160
CEI (Italian Bishops' Conference) 93
Centeno, M.A. 18, 27
chaos, and tourism 23
China Pakistan Economic Corridor 186
China–Vietnam border 178
Chiovenda, M.K. 63
civilizing process 26–7
co-existence 27, 78
Cohen, N. 129
Cole, S. 161
collaboration 79–80
collective identity 74, 82
collective memory 72, 73, 74, 75, 79
Colombia
    cross-border tourism 179
    researching PTT in 123–4, 128, 129,
        131
    tourism and peacebuilding 24–5
colonialism 25, 28, 77
Comaroff, J. and J. 19, 20, 25
commercial tourism practices 197
communication 109, 152
communist heritage, policy strategies 57,
    58, 59, 61, 62
community-based tourism 10, 24, 123,
    125, 126
commuting technology, advancements
    in 107–8
comparative studies 154, 203
complex contagion 111
complex systems perspective, peace and
    conflict 105–117
compromise strategy, CSR-peacebuilding
    196
conflict 2, 3–4
    complex systems perspective
        105–117
    gender and 159
    internal and external periods 23
    intractable 126
    media and animosity 36
    and research ethics 129
    tourism as an aggravator of 19, 30
    tourist arrivals and reduction in
        21, 22

transformation 5, 6
    see also cross-border conflict;
        inter-ethnic conflict;
        international conflicts
conflict avoidance 21
conflict resolution 5, 6, 24, 159, 177, 196
connectivity 108, 111
contact hypothesis 1, 7, 9, 10, 11, 20–21,
    141
contagiousness of violence 110–111
containment of violence 110
contestation, memory and 72
controversial cultural heritage 56, 58,
    63, 64
controversial historical events 72–3
cooperation 7, 8, 9, 22, 115, 139, 152, 157,
    160, 175, 176, 179, 185, 186, 187,
    200, 203
coping strategy, CSR-peacebuilding 196
corporate social responsibility (CSR) 11,
    12
    contribution to peace (study)
        193–204
        conclusions and implications
            202–4
        findings 200–202
        methodology 198–200
        relevant studies 194
        theoretical background 195–7
COVID-19 pandemic 30, 51
Crespo-Sancho, C. 157
critical theory 25, 49, 52, 63–4
Croatia 71
cross-border cohesion 181
cross-border conflict 108–9, 179, 184
cross-border cooperation 175, 176, 179,
    185, 186, 187
cross-border integration 176, 179, 180,
    191
cross-border tourism 175–6, 178–85, 186
CSR see corporate social responsibility
cultural affinity 176, 180–81, 185, 186,
    187
cultural boundaries 180
cultural heritage 92
    and peace, need for research 11
    policy choices for dealing with
        57–62

preservation 10, 50, 56, 57, 58, 59,
    60–62, 63
symbols and sharing of 91
see also heritage tourism; public
    monuments
cultural similarity 181
cultural superiority 27
cultural tourism 98, 179, 184
cultural trauma 74
culture(s)
    cross-border integration 180, 181
    gender roles and norms 165
    as a medium for peace 184
    of peace 17, 18
    quality of contact 21
    reframing of 71
cycling routes 179
Cyprus
    dark tourism (study) 74–82
    see also Greek Cypriots; Stelios
        Philanthropic Foundation;
        Turkish Cypriots

Dalby, S. 124
Dallen, T. 23
D'Amore, L.J. 7, 89, 91
dark heritage 24, 71, 76, 77, 80
dark tourism 56, 63
    contribution to peacebuilding 74
    Cyprus (study) 74–82
    literature review 70–74
    motivation 23
    supply 69–70
'dark-darker framework of dark tourism'
    69
debates 1–2, 7–9, 11, 91, 140
debordering 177, 181, 185
defamating effect, of media 41–2, 43, 44
dependency, tourism and 25
Derrida, J. 73
desensitization 25
destination labels 81
destination management organizations
    (DMOs) 79, 80, 81
destination resilience 19
destinations
    border tourism 175
    cultural similarity and selection of
        181
    distance and selection of 182

monument destruction and sterility
    of 62–3, 64
post-conflict 22–6, 30–31
destroyed heritage, retained as
    a reminder 58–9
'destruction of heritage' policy 58, 59
development programmes 166
Di Giovine, M.A. 92
dialogue 9, 10, 11, 50, 81, 82, 121, 186,
    203
diffusion models 116
diplomacy activity 6, 7, 160, 195, 197
'dirtiness' of peace 126, 128
discourse(s) 23, 74, 126, 127, 130, 134,
    161, 165, 166, 179, 196
disempowerment 129–30, 162
Disneyfication 81
distance, and destination selection 182
distance decay/distance desire 182
distributive justice 6, 49, 193
divided communities 7, 8, 74–5, 76, 203
divine presence, works of art and 99
double burial 23
Douglass, F., statue 55–6
Dredge, D. 160
Duffy, L.N. 162

ecclesial cultural parks (ECPs)
    governance 97, 100
    and inner peace (study)
        discussion and conclusion
            99–101
        methods 93–5
        results 95–9
        theoretical background 90–93
    mission 96–7
    organizational model 96
    as territorial systems 96
economic costs
    of containment of violence 110
    of preservation 59–60
economic growth 29, 161, 166
economic prosperity 17, 18, 19, 20, 24, 29
economic support, cross-border tourism
    180
economy
    tourism and the 1, 19, 21, 139, 186–7
    war and the 26, 27
    see also alternative economy; global
        economy; sharing economy

ecotourism 10, 125, 133, 162, 184
ECPs *see* ecclesial cultural parks
education 10, 17, 140, 159, 161
        see also peace education; tourism
            education
educational heritage 92
Elias, N. 18, 26
elite tourism 98, 100
emotion(s) 91, 130, 131–2, 133, 151, 152
empathy 20, 23, 132, 152
employment 1, 10, 96, 153, 158, 161, 162
empowerment, female 157, 158, 159, 161,
        162, 163, 164, 165, 167, 177
enclave tourism 177
engagement strategies,
        CSR-peacebuilding 196
environmental peace 91
environmental preservation, and peace
        10
EOKA-B coup 78
'ethic of solidarity and commitment' 134
ethical business conduct 197
ethics 44, 128–30
ethnic minorities 8, 10, 19, 20, 153
Ethnicity Inc. 19
ethno-nationalist sentiments 76
ethnocentrism 20, 21, 36
Europe 25, 27, 72–3, 108, 166, 179
        see also individual countries
European imperialism 28
Everingham, P. 160
exponential random graph models
        (ERGMs) 115
external factors, in future research 12
external valuation 195
extremists/extremism 108–9, 110, 111,
        114

failed/fragile states 19, 21, 24, 25, 203
fake news 35, 42, 43
Farmaki, A. 8, 9, 10–11, 77, 196
feedback loops 106, 109, 110, 111, 112
female leadership 165
feminist economics 160–63, 164
Fernández Herreira, A. 89
field notes 129
Finland–Sweden border 179
Floyd, G. (protests/riots) 50, 51–2, 53,
        56, 64–5
Fog, A. 35

Foley, M. 69
forgiveness 10, 124
fortifying effect, of media 42, 43, 44
Foucault, M. 28, 29
fragmented networks, and violence
        111–12
Frank, A. 134
Frankfurt School 49, 52, 63–4
Friedrich, M. 70
fuel tourism 177
funding/non-funding of preservation
        58, 61

Galtung, J. 5, 98
game theory 116
Gandhi, M., statue 56
gender approach to PTT 157–68
        conclusions and implications 167–8
        feminist economics approach
            160–63
        progressing the research agenda
            164–7
gender equality 157, 159, 160, 161–2,
        166–7, 168
gender essentialism 162–3, 166
gender gap 157, 163, 164
gender inequality 159, 160, 161, 165–6
gender relations, economic organisations
        163
gender responsive peacebuilding 159–60
gender roles 158, 159, 160, 162–3, 164,
        165, 166, 167, 168
gendered stereotypes 161, 163, 165, 166,
        167, 168
Germany/German heritage 57, 58, 59,
        62, 71
German–Poland border 177
Gilgit Baltistan region 184–5, 186
global economy 1, 2, 110
global events/crises 22, 161
global justice 51
Global Peace Index 127
global tourism 8, 10, 71, 106, 140
globalization 20, 107–9, 110
government assistance, in recovery 24
grassroot peace processes 159, 198
Greek Cypriots 74–5, 76, 77, 78, 79, 198
greenways 179
Guasca, M. 24
Guia, J. 178

guilt (researcher) 133

Habermas, J. 73
Haessly, J. 17
Halbwachs, M. 72
Hansen, T. 91, 100
harmonious borders 178, 180, 181
Hawkins, D.E. 197
heritage 23, 92
    see also cultural heritage; dark
            heritage
heritage tourism 71, 81, 92, 177, 178,
        180–81
heritagization 80, 81
historical events, interpretation of 72–3
historical heritage 92, 100
historical narratives 73, 75, 76, 77, 78–9,
        81–2
Hoeffler, A. 4
holistic approach, to positive peace 5
holistic dimension, tourism–peace
        relationship 152
Holocaust 71, 72–3
Holocaust Museum (Washington) 69
homophily 111, 114, 115
hospitality industry, gender equality in
        166
host-guest relations 20–21

'ideal tourism worker' 163
identity(ies) 3, 71, 72, 74, 78–9, 82, 92,
        110, 129
incentivization, cross-border tourism 180
income 153, 162, 164
independence, female socio-economic
        162
India 164
India–Pakistan border 176, 179–80,
        183–5, 186
individual choice, myth of 164
inequalities
    and conflict 3
    female empowerment and
            minimisation of 158
    gender and production of 158
    positive perceptions and elimination
            of 153
    tourism and 1–2, 10, 91, 157, 160,
            167

    see also gender inequality;
            socio-economic inequalities;
            structural inequalities
influential nodes, detection of 116–17
informants, impacts of PTT research on
        128–33
information and communication
        technologies 108, 110
information provision, media and 35,
        37–8
infrastructure 110, 122, 178–9, 197
injustices 8, 10, 125
inner peace, ECPs and (study) 89–101
institutional support, cross-border
        tourism 180
INSTRAW Gender, Peace and Security
        (UN) 157
inter-ethnic conflict 19, 20, 21
interactions 82, 114, 186, 195, 200
intergroup dialogue/contact 9, 10, 11, 50,
        186, 203
international conflicts 35, 114, 115
International Institute for Peace Through
        Tourism (IIPT) 124
international standards, adoption of 197
international tourism, and proximity of
        destination 182
interpersonal communication 152
interpersonal safety, PTT research 128,
        129, 134
interpretation/reinterpretation 72–3, 74,
        76, 77, 81, 127
interstate war 108
intractable conflicts 126
invisibility of gender inequality 165–6
Iraq 111, 112, 114
ISIS 56, 111
Israel–Palestine context
    PTT research 122–3, 124, 126, 129,
            130, 132–3
    tourism 80, 177, 178
Italy 58
    ECPs and inner peace (study)
            90–101
Ivanov, S. 57

Jamali, D. 196
Johnson, M. 198
Johnston, T. 70
Joseph, J. 203

justice 5–6, 159
    see also distributive justice; social
        justice

Kalisch, A.B. 161
Kartarpur Sahib 184
Kashmir 183–5, 186
Kelleher, A. 198
Kelly, I. 17, 140
Kerr, R. 6
Khalilzadeh, J. 115
Kim, S.S. 7
knowledge, need for contextual 127
Kobayashi, A. 133
Königsberg bridges problem (Euler) 114
Königsberg Royal Castle 58, 59, 62
Korstanje, M.E. 28, 29
Kulakoğlu Dilek, N. 143, 152
Kvale, S. 128

labelling 126
language 9, 21
Laos 186
Latin America 27, 179
    see also Colombia
'leave to rot' policy 57, 58–9, 62
Lee, C.K. 70
Lee, R.E., statue 58, 59, 62
Lenin's mausoleum 57, 58, 61
Lennon, J.J. 69
Levy, S.E. 197
local communities
    CSR contribution to 195, 197, 203
    exclusion from tourism revenues 8
    impact of PTT research on 128, 130
    involvement in peace education
        practices 203
    sensitivity towards disadvantaged
        52–3
Lomazzi, V. 166
low income 153
Lynch, P. 7, 23

McIntosh, A.J. 121, 132, 133
McKercher, B. 70, 98
McKinley, W. 29
macro ethics 129–30
macro-level theories, of conflict 3
mainstream economics, and gender 164

Mansfeld, Y. 26
Maoz, Z. 115
Marcuse, H. 63
mass media 35, 41, 45
mass tourism 1, 8, 91
media
    animosity and tourism 37–8
    animosity and tourism (study)
        discussion and conclusions
            42–5
        findings 39–42
        methodology 38–9
    footage of George Floyd incident
        51–2
    role and criticisms 35–6
meditation 100
memory 72, 73–4
mentoring 166
meso approach, conflict studies 4
metaphorical perceptions, peace-tourism
    relationship 140, 142–54
micro ethics 128–9
micro-level theories, of conflict 3
Miles, W.F. 69
Mirshak, R. 196
mistrust 8
mnemohistory 72
Mobekk, E. 6
modelling complex systems 106, 115, 116
Mooney, S.K. 165
morbid consumption 25
Morgan, N. 24
Moufakkir, O. 17
multilayer networks 115
Muñoz de Escalona, F. 28
museums 10, 69, 77, 78
myths, deconstruction of 73

narratives
    of PTT research 129–30
    see also historical narratives;
            national narratives; tourist
            guide narratives
national barriers 21
national identity 78–9
national narratives 77
national tourism organizations 187
nationalistic sentiment, as an obstacle to
    PTT 7–8
natural heritage 92

nature 99
negative peace 5, 17, 105, 177
neighbouring destinations 182
neo-Marxism 49
network science 106–7, 109, 110, 111, 112–13, 114–15, 116–17
new narratives 81–2
news, media shaping of 44
Nibigira, C. 24
Nica, M. 23
niche tourism 10, 11, 22, 98, 99, 100
normative approach, PTT debate 122–6
norms 125, 131, 162, 164, 165, 197
Novelli, M. 24

OECD 161
Oetzel, J. 195
Olick, J.K. 72
organized interests, in preservation 61
other(s) 20, 25, 76
outsider role, PTT research 132–3

Pack, S. 19
Pakistan see India–Pakistan border
Palestine see Israel–Palestine context
Papadakis, Y. 76
Papavasiliou, V. 78, 79
Passerini, L. 72
past experiences, and animosity 40, 43, 44
peace 2, 4–6, 17
     border and cross border tourism 177–8, 183–5, 186
     complex systems perspective 105–117
     concept of 122–8
     culture of 17, 18
     subdivision of 91
     sustainable development goals 2, 6, 193, 195, 201
     tourism as benefitting from 8
     see also inner peace; social peace
peace activists, researchers as 133
peace awards 201–2
peace education 18, 142, 203
peace of mind 92, 99–100
peace parks 10, 179
'peace sensitive tourism' 91
peace studies 122

peace tourism 89, 90, 91, 98, 128
peace tourism studies 20–21, 26, 141
     future research agenda 29–30
     methodological problem 18, 28
peace-through-tourism (PTT)
     and animosity 36–8
     and CSR 197
     in Cyprus 78–9
     debates/criticisms 1–2, 7–9, 11, 90, 91, 122, 140
     gender approach 157–68
     rationale behind proposition 1
     requirements for 9–11
     research
          contribution of research 133–5
          future agenda 11–12, 134–5
          impacts on informants and researchers 128–33
          ontological and epistemological challenges 122–8
peace-tourism relationship 105, 139
     complexity of 107
     metaphorical perceptions (study) 140, 142–54
peacebuilding
     CSR as tool for 193, 196
     denial of agency 126
     gender and 158–60, 167
     inclusion of tourism educators in 152
     need for various actors in 6
     tourism and 1, 9, 10, 17, 21, 25–6, 63, 74, 79–81
peacewashing 126
peer-to-peer accommodation platforms 10
Peleg, S. 3
perceived reality, media and 36
perceptions, of peace-tourism relationship (study) 140, 142–54
perceptual change 7, 9, 11
phenomenology 143
philanthropy 197
phoenix tourism 7, 23
pilgrimage routes 96, 100, 184
Pinker, S. 20
planned resilience 19
plurality of peace 122, 124–5
policy
     eradication of inequalities 10

and gender 163, 166
and peacebuilding, future research 12
PTT research and influence on 134
regarding public monuments 57–62
political borders/boundaries 180, 185
political ideology 36, 37, 40, 43, 44, 59, 61, 62, 63, 76, 181
political influence 7, 8
political stability 17, 19, 20, 21, 22, 24, 25, 27, 30, 75
politico-economic conditions, and gender 164, 165
politics, and interpretation of historical events 73, 76
Poria, Y. 57
Portugal 163, 164, 166
positionality (researcher) 127, 131
positive approaches, PTT research 127
positive peace 5–6, 17, 105, 177–8
Post Conflict Heritage and Postcolonial Tourism 25
post-colonial theory 25
post-conflict emotion 91
post-conflict tourism 18, 20, 23
    destinations 22–6, 30–31
    as a divisive factor 8
    prevention and 22
post-memory 73–4
poverty/relief 20, 22, 24–5
power 63–4, 109–110, 111, 112, 162, 163
    see also disempowerment;
        empowerment
Prats, L. 178
Prayag, G. 19
presence, peace as a 17
preservation 10, 50, 56, 57, 58, 59, 60–62, 63
prevention, and post-conflict tourism 22
Prideaux, B. 7
private sector 11, 154, 193, 194, 197, 201, 202, 203
procedural justice 6
profit-orientation, of tourism 1–2, 20, 91
'protection of heritage' policy 57, 58
proximity 114, 182
proxy measures, observing state preferences 114
PTT *see* peace-through-tourism
public monuments, destruction 50, 53–7

the spark(s) leading to 51–3
public opinion, media shaping of 35, 36, 44
public-private partnerships 203

qualitative research 20, 127, 130–31, 134–5, 143, 144
quantitative research 20, 127–8, 131, 133, 154, 203

racism 50, 52, 53, 56
rational economic woman 165
Rawls, J. 49
rebellion groups, cross-border conflict 108–9
rebordering 177, 185
reconciliation 1, 6, 7, 11, 24, 37, 63, 71, 100, 124, 159, 203
recovery 23, 24
Reddy, M.V. 23
Redekop, P. 100
reflexive writing 134
relational dimension, tourism–peace relationship 152
relational peace 91
religious tourism 23, 81, 181, 184
'remove from view' policy 58, 59
representation 72, 129–31
research ethics 128–30
researchers, impacts of PTT research on 128–33
resentment, as an obstacle to peace 8
resilience 18–19, 23, 26, 110, 161
responsible tourism 91
restorative justice 6
retention of destruction, as a reminder 58–9
risks, PTT research 128, 129, 132
Robbins, J. 72
Roosevelt, T., statue 58, 59
rural development 182
rural women 162, 164
Russia–Ukraine war 30, 36, 38–45, 140, 142

sacred/sacredness 89–90, 97, 100, 184
safe environments 141
safety risks, PTT research 128, 129, 134
Sánchez Sánchez, A. 89

Saudi Arabia 165
scenario simulation 116
Scheyvens, R. 162
Schwartz, S.H. 91
Seaton, A.V. 69
Second World War 18, 71, 72–3
self-organized system of systems (SoS) 113
sensitivity, in research 124, 125
shalom 99
shared enemy 115
sharing economy 12
simple contagion 111
simulation 116
situational animosity/affiliation 37, 43, 44
slavery heritage 70, 71
snowball sampling 94, 129
social agents, businesses as 193–4
social change, PTT research and 133
social cohesion 195
social identity 3, 72
social ideology, preservation of culture 61, 62
social justice/movement 49–50, 51, 52, 53, 63, 64, 98, 124
social media 35, 36, 37–8, 41, 42, 44, 45
social network analysis 114–15
social peace 98, 139
social physics 106–7
social power 162
social reproduction economy 164, 165
social stability 10, 176
socio-cultural gaps, tourism and widening of 8
socio-economic benefits, of tourism 10, 141, 176
socio-economic development 92, 96, 125, 159, 195
socio-economic inequalities 1–2, 10, 11, 91, 157, 160
Spain 19, 164
specialized tourism 79, 80, 81, 82, 91
spirituality 89, 96–7, 99, 100
Srinigar 184–5
stability
    tourism and 8, 22, 24
    see also political stability; social stability
stable animosity/affiliation 37, 43, 44
stable peace 125

stakeholder perspectives, CSR contribution to peacebuilding 200–201
stakeholders
    ECPs and inner peace study 93–4, 95–9, 100
    intractable conflict and PTT research 126
    perceptions on peace-tourism relationship 154
state preferences, and interactions 114
statistical models 115
steering effect, of media 40–41, 42, 43, 44
Stelios Philanthropic Foundation, contribution to peace 194, 198–204
stereotypes/stereotyping 7, 8, 25, 26, 71, 161, 163, 165, 166, 167, 168
Stergiou, D. 8, 10–11, 196
sterile landscapes, destruction and 62–3, 64
Stone, P.R. 69
structural inequalities 5–6, 153, 159, 160, 167
structural theories, of conflict 3, 4
Stylianou-Lambert, T. 77
sustainable development 6, 90, 96, 167, 193
sustainable development goals (SDGs) 2, 6, 52, 161, 193, 195, 201
sustainable peace 6, 159, 185, 186, 187
sustainable tourism 184
Swain, M.B. 162
Switzerland 177
symbols/symbolism 57, 91, 201, 202
Syria 111, 112
system of systems (SoS) 113
Szoborpark/Statue (Hungary) 58, 59

taxation 20, 25
technological breakthrough/innovation 18, 26, 28, 29, 107–8
terrorists/terrorism 26, 28, 29, 114, 176
Thailand 186
thanatourism 69, 70
Theidon, K. 133
thematic analysis 95
third-generation phenomena 73–4
third-party language, and intergroup dialogue 9

tolerance 63, 122, 153
Tomljenovic, R. 20
tourism
    complex systems perspective 107,
        113
    as a divisive factor 8, 11
    and the economy 1, 19, 21, 139,
        186–7
    global events and effects on 141–2
    need for safe/peaceful environments
        8, 141, 153
    negative impact of destructive mobs
        56–7
    outputs/benefits 10, 139, 141, 153,
        176
    and peace *see* peace; peace tourism;
        peace-through-tourism;
        peace-tourism relationship;
        peacebuilding
    problems generated by 19
    resilience to external crises 18–19
    war and development of 18, 26
    see also border tourism; cross-border
        tourism; dark tourism;
        peace tourism; post-conflict
        tourism
tourism education 140, 142, 152, 153,
    154, 203
tourism entrepreneurship 128, 166, 177,
    203
tourism labour 161, 163, 165
tourism students, perceptions (study) 140
    discussion and conclusion 151–4
    findings 144–51
    methodology 142–4
tourism-centric approach 181
tourist guide narratives 78, 79, 80, 81
tourists
    host-guest relations 20–21
    impacts of PTT research on 129
    motivation 21, 23, 44, 77, 101, 177,
        182
    subjectivity/perception 80
Track I/II/III actors 6, 7, 160
trade/tourism 105, 107, 108, 113, 114,
    115, 116
transdisciplinarity 125, 134
trauma 73–4
Travel for Peace 139
travel writing 21

troubled pasts, memory representations
    of 72
Turkey 7, 111
    see also Cyprus; tourism students,
        perceptions (study)
Turkish Cypriots 74, 75, 77–8, 79, 198

United Kingdom 51
United Nations 90, 114, 157, 159
    Agenda 2030, SDGs *see* sustainable
        development goals
United States 50, 51–2, 53–5, 59, 62,
    64–5, 107, 108, 111–12
US–Canada border 177, 179

validating effect, of media 39–40, 42–3,
    44
values 3, 17, 27, 37, 57, 61, 64, 65, 77, 89,
    90, 165, 179, 185
Van Broeck, A.M. 24
Vanneste, D. 24
victims/victimhood 41, 44, 58, 73, 77,
    123, 124, 130, 159, 167
violence(s) 20
    and conflict, complexity of 109–112
    multiplicity of 125
    network diffusion 116
    reduction of, worldwide 20
    self-control 27
    women as victims of 167
volunteer tourism 10, 160

wage gender gap 163, 164
war 17–18
    and development of tourism 18, 26
    and the economy 26, 27
    gender and 159
    impact on tourism 141–2
    and social, technological and
        political development 27–8,
        29
war tourism 20, 22–3
water, tourism and gender 167
Webster, C. 57
West/Westerners, cultural preservation
    63
Winter, T. 25
Wintersteiner, W. 91
Wohlmuther, C. 91

women, and peace 157–68
works of art, and divine presence 99

Yankholmes, A. 70